BRUJAS

BRUJAS

THE MAGIC AND POWER
OF WITCHES OF COLOR

LORRAINE MONTEAGUT, PhD

CHICAGO
REVIEW
PRESS

First hardcover edition published in 2022
First paperback edition published in 2023
Published by Chicago Review Press Incorporated
814 North Franklin Street
Chicago, Illinois 60610
ISBN 978-1-64160-995-1

Portions of the chapter "The Moon Coven" have previously appeared in an article by the author, "The Wild Self: What Is Wild to One Is Home to Another," *Appalachia* 72, no. 1 (2021): Article 15.

The poem "Emerge" is from Yuki Jackson's unpublished series Mark of the Beast, pt. 8. Used with permission.

The Library of Congress has cataloged the hardcover edition under the following Control Number: 2021938740

Cover and interior design: Sadie Teper
Cover illustration: Kimberly Rodriguez, a.k.a. Poeta Goddess

Printed in the United States of America

For my abuelitas,

Elsie, Elvira, and Ninoska

A NOTE TO THE READER

Poeta Goddess created the cover illustration for this book. She begins each design with an intention and channels the images "to remind folx of their resilience, magick, and power." She writes a line of poetry or a prayer to accompany each design. For this one, she offers you this invocation:

May my Art be the light to lead me home.

Before you proceed, I invite you to say the words to yourself. Drop into your heart. If you have a physical copy of the book, you might consult the cover as you would a tarot card. Let judgment and expectation fall away. Pause here.

What arises for you?

The cover image says *folklore* to me. A figure draped in a veil holds a candle, and the wax drips between their fingers. They've been there a while, trying to create a connection. They stand with their back to their altar, smoke billowing in a chalice, candles flickering with the breath of ancestors. Behind them, a portal has opened, but the figure doesn't quite notice. They are intent, face downturned, a look tender and nostalgic for homelands they feel but have never known, where story lines are unbroken and exile is never necessary and nobody has to hide who they are.

When I started writing this years ago, I turned to face the past. I reached for my *abuelitas*. They reached back through the ether between us. I learned about generational shadows, the traumas that are kept secret and passed in silence down family lines. The shadows of my line clarified into patterns and lessons as I wrote. There was so much power waiting for me. In the midst of this project of recollecting, I had become part of a spiritual community of brujas who are also connecting to their ancestral traditions and breathing new life into their pasts.

Brujas are the new generation of spiritual activists and teachers and healers.

The Spanish word for witch is not simply a straightforward translation of the English. *Bruja* ("brew-ha") is the word for "female witch," and *brujo* means "male witch," but the terms connect to different traditions and histories than that of the Anglo-Saxon witch. They instead refer to the traditions of West Africa that made their way to the Caribbean and the Americas through slavery, and to the traditions of the Indigenous peoples of the Americas, who were displaced and forced to assimilate to the cultures of European colonizers.

The term *brujx* ("brew-hex") is growing in popularity and mirrors the new *Latinx* ("la-teen-ex"), encompassing the female and male terms and extending to include gender nonconforming practitioners. It sets the new generation of practitioners apart from the older notion of *brujería*, or witchcraft, with its closed traditions and histories of stigmatization and oppression. Brujxs are part of a larger group of witches of color who are reclaiming the spiritual traditions of their families' homelands.

All of these terms—*witch, witches of color, brujas, brujx, Latinx*— are complicated and contested. There is no set definition for any of them, and there's disagreement about who we are talking about when we use them. *Witches of color* is similar to *people of color* in that it includes anybody who isn't White, but there's no consensus about whether these terms include White Latin Americans or White-passing people like me. And not all witches of color identify with the terms *bruja* or *brujx*, especially if they don't have a direct connection to Spanish-speaking countries or the Afro-Caribbean diaspora.

Some people are adopting *Latinx* because it challenges the patriarchal structure of the Spanish language and is inclusive of gender-nonconforming folks. But the Latin American experience is not a monolith, and many resent the new term they feel is being foisted on them by a privileged minority. (My Colombian mother and Cuban father would never use the term, if they've even heard it.) Though I often use it myself, I ultimately take issue with the reference to Latin *anything*, as I see it as another form of European colonization of a vastly diverse set of peoples. Throughout the book, I favor what individuals like to be called. That's usually connected to where they are from, specifically their countries, their communities, or their tribes.

A NOTE TO THE READER

Every good witch knows that words are spells. As magic is flowing, so is the language we use. It's OK to not have the perfect word sometimes because language is flawed and cannot always encompass all the possibilities. What's important is that we remain conscious of the words we speak and transparent about why we choose to use certain words. I've decided to call this book *Brujas*, since it's more recognizable and easier to pronounce than *brujxs*, but I mean it as a fluid term that includes magical people of all gender identities and orientations.

This book is for all those who want to learn about or practice ancestral magic and magical activism. Though the stories and research I present center on brujas and the histories of the Afro-Caribbean diaspora and Indigenous people of color, anyone can adapt the information and rituals to consciously explore their ancestry, develop sustainable practices to heal themselves, and reclaim their magical powers.

The first part of the book features some of the ancestral traditions upon which the bruja is based, the second part explores the different kinds of activism brujas are engaged with, and the third part is about the businesses, practices, and networks of the modern bruja. Each chapter focuses on a specific topic and a different bruja practitioner. I also offer my personal stories because I believe they are things we might share in common, and they provide a model for how to reflect on the topics in relation to your own life.

I encourage you to use this book however it helps you most. You might read in order if you're the type who likes to follow a narrative. Or you could skip around to topics or brujas you're interested in. At the end of each chapter are ritual exercises to help you initiate steps along your own spiritual path, as well as more resources from witches of color or other practitioners of ancestral spiritualities. Since astrology is increasingly accessible to spiritual seekers regardless of their ancestral traditions, I've associated each chapter with an archetype of the zodiac in the order they appear on the astrological wheel. You do not have to be fluent in astrological symbology or even believe in astrology's divinatory potential to use these sections. They are meant as introductory tools for reflection and to inspire your rituals or altar items.

For instance, if you're prepping for a ritual honoring the full moon in Scorpio, you might flip to the end of chapter 8 for a quick reference of an element or affirmation to employ in your practice. For you astrology enthusiasts who know your birth charts, you might take the journal prompts a step further. Look to the house where a particular sign falls in your chart and note whether you have any placements there. The houses of astrology represent areas of life, and the planets represent our drives. This is only *a* book, not *the* book, on brujas. I recommend you explore the resources I've included for further study and the work of other practitioners to dive more deeply into the topics I introduce. Attend workshops, subscribe to their YouTube channels or their Patreon accounts, and share the wealth of knowledge they have to offer. In this way, you can become a part of this growing bruja movement.

The book closes with a poem by Yuki Jackson, part 8 of a series she wrote called Mark of the Beast that documents her journey of self-acceptance. It employs the Buddhist myth of the daughter of Sāgara the dragon king, ruler of a divine race of half-serpent and half-human beings. At eight years old, she had unparalleled wisdom and could see to the root of any matter. She appealed to the Buddha to attain enlightenment, but she was rejected because she was female. She then changed her body to a masculine one and embraced enlightenment of her own accord. The poem felt like an incantation when I first read it, binding our stories together with a closing spell.

Our stories, mythical or biographical, are sacred. I have so much love and respect for the practitioners who opened their hearts to me. Their stories and support have gotten me through a grief period and encouraged me to keep at my art, however slow it was in coming. This book is theirs as much as it is mine. I have based all the stories in the book on personal interviews and correspondence and on workshops and events I have attended. I also honor the many brujas that I did not have the opportunity to include. I look forward to meeting you.

I hope that wherever you are on your path, you'll be kind to yourself and take it slow. Rest often. Enjoy the little things. Know that with intention and steady discipline, you'll make the connection you're looking for. When life gets hard, open to love. This is your artistry and your birthright. Opening your heart is the most courageous thing you can do because it requires you to also open to pain, to process and transmute it, in order to make room for joyful expression.

The art is here, in this process, not in the end product. Trust. There is time yet for what you wish to create. Turn to the ancestors.

Content Warning: This book contains references to anxiety, death, depression, domestic abuse, drug use, sexual assault, suicide, police and gun violence, racism, and other potentially disturbing topics.

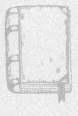

I

A MAGICAL ANCESTRY

"I touch my own skin, and it tells me that before there was any harm, there was miracle."

—adrienne maree brown, *Pleasure Activism: The Politics of Feeling Good*

THE NEW BRUJAS

By the time Sabel Santa arrived in Carolina, Puerto Rico, a municipality east of San Juan, she was mute. She was two years old. Her family was perplexed because she had just begun to speak her first full sentences of English in the United States, where she was born. They tried coaxing her into talking again, to no avail. Sabel would not speak.

It was 1987, the same year King Juan Carlos and Queen Sofía of Spain visited Puerto Rico to plan the commemorative event for the five hundredth anniversary of Columbus's "discovery" of America. Just before their public appearance, five bombs went off on different areas of the island. One of the bombs caused property damage to the Bank of Boston, a couple miles from Sabel's grandmother's house in Villa Carolina.

Sabel's mother had left her father behind at the military base where he was stationed. Her grandmother took Sabel and her mother in, and they were once again an unbroken matriarchy. Sabel had the brown skin of her mother's line, her inheritance from the West Africans who were brought forcefully to the island in the 1500s.

Her grandmother was an eccentric woman. She didn't go to church like the other ladies in the barrio. She sensed when people were on their way over. She talked to plants. The objects in her kitchen were all enchanted to her, and she put her nurturing energy into everything she cooked, which would sustain the bodies of her descendants. For a while, she was Sabel's best friend. With her grandmother, she didn't need to speak. They communicated without words. Her grandmother would fix her eyes on Sabel, and Sabel understood and would nod or shake her head.

Sabel intently observed the world around her, new to her but old to her family. The buildings with their flat roofs and wrought-iron geometric patterns. The patron saint festivals for San Fernando, yet another Spanish king. Her neighbors, shouting and dancing and fighting and loving. A thrumming of magic barely perceptible, whispering.

Months went by, and Sabel began to speak again.

In Spanish.

Throughout the 1970s and '80s, there were isolated bombings on the island and on the mainland to protest Puerto Rico's status as a commonwealth under the United States. Most resulted in no injuries or casualties, but they were a constant reminder of the people's unrest in a land that had been colonized by Spanish powers since the late fifteenth century, before the United States invaded during the Spanish-American War in the late 1800s.

There were other forms of resistance. Brujería was first documented on the island in the 1500s, as a response to the colonizers' religion and as a method of keeping Indigenous and African traditions alive. Providing private modes of healing and dissent, brujas and brujos stepped in to help the people when governments and mainstream medicine fell short. These were not always peaceful practices. They were responses to violence and oppression and often required sacrifices, so they were easily denounced by the Catholic Church and the government as devil worship. Many descendants of these traditions were successfully converted to Christianity and condemned their own ancestry, and the stigma lives on today. But since brujería wasn't a religion with established institutions or hierarchy, its grassroots rituals were difficult to identify and stamp out. Brujería survived in the shadows.

Next door to Sabel's grandmother lived a so-called bruja, and though Sabel's grandmother was clearly an intuitive herself, she forbade Sabel from visiting. But Sabel couldn't help herself from getting close. She was fascinated by the decapitated birds hanging outside her neighbor's door. What could they be for? What else was inside? Somehow she knew that there was more to the "witch" than her grandmother said, that these people who lived just apart from the rest of them and made strange sacrifices were not necessarily evil. The way of the bruja was a current that flowed under everything on the island, beneath the Spanish names and customs—something far older, full of mystery, misunderstood.

Sabel began collecting occult objects of her own, crystals and spell books and tarot cards, and she created her own rituals. When she was thirteen, Hurricane Georges hit Puerto Rico, and Sabel energetically absorbed the force of the wind and the rain, believing it to be her magical initiation.

A MAGICAL ANCESTRY

At the same time, one thousand miles away in Florida, another thirteen-year-old was getting ready for the same storm. I pushed my furniture to the middle of my room and tucked my prized possessions into the closet that held all of my secrets. I remembered Hurricane Andrew and how I'd been too little to save my things when parts of the roof flew off and the windows all broke and the carpets flooded. I should've been scared. I'd never admit it, because I knew what a hurricane could do—how it could take your home or your loved ones in a blink—but the truth was, I was always excited when a storm was on its way.

Each storm feels like an inheritance. Before a storm hits, the barometric pressure plummets, and the air feels both full and empty. The skies become an otherworldly green grey, and the wind assumes a harsh whisper. Then comes a trance of water and wind, hands of gods mixing everything together, strengthening the undercurrents. The past emerges to the present, and they become one, and you can remember things long forgotten, things maybe you'd never been taught but somehow you carry, like how to keep possessions light and when to run or when to hunker down. Like how to rebuild after the storm, that emissary of nostalgia carrying the tears and sweat of our ancestors hundreds of miles to rain down on us.

Brujas hold this reverence for hurricanes. Maybe it's because they follow the trajectory of a great ancestral migration, originating from the coast of Africa, running through the Caribbean, some dying down, some gaining strength, before settling in the United States. Hurricanes are a reminder to keep moving, to find higher ground, to survive.

Sabel's story hums between binaries: Black and White. Spanish and English. The occult and Catholicism. Colonized and colonizer. Her in-betweenness is her special mark. The bruja contains all these identities, allowing Sabel a fluid movement between them.

★ ⭐ ★

When we moved to our new home in the suburbs of West Kendall, Florida, I started to have the alligator dreams. In the dreams I am dressed in white, walking barefoot across a vast swamp. I'm trying to make it to a shoreline a few feet out of reach, but it keeps moving of its own volition. Along the way, I step on the heads and bodies of stonelike gators. The water is opaque milk, and there is a penetrating fog. If I'm slow and intentional with my steps, the gators remain stone. If I hesitate in fear, they start to move and snap at me. In some dreams, panic takes over, and I freeze on one of the gator heads, eternally encircled by the reptilian force of the swamp. In others, I slip and fall into the water, and I'm torn limb from limb.

I still have the dreams, though I haven't lived in West Kendall in nearly twenty years. It is the closest thing I have to a homeland, this unincorporated part of Miami-Dade County. Abutting the eastern border of the Everglades, West Kendall is named for the European merchant who bought it in the late 1800s. Ours was the first house in our development, Sunny View Homes, the helm of the area's suburban boom in the 1990s.

I was nine when we moved there. I was a tomboy, with knobby knees and a nose like a bird's beak. The grown-ups, mostly South and

Central American and Caribbean immigrants like us, stood on the foundations of homes that would bear the broad strokes of the Spanish Colonial style, what they'd collectively decided was the mark of progress. They reviewed their cookie-cutter plans, pointing here and there.

I perched on the roof and followed the sun as it set on the interminable marsh, clouds towering milky pink and yellow on the horizon. All around were U-pick strawberry fields, rows and rows stretching west to the swamplands. I ignorantly thought the Everglades a wilderness. I didn't know it had long been home to nomadic migrant workers and Miccosukee.

Then more neighbors came, and mazes of stucco houses all the same, and the strawberries were paved over. Our suburb became indistinguishable from all the others. It was sunny, but in a bad way. Without the swamp to absorb the light, the roof view turned to a blinding whiteness, the beam of an alien ship keeping everything in suspension. Barred from nature, I craved relics of the old Florida of my imagination. I was so close to it, to Big Cypress and the ancient alligators and the collective memory of the Seminoles who knew every mangrove, every dome. I might as well have been a world away.

There were two Floridas, one humming, trapped under the weight of the other.

Years went by, and I could feel the hormones making space inside of me—for what, I didn't know. I pressed my face to the heat of the pavement to listen for the old magic beyond the burning of my ear. Nature became synonymous with the past. I didn't want to grow up and forget the swamp. If I could somehow channel it, I might spare myself an adolescence of suburban mundanity. When I smelled a storm coming, I sat ready on the roof, my arms to the sky, half pretending I controlled the thunder, half hoping lightning would strike me and I'd get powers.

My little brothers shared a room where they created an insular world, so I explored on my own. My closet was your ordinary preteen confessional, the walls covered in posters my mom wouldn't like out in the open. Alien-like as he was, with breasts and a bony bump where genitals would be, Marilyn Manson's *Mechanical Animals* album cover was particularly offensive to conservative sensibilities. Nothing was a solid line—not gender, not species, not genre. I excused the violence he portrayed as "artistic," unaware of the real abuse he inflicted. He made me feel like I could be anything, love anyone. Behind the posters were the names of crushes and symbols I'd made up as placeholders for words I didn't yet have. I could only write them in total confinement, doors fully shut. Though they pressed me to the wall, I was safe in my altar of clothes and cracked light, away from the overexposed photograph that was my waking life.

Darkness called in a richness of forms I wished I could unsee. One scared me to the core: a shadow that materialized into a witch in the corner of my room, all static and dark matted hair like the girl from *The Ring*. If I let my guard down, she would advance. Once, she got all the way to my chest and clawed to get in, and I felt myself coming untethered from my body.

Panic became a familiar visitor. Over time, I learned how to keep the shadow in her corner with my willpower. When she appeared, I had the weird feeling that I'd asked for this, like it was a wild offshoot of my imagination that had grown a will of its own. My terror pushed away any wish of magic, and when the sun rose, I was happy to look out my window onto the boring street with the boring little houses all the same. But then the fear would wear off, and I'd start experimenting again, chanting made up words into the air, inviting spirits to speak with me.

I didn't yet know that this mundane existence my family had created was the product of careful decisions to separate us from the worlds of chaos from which we'd come. I didn't know that I was opening a door my ancestors had intentionally closed, that the strange shadow in my corner would continue to grow in strength.

My parents were born in Colombia and Cuba, which didn't set me apart from the other kids at school, who were mostly children of immigrants themselves. But I had a sense that there were secrets my family wouldn't tell me, and for some reason, I was afraid to ask. Besides some old photos, they brought no heirlooms that I could use to access family memory. To them, progress was a constant newness, the cold and hard aesthetic of Miami in the early 1990s: glass walls, marble floors, granite countertops. Even our decorations were marble, like the little eggs my parents placed on pedestals around the house. We weren't allowed to play with them, but sometimes I would sneak them into my palm, feeling their weight as I warmed them, imagining I might one day hatch a baby alligator made of alabaster.

We'd routinely throw out perfectly good stuff to make room for new stuff. I think of all those shards of recyclable material in the landfill. Maybe now, decades later, they're finally escaping their temporary prison and returning to the earth. What if the shadow I see is energy, old memory, trapped like the tons of our things that can't decompose, contained as they are in all that plastic? Can I undo whatever curse is holding it in place and set it free?

As a teen I swung on an accelerating pendulum of fear and ennui. That's when I decided I would absorb the shadow and become a witch myself—one sweaty morning, paralyzed in my bed, overwhelmed by my changing body. Being a witch was the solution to all my problems. I'd once and for all refuse the sterile life around me, the endless big-box consumerism and the nine-to-fives. I'd learn the skills I needed to face the shadows, like Sailor Moon and Buffy the Vampire Slayer.

I escaped my awkward reality through the fantasies of pop "occulture." To my excitement, the witch had arisen as an icon of goth and grunge subcultures in the late '90s. Suddenly, being a witch was just the right degree of taboo for a rebellious teen. The witch was the only aesthetic that fit my in-betweenness, and like a whole subset of girls of my generation, I dressed like the witches from shows like *Charmed* and movies like *The Craft*. Dog collars and baby tees. Flowy skirts with combat boots. I wanted to get deeper than superficial experimentation, but I wasn't sure where to turn for spiritual guidance.

I wrangled my few friends into a coven. (It really takes off if you mimic a fictional one and each choose a character.) We sat in circles and chanted our poems as spells. We concocted smelly potions that we sprayed onto the lockers of the girls we didn't like. We hexed the exes who broke our hearts and reserved the nicer-smelling potions for love spells. And we had crystals, of course. Each kind of crystal imbued us with different powers, we said. We didn't care to find out if this gorgeous pyrite that increases intelligence might have come from a mine letting loose millions of gallons of acid into drinking water.

We were just girls. We were the children of immigrants. I was the whitest of them all, which I got from the relentless Spanish genes on my father's Cuban side. I was called *gringa* and *mona*. My Colombian cousins on my mother's side were darker and gorgeous, with deep, dark eyes and thick hair. My skin felt so thin in comparison to theirs, which never burned. Two of their mothers, my favorite aunts, were inseparable, and I thought them Amazonian goddesses. For a time, they shared a master bedroom from which they reigned the house like a pair of queens.

I could live in the curve of their hips, the forest of their hair. They told me I was beautiful for my light skin and green eyes and that these things would take me far. That's what I had to do, they said—get ahead for the family. But I felt small and exposed next to them, like a snail without its shell. Looking White *did* help me assimilate to American life faster than my cousins. White was new, a passport. Over time, Spanglish was the most I could muster of my mother tongue.

Now, I see Spanglish as a spellwork of sorts, a rejection of two colonizer languages in favor of something in between, something my own.

One night, my mother and aunts took me to Catholic mass where people dropped to the floor with the Holy Spirit. After, at a house nearby, they made me stay outside as they consulted someone dressed all in white. They appeared with something wrapped in burlap (and covered in blood?) and they told me not to tell anyone where we'd been. In my family, brujas were associated with dark magic and openly shunned, so they were sought in secret.

Years later, I drove around town in search of brujas myself, but nobody had "witch" just written on their doors, so I had to be satisfied with the esoteric book shops run by older White ladies whose histories and homelands were so different from mine. They wore loose, flowing clothes and kept cabinets of herbs I'd never heard of and displayed books and books about Wicca.

I built my magic on my own. I read all the books I could find, science and new age ones alike. Learning about the force of an alligator's bite felt the same as learning about the planets of astrology. I held on to the word *bruja* because it was more right than the witch I associated with paganism, but I didn't identify with it openly because my practice wasn't the brujería that seemed to equally scare and attract my family.

As an initiation of sorts, I carved the word into my closet of secrets: B R U J A. I didn't know it, but I was one of thousands of dormant little witches all over the country, and years later, we would start to show ourselves.

★ ✸ ★

Every couple of decades, the witch syncs up with feminist movements. In the 1960s and '70s, the witch was rebranded as a symbol of women's rights, antiestablishment politics, and environmental stewardship. In the late 1990s, the witch embodied a segment of a generation of teens pushing the boundaries of fashion, sexuality, and mental health awareness. In the 2010s, as a new intersectional feminism emerged, so did the new witch. She stands at the borders of complicated racial, class, and gender identities. She's a reflection of the feminism of these times, always shifting in response to political, social, and environmental problems.

During this time of great political and environmental upheaval, the witch is back and stronger than ever. Maybe this time, she's not just a fleeting trend. Pam Grossman, author of *Waking the Witch* and host of the popular podcast *The Witch Wave*, suggests that the witch is here to stay, as she's a reflection of a new wave of feminism that is not likely to subside but to grow and evolve as we continue to challenge our institutions. A March 2020 *Atlantic* article, "Why Witchcraft Is on the Rise," makes the case that interest in the supernatural increases during periods of instability marked by distrust of the establishment. Days after I read the article, the country went into lockdown for the COVID-19 pandemic, and later, Black Lives Matter protests disrupted every city in the nation. Witches took to IGTV and TikTok to hex police officers and cast protection spells over protestors.

Witchcraft is "out" in the public eye more than ever. There was even suggestion that one of Kamala Harris's family members would sage the Capitol after President Joe Biden's inauguration, to clear the negative energy from the Trump supporters who had stormed it.

Not long ago, witchcraft could get you killed. *Witchcraft* was a bad word, a dangerous word that colonizers used to demonize Indigenous practices or denounce progressive ideals. The word *witch* is derived from Old English, and it was largely used by those in power to call out and persecute people throughout history. *Witch* was thrown like a curse onto those who lived close to the land, who fulfilled the roles of healers and spiritual guides for their communities. Some were labeled witches even when they had no tie to magic. They were persecuted in the tens of thousands for living outside social norms—for doing men's work, for experimenting with healing modalities, for being queer, for threatening church and state. They stood on trial across Europe and, famously, in Salem, Massachusetts. They were blamed for illnesses unknown, misdiagnosed as demonic possession and witchcraft.

The cure was banishment or execution.

In the mid-twentieth century, the witch began to shed its negative connotation as Pagan Witchcraft and modern-day Wicca developed in England and took root in the United States shortly after. In the 1970s the Reclaiming movement in San Francisco centered the Goddess in political activism, forever binding the feminist with the witch, and Wicca is now observed as an official religion in the United Kingdom, United States, and Canada. Feminists have succeeded in taking the word *witch* back from the mouths of persecutors, and they have brought hidden practices to the open, in defense of many ways of life. The witch is no longer the Halloween caricature, the one with the pointy hat and the mole and the cauldron.

Feminist witches are breaking free of stereotypes and religious stigma. They are figures of empowerment. Their magic is associated with natural science, self-care rituals, and activism. They have expanded beyond Europe and Wicca, representing a new age of spirituality that blends many backgrounds and rituals and follows no dogmatic rules.

A MAGICAL ANCESTRY

The story of the feminist witch continues to be refreshed, reflected most recently in television reboots like *Chilling Adventures of Sabrina*.

But as mainstream feminism still struggles to fully adopt intersectionality in practice, so does the mainstream witch, which centers the White cisgender female experience. The Anglo-Saxon witch is not everybody's witch.

Witches of color—comprising Black, Afro-Caribbean, and Latinx witches and spiritual practitioners of Indigenous ancestry—are increasingly reclaiming their ancestries and speaking out against the internalized colonialism, cultural appropriation, and spiritual consumerism that mars mainstream spirituality. At the heart of the trend is an enduring yearning among witches of color to reconnect to the old ways of their ancestors. While some grew up initiated into family religions, many have been disconnected from their ancestral practices for a generation or more, so White spirituality sometimes serves as a sort of scaffolding for mystical exploration.

Though Wicca is a religion distinct from witchcraft (which is a practice), many witches of color have turned to Wicca or other pagan religions for their established rituals and days of observance. Some begin their spiritual exploration through yoga, leading them to Eastern religions like Hinduism and Buddhism. Some enter through new age spins on established practices like tarot or astrology. They often mix these things with the Christianity or Catholicism they were indoctrinated into in childhood.

As their online communities grow, witches of color are gaining confidence in the unique perspectives they have to offer. Though they might draw inspiration from and develop in response to the popular White witch, they reject the whitewashed "love and light" spirituality that pervades social media. Instead, they nurture conversations about shadow work, which involves honestly facing fears, traumas, and death. More and more, they are paying homage to the rich histories of their specific tribal and homeland traditions and speaking out.

Some of them, like Sabel, are calling themselves brujas. Brujas are born in the US. They are born in the Caribbean. They are born in Mexico, in Central America, in South America. Their skin is brown, red, yellow, white. They speak Spanish and English and Creole and Nahuatl. They are female. They are male. They are gender nonconforming. They are queer. They are Catholic. They reject Catholicism. They have ancestors of Yoruba. They were brought up with Indigenous wisdom. They have been disconnected from their homelands. They feel a calling to magic, so they reach for what they can. There's one thing they all have in common: the power of their ancestors, which runs through everything they touch.

Brujas know that the land Columbus stumbled on was far from the "New World," that the systems of our world were built on the lands of people who were around for centuries before the colonizers arrived and through the sweat of the enslaved people brought across the ocean. Brujas know that their memories exist on the land of their ancestry, in the rocks and soil and waters of their past. Power is not an individual possession.

It comes from the ancestors.

INITIATION RITUAL

Everybody has ancestors and the ability to connect with them. To become initiated into your unique ancestral path, you must first open the line of connection between you and your ancestors. If you have access to a tradition or religion that you are connected to through your ancestry or community, you might ask an elder or mentor what steps you can take to become formally initiated onto your path. But you do not need external validation to begin your practice. All you need is the intention to embody the spirituality of your ancestors, whatever that looks like for you.

This can feel scary, like "coming out," especially if your family has a negative view of magical ancestral practices. Coming out is not usually just one moment but a series of moments that range from the most private time alone to public declarations. Follow your intuition about what you're ready for.

The only point of caution I will offer is that you remain true to what is yours. There is no need to assume the culture or ancestors of others with whom you're unfamiliar. When you are first starting your practice, choose ancestors you have known and loved. Not all ancestors are helpful or easy to work with. If you do not feel connected to your own blood ancestors, there are always helping spirits that you can access through your own cultural connections. Do you have teachers and mentors in your community? Who were their teachers? Do you study a particular lineage of philosophy or spirituality? Perhaps there are historical figures you can turn to. Ancestors sometimes appear to us outside our blood family. Maybe they aren't even human. Traditionally, ancestors are spirits of the dead, but for our purposes, ancestors can be deities or plant spirits or even imagined or fictional characters who feel ancestral. Whatever your entry point, ancestral magic is stronger when you have an organic connection to your ancestors.

You might try this simple ritual first, adding or removing elements as you see fit. All initiation and intention rituals are most powerful around new moons, when the sky is dark. You will need paper and pen, a mirror, a candle, a lighter, and a safe surface on which to burn paper, like an ashtray.

1. Find or create an artifact that reminds you of the ancestor or the ancestral practice that you would like to connect with. This could be a photograph or an heirloom. It could be a book written by someone in your ancestry or from your spiritual tradition. It could be something you find on a nature walk.

2. On a piece of paper write down what tapping into your ancestral magic means to you. This might include details about your ancestry and how you plan to reconnect to it. You might include a spiritual leader you wish to emulate, a specific practice you want to learn, or a personal or family difficulty or trauma that

you would like to transmute. Be specific and include a time frame if it applies, as all intentions are more powerful when you are clear.

3. Light a candle. This can be any candle, or it can be something that represents your ancestry, like an altar candle to a specific deity. Or you can choose a color that represents you in some way. When in doubt, go with a white candle, which represents clarity.

4. Stand or sit in front of a mirror in a safe, well ventilated, and private space with your ancestral artifact, candle, and written intention. This might be at your altar if you have one. If not, no worries! You'll learn how to set up your ancestral altar in the next chapter. If you already have other ancestral objects on hand, you might also want to set those in front of the mirror.

5. Take a few deep breaths as you look into your eyes. Then light your intention with the flame of the candle as you speak, "Ancestors, I call you to me for guidance and support. Ancestors, I call you to me so that I may honor you." You may adjust this or use your ancestors' names. Do what feels natural.

6. Drop your intention in the ashtray and sit with it until it burns, relighting if necessary. You can repeat your mantra, or you can hold an image of an ancestor in your mind. You might sit the whole time the candle burns if it is a small one, or when you're done, you can snuff it out and relight later as needed. Take this time to thank your ancestors before you close your ritual.

You can repeat this ritual any time you feel your connection to your ancestors waning or when you would like to initiate a particular step along your spiritual journey.

ARIES: THE SPARK

Aries is the first sign of the zodiac, so it is the initiator, associated with courage, drive, and passion. It rules the first house of the astrological wheel, which corresponds to beginnings, early childhood, appearance, and identity. Arians are eternally childlike. They are sometimes mischaracterized as reckless, but they are sensitive to injustice and will fight to protect those they love. Use the power of Aries when you need a little spark to initiate a project or goal, or to call in positive energy, authenticity, and an innocent love of the world.

ELEMENT: Cardinal fire

PLANETARY RULER: Mars

AFFIRMATION: "I am"

FOR YOUR ALTAR: Peppers, spices, fire, warrior deities, the ram, red and orange stones, stimulating scents

JOURNAL: Write a list of the identities you've assumed throughout your life. Try to write them as they come to mind, without editing them. When you are done, take stock. Have you outgrown any of your identities? Which feel like they come from inside, and which feel imposed by others' expectations? Do any conflict? Is anything missing? Is something new emerging?

INITIATION GUIDES

Tarot and astrology are rich entry points for the beginning bruja. I recommend visiting The Hoodwitch (@thehoodwitch, thehoodwitch .com), run by Bri Luna. The Hoodwitch offers astrology and tarot readings, but the real power of the platform is in the way it helps new witches and brujas embrace "everyday magic" with confidence and power.

For more information on rituals, check out Michael Cardenas of Olde Ways (@oldeways, oldeways.net), a clairvoyant and medium who posts invaluable tips about altars, energy work, and rituals. He also offers spellwork and group service rituals.

If you're looking for a tarot deck, consider decks by creators of color, like The Afro Tarot, The Hoodoo Tarot, or the AKAMARA. Reference @browngirltarot for a full catalogue of "melanated decks."

OCCULT POWERS

At age ninety-six, Elvira Llaurado had long reigned as our family's tiny matriarch. I loved her not only because she was my nicest abuelita, but also because she was so old. Her hair was a perfect white poof; her eyes had gone light blue with cataracts. She remembered everything—birthdays, anniversaries, phone numbers. I knew that she held a world of memories, strange things that weren't documented in the few photo albums I'd already scoured. But like so many older Cubans in Miami, she didn't speak much of the past.

She had been a spirit medium in Santiago de Cuba in the mid-1900s, and I tried asking her about the shadow in my room once. She had given up channeling spirits when her daughter, my grandmother Elsie, died of cancer in her early forties, before my birth. I didn't have details. When I finally summoned the courage to ask her about the shadow, near the end of her life and the beginning of my adulthood, she told me to close my eyes and pray when the shadow appeared. She never told me who to pray to. Her life and work in Cuba would remain a negative space in my history, like the dark spots in an old reel of film, indicators that something went missing in the changeover from our past to our new way of life.

What I knew of her came mostly from my father's stories, but he was recalling memories from a distant childhood. They seemed like dreams to me. When he was a kid in Santiago, a stranger looked into his rare green eyes, speaking what my father couldn't have known was a spell.

"Que bonitos ojos tienes."

What pretty eyes you have.

The next morning, he couldn't open his eyes. Over the following weeks, his parents and grandparents took him to every doctor they knew, but none could get his eyes to open. Suspecting black magic was at play, Elvira called on the support of other spirit mediums, known to my father as "the circle of brujas."

They placed my father in the middle of their circle and chanted prayers to lift the spell of the evil eye until, finally, his eyes opened. He remembers seeing a hazy ring of women towering around him, dressed all in white, his grandmother in the center.

The way Elvira looked the last time I saw her is a visual heirloom. She sits calmly in a rattan chair, a luminous royal, her past full of colonial drawing rooms and mythic spiritual battles forever unknown to me. She already sees the afterworld to which she is headed. I run my thumb along the little bones of her hand, and that's what stays with me the most, the way her skin easily slips along her skeleton, a thin veil ready to part.

Just close your eyes and pray, I hear her tell me again and again, and rose-colored visions of secret rituals dissipate in the harsh light of the ordinary world. Something bad had happened many decades before to make her leave her practice, something she took to the grave. When she died in 2006, a thread of my ancestry was torn.

The ways of the old country were lost to me.

✶ ✹ ✶

Cuba is really the land of the Taíno. Many words that conjure the Caribbean and the US South are Taíno words. Mangrove. Iguana. Tobacco. Hurricane comes from the Arawakan word *huricán,* the god of evil.

It was easy enough to associate the one-hundred-mile-per-hour winds that tore through their homes with a bad entity; what was less clear to the Taíno was that the Spaniards that landed on their shores in 1492 were a far more destructive force for which they didn't yet have a name.

The Taíno were the largest group of Indigenous people of the Caribbean. When Christopher Columbus encountered them for the first time on his exploration of the "New World," he erroneously called them "Indians" because, well, he thought he'd landed in Indonesia.

Archaeological evidence suggests that the Taíno originated from the Amazon Basin or the Andes before they migrated through Central America to the Caribbean. They were a matrilineal society that worshipped goddesses and ancestral spirits, which they called *zemí.* They loved nature as they loved their bodies, with a practical reverence for the way it sustained their precious, temporary lives. They created physical zemís to represent the spiritual forms they worshipped, and their rituals were beautiful and heart centered. Women were the leaders, made the decisions, and established the family lines. Columbus's account describes them as "always smiling."

On his second voyage to the Caribbean, he exploited this kindness, requiring each Taíno individual to pay him an *encomienda*, a tribute of gold every few months. They were also forced into hard labor with the "reward" of conversion to Catholicism. Those who did not cooperate were punished by mutilation or death. Many died of famine and disease from overwork on new sugar plantations. If they fled, they were hunted down, and women, once free and powerful, were raped and sold.

Within decades the Indigenous population of the Caribbean was all but gone, as European colonialists overworked, abused, infected, starved, and executed the Taíno. With their numbers dwindled to nearly nothing, the Spanish crown and the Catholic Church gave the blessing to use slave labor to keep the sugar industry going, which led to the first documented forced removal of people from Africa.

Millions of Africans were enslaved and taken to the Caribbean in the ensuing centuries. One of the largest groups were the Yoruba people from Western Africa (present-day Nigeria, Benin, and Togo), who had a strong oral tradition that they were able to preserve despite separation and fragmentation across the islands. Their traditional religion, Orisha-Ifá, forms the foundation of the most practiced Afro-Caribbean religions in the United States and across Latin America today, including Cuban Lucumí/Santería, Haitian Vodou, and Brazilian Candomblé.

The transatlantic slave trade also spread decentralized African folk practices like plant medicine, rootwork, divination, and the worship of Vodun, or "spirit" in the Fon and Ewe languages. Across the Caribbean and the United States, the African veneration of ancestor spirits and nature has contributed to many other religions, such as Palo (also known as Palo Monte, Palo Mayombe, and Las Reglas de Congo) and has influenced spiritual systems of healing, like Obeah, Espiritismo, and Hoodoo.

Because of the African tendency to add to their spiritual practices when in contact with other religions, and because their traditions have been passed down orally, it's not easy to untangle the threads of the mainland African traditions from all the religions and systems of spirituality they've influenced. Before the slave trade and the horrors of colonialism on the African continent, the African orientation to spirituality was largely open and inviting. Over time, Africans needed to keep their ancestral traditions secret in order to preserve them against the powers of colonialism and enslavement.

The West African cosmos, which is still one of the greatest sources of the Caribbean imagination today, includes interactions between divinities, spirits, ancestors, humans, animals, and natural forces. All religions and systems that descend from this cosmos are ancestral based; the dead and living can communicate, and the ancestors can influence human affairs. In the Yoruba tradition, Olodumare is the supreme being who placed *orishas*, or deity spirits, on earth.

THE SEVEN AFRICAN POWERS

There are countless orishas in the Yoruba pantheon, but a handful have risen above the rest, powerful archetypes that have helped people connect to the divine. These are known as the "seven African powers." Because African wisdom was passed down orally and there is no written text, you'll see their names spelled in a variety of ways. If you want to learn more about the orishas, The Ashe Shop (@theasheshop) is a great resource.

Elegua, also known as Eshu or Legba, is often called the trickster orisha and represents the beginning and the end of life, or the opening and closing of paths. Elegua is called on first in ceremonies because he holds the doors to communication with other orishas. His colors are red and black.

Obatala, blessed by Olodumare to create earth and mankind, is said to have saved humans from destruction time and again. He is associated with the head and dreams. His color is white, and he is patron of the ceiba tree.

Yemaya, or Yemoja, is the great mother who rules over the seas and all life-giving water. She is nurturing and can be terrifying when protecting her children, manifesting as floods or tidal waves. Her colors are blue and white.

Shango is the orisha of fire, lightning, thunder, and war and the patron of drumming and dancing. He is a royal ancestor of the Yoruba people, and he represents beauty and passion. His colors are red and white.

Oshun is the orisha of love and sweetness. Yemaya, her older sister, granted her dominion over rivers. She represents joy and exuberance. She is the youngest orisha, and she is sometimes called the queen of the witches. Her colors are yellow and gold.

Ogun was believed to be the first orisha to descend to earth. He is often portrayed as a blacksmith, and his symbols are iron, the dog, and the palm frond, as he was said to clear the forests on earth to make way for the orishas.

Oya, sometimes syncretized with Ochossi and Orunmila, is the orisha of winds and storms, and she brings change to humans. She is the fiercest of the female orishas and fights alongside Shango. She guards the boundaries between life and death. She wears a multicolored skirt, with which she creates tornadoes.

Orishas carry the cosmic energy, *ashé* (which translates to "so let it be," often said at the end of prayers or for emphasis). When children are born, an orisha accompanies them, known as the guardian of their head. Possession is a routine part of communicating with *egun*, the spirits of ancestors. In Santería, priests (*babalawo*) and priestesses (*iyalawo*), who have gone through the initiation of *kariocha*, allow themselves to be possessed while in trance for the benefit of their communities. The orishas speak through them, becoming manifest through the body (called the caballo, or "horse") of a living being. It is a kind of sacrifice on the part of the *santero*, or the practitioner of Santería, to give up individual consciousness in order to facilitate communication between the spirits and their audience.

It's said Olodumare placed orishas on earth to mediate for humans. Indeed, the Caribbean was in need of spiritual mediation. It experienced a storm of change, as the Indigenous people were expeditiously replaced by very different peoples from across the Atlantic Ocean. For these terrible reasons, its earth is enchanted, as it absorbed the bodies and stories of millions of people whose ancestral lines were disrupted. Most were not properly honored in death, and to this day, we walk on their unmarked graves.

To come from this land, then, is to carry unfinished business.

Juliet Diaz speaks to plants.

When she was in grade school, her teacher pulled a plant out of the dirt to show the class the root system. Juliet had gotten herself to the plant's level. She was zoomed in, studying the hairs and the veins. When her teacher pulled at the plant's roots, she saw a mist form around it, like a watery aura, and through her left ear she heard screeching, like she had tapped into some new frequency. She understood that she was hearing the plant hurting, and she felt the pain herself. She started yelling for her teacher to stop, saying the plant was crying.

All the kids just stared.

"Don't you hear it?" Juliet asked.

That's when she realized that nobody else communicated with plants the way she did. From then on, she would hear the "negative" communication through her left ear and the "positive" communication through her right ear. It was not just plants. Juliet could sense spirits of all kinds: nature spirits, animal spirits, and the spirits of humans who have passed. It was overwhelming at first, because she didn't know how to control it. Her mom didn't understand.

"No seas tan loca," her mom would say. *Don't be so crazy.*

It was the 1980s in New Jersey. Her mother had a lot going on. She had arrived from Cuba on the Mariel boatlift, the mass emigration of Cubans to the United States. Juliet's father got into dealing drugs, and they were on welfare and always moving around to different project housing. The building Juliet remembers best was the Thirty-Ninth Street projects in Union City, a seven-story brick building surrounded by cemeteries. They provided hours of refuge from the busy streets. She retreated to them the way most kids took to parks or forests, creating a world of her imagination, watering the moss that covered the gravestones, returning home covered in dirt.

In 1986, when she was five years old, her father was killed in a drug-related execution. She was questioned by federal officials. Juliet doesn't know exactly what happened, but she was aware of the violence always on her periphery. Some of the men who lived in the projects were worse than others. She was sometimes scared to be alone with them. There are many things she still can't speak of. In moments of deep pain, Juliet escaped to a place in her mind, a jungle with a huge cliff with a raging waterfall. It was loud by the cliff. She allowed herself to be enveloped by the roar and the mist of her imagination.

When she was seven, Juliet tried to kill herself. She was having feelings far more complicated than what people thought a young person capable of at her age, and she had nobody to talk to about them. She felt that she didn't belong. She didn't understand how to communicate with people. She could hear their thoughts, but people would rarely say what they were really thinking. She learned to stop trusting them.

So one day, she walked up to the roof of her apartment building and stood on the ledge. A child with Down syndrome had just jumped out from the sixth floor and died, so she knew it would work. The ledge became the misty cliff, beckoning. The roar of the water filled her ears. She leaned forward to let herself fall and be swept away by the current.

Then a great wind came and knocked her onto her back. She landed hard. She lay looking up at the sky, and she saw yellow and white flowers falling, raining down on her and swirling around her body. They enveloped her like a hug. She heard "You belong here," and when she turned, there was moss on the ground, like the kind on the cemetery stones. Her tears were watering it.

"Don't ever do this again," she heard a voice say.

From then on, Juliet saw the magic in the earth. It raised her in the absence of her parents. The cemetery was her wonderland, full of animals and plants to explore. She remained close to her dead, and it felt like a gift. Her dad was buried there. They couldn't afford a gravestone for him, so Juliet marked the grave on her own with sticks and rocks. It was her first altar.

Try as she might, she wasn't able to make a connection with the spirit of her own father. But she promised her spirits, whom she talked to regularly, that she would never try to kill herself again. She would have to fight to keep that promise.

The ancestors had work for her.

★ ✹ ★

When Elvira's daughter, my grandmother Elsie, graduated with her teaching degree, she left her home in the heart of Santiago to teach the children of sugarcane farmers in the countryside, in a town called La Maya. Elsie's father was the harbormaster of Santiago, and her parents expected her to "marry well" into the upper-middle class. Instead, she married my grandfather, the youngest son of a sugarcane farmer. I like to think that in her was a streak of the revolutionary spirit that had permeated the surrounding Sierra Maestra, where Fidel Castro's forces hid while they gained strength.

The wooded countryside of Cuba has always represented resistance against the government. Long before the wilderness was a refuge to Castro's revolutionary forces, it was home to a large number of escaped Africans that the enslavers came to call *cimarrones*—wild ones. They formed communities in the thousands that freely practiced Lucumí, or Santería.

The word *Santería* started out as a derogatory imposition by the Catholic clergy in Cuba to distance the worship of African "saints" of Yoruba from the Christian god. Over time the term has shed its negative connotation, and many practitioners use it to describe the blending of Yoruba and Catholic pantheons. Santería has many names, including Regla de Ifá, Regla de Ocha, and Regla de Lucumí. It's believed that there are more practitioners of Santería than there are Catholics in the Caribbean. Since many saints and orishas have similar associations, Afro-Cubans have masked their worship of orishas with worship of

33

the saints, and they adopted Catholic rituals. This has preserved the Yoruba pantheon and the rituals that were made illegal for so long.

But in the rural parts of the island, Santería survived. To walk into the woods was to walk into the world of the orishas.

Elsie might have heard whispers of this spirituality from the dozens of children she taught around the countryside, but she was not connected to the spirituality of her mother. She was focused on her work, eager to help her students gain at least a basic level of literacy so they could keep up with the advances in the urban areas.

In December 1958 the rebel air force, led by Castro, fired down onto President Batista's soldiers in their headquarters in La Maya, forcing Elsie to flee with her husband and son, my father, who was one year old at the time. They rode a horse out of La Maya and crawled into a drainpipe at the outskirts of town and waited for the battle to end. Castro swept the nation. His troops marched into Havana waving the flag of the trickster orisha Elegua, a flag of the people. But when Castro solidified his power, the government distanced itself from Santería and imprisoned its followers, fearing that it could be a vehicle for counterrevolution.

As the years passed, it became clear to Elsie that things would only grow worse for her family. Castro had not kept all his promises, and life wasn't getting better as far as she could tell. She felt her freedom slipping away. She had to let the children and her land go.

She sent my father on one of the first Freedom Flights to Miami, and eventually, she also went into exile, leaving behind the little school in the countryside for an unknown life in the United States. But a disease had been quietly growing inside her. Not long after settling in

New York, she was diagnosed with ovarian cancer. She died in 1974, at the age of forty-one.

A few days later, Elvira would try to contact her daughter Elsie from the dead. It would be her last séance.

Like a lot of old-school spiritual practitioners, Elvira would probably object to my calling her a bruja, and I wonder what she would think about my "reclaiming" her practices. She practiced Espiritismo, a spiritual system that she used while maintaining her status as a Christian. Espiritismo in Cuba is closely related to the Spiritism movement of nineteenth-century Europe founded by Allan Kardec, which was on the rise at the same time as Victorian science and invention. Kardec's Spiritism is characterized by a belief in the afterlife, in reincarnation, and in spirit guides. There is a distinct material and spiritual world, and the spirit medium accesses the spirit world through her guides.

By the late nineteenth century, séances were all the rage in Europe and the United States, and some spirit mediums even took their show on the road, entertaining the middle and upper classes alike in drawing rooms around the world. These ideas also appealed to liberal, urban populations of Latin America, especially Brazil and the Caribbean countries, which were officially Catholic. Catholicism already centered on a belief in saints, and Spiritism created a bridge between mainstream Catholicism and Indigenous- and African-based religions, forming a syncretic spirituality that stressed the importance of the dead, ancestors, and spirit guides.

The Latin American iteration of Spiritism was more political than its counterpart in the global north; in many ways, it was a reaction to the Catholic Church's collusion with corrupt governments. Espiritismo became a resistance to the oppression of more overtly African practices, but in some ways, it hypocritically adopted the methods of the colonizer, whitewashing rituals to serve middle- and upper-class whims and economies.

In Cuba the Afro-Cuban traditions lent Espiritismo, also known as Mesa Blanca (white table), its language for describing the spirits of the dead and orishas, as well as its rituals of dancing and chanting for the ancestors. The *misa espiritual* (spiritual mass), used to invoke the dead and possess the living through song and prayer, is at its core an Afro-Cuban rite that united the lower and middle classes of Cuba.

Espiritismo de Cordon is a branch of Espiritismo practiced in the Oriente Province, where Elvira grew up. In Cordon, which literally means "cord" or "string," trance and ritual are more central than in other traditions of Espiritismo. Each practitioner possesses a chain of spirits, and to access those spirits, rituals are carried out with a circle of practitioners who hold hands, dance, and chant together. This is consistent with the rituals my father told me he witnessed as a child.

Spirit mediums, or *espiritistas*, like my great-grandmother connected the living with their deceased loved ones with the help of *muertos*, the spirits of once-living humans. These spirits appear to the mediums during their initiation and act as gatekeepers to other spirits. During a séance, there are multiple mediums—the muertos and the espiritista—and they seem to merge into one being as the medium falls into trance. My father remembers Elvira transforming into her muertos during her séances. It was as if someone else emerged from deep inside of her and pressed up against her skin, with their own expressions and mannerisms. Cordon practitioners usually undergo a strong initiation. Some have reported seeing shadows before initiation, and after training in ritual technologies, the shadows clarify into specific entities. The medium animates a shared past between these entities and the community, enacting stories that are unfinished and untold. During a misa, the medium works to find resolution in these relationships and stories.

Mediumship is a performance between the medium and the spirit world, often of grief, to help the living carry on.

On the night after Elsie's death, in Elvira's new home in Brighton Beach, New York, she called for whiskey and a cigar in voices that weren't her own. They were the voices of her spirit guardians, an Afro-Caribbean couple who spoke deeply accented Spanish. When they spoke through Elvira, her face changed, and she was no longer the subdued lady that everyone in the family turned to for guidance. She was unpredictable. She was loud. She was too much contained in too little a body.

She sat at the head of a table covered in a white cloth, candles burning throughout the room. Her husband, son, and grandson sat around the table, waiting for her to make a connection. After her guardians consumed their ritual whiskey and cigar, they began the call to Elsie.

Before long, they made a connection, but the voice coming through was not Elsie. It was something angry and desperate for a body. The candles flickered, casting strange shadows on the wall. Elvira's guardians were yelling. They couldn't control the angry spirit. Elvira's body lurched onto the table, then careened back toward the wall. She was tossed around the room. Then she fell to the floor.

The connection was severed. Elvira never channeled again.

In our exile, we cut the thread between us and our family in Cuba. I wonder if something about the transition hurt Elsie, like a curse. My parents tell me that shortly after I was born, Elsie came to visit me from the afterlife. They watched as the chair next to my crib began to rock on its own, and they just knew it was Elsie. My dad gave me her name. *Lorraine Elsie.* I think when we are named after ancestors like this, we are meant to live the life they couldn't.

I'd like to say that I have called on Elsie as an ancestor spirit, the way I call on her mother, Elvira. But her death broke the ancestral chain, and I have felt the weight of carrying her name. She is more of a haunting than a guardian spirit.

Elvira's grief had torn her open and left her vulnerable to attack. Who knows what she experienced in that last moment with the spirits, as she desperately tried to reach her daughter one last time? What happens when the thread of a family line breaks, when someone dies too soon? When goodbyes cannot be said and wisdom cannot be passed down?

Where does all of that energy go?

The word occult has its roots in the Latin *occultus*, meaning "hidden, secret." In many occult practices, the rituals that are concealed and kept private are said to contain the most power. Throughout the Caribbean and the Americas, the practitioners of African and Indigenous traditions have occulted their magic for centuries by mixing it or masking it with the dominant religions of their regions, especially Catholicism.

They have done this to avoid persecution, to privately defy the powers that ruled the public sphere, or to assimilate to their colonizers' worlds and to the places to which they moved in exile.

This mixing might be the reason the Taíno didn't fully die out. It was originally believed that they became extinct following European colonization and the introduction of the slave trade. However now scholars believe that the Taíno only withstood a "paper genocide," as the Census excluded them, but they continued to mix with other ethnic groups. Recent DNA testing has proved that there is Taíno blood in many living people throughout the Caribbean and their descendants in the US.

Juliet Diaz is one of them.

Although the Taíno population did not survive colonialism as a distinct ethnic group, their culture survives in the rituals of Afro-Caribbean religions. Witchcraft might have meant something different and more sinister to original practitioners of Afro-Caribbean traditions, but now it's increasingly used as an inclusive term that summons Indigenous ancestral power. This reclamation has been happening for some time within European witchcraft, and now, as African traditions are coming out from hiding, a new generation of practitioners is reclaiming the terms *witchcraft* and *brujería*, associating them with positive healing practices.

Juliet has transformed her sensitivity into a living, working as a spiritual medium and forming communities of witches and healers through her various platforms. Her first book, *Witchery: Embrace the Witch Within*, is a bestseller in the magical community. She has a big following on social media, where she shares her talents for seeing spirits and her extensive plant knowledge. In her second book, *Plant Witchery*, Juliet distills the wisdom of her years of experience with plants. She has over four hundred plants herself, which line the walls of every room of her home.

But not everything has been easy. Juliet was recently diagnosed with lupus, and the disease affected her thyroid gland. Her mortality continues to challenge her, but she now sees illness as a spiritual opportunity. She thinks getting sick was a sign from her ancestors that she was working herself into the ground, doing too much at once. She's taken the hint and started to slow down and care for herself.

"I want to show my kids what it means to heal," she says.

She teaches them the ways of the Taíno, that they are nature, manifested. Nurturing their bodies is the first step in healing their peoples' past, though some wounds never fully heal.

Juliet has been initiated as a *bohuiti*, or "healer," of her tribe, Higuayagua. She was recently profiled in a National Geographic photography series of the surviving Taíno people. Her existence proves that ancestral magic can be kept safe despite every effort to eradicate it.

"They named me Bawainaru, which means 'Ocean Woman,'" Juliet says. "People know me for plants now, but that name is so perfect, because I've always had that strong connection to water."

On January 18, 2019, at the first Indigenous Peoples March in DC, Juliet spoke to the crowd. "All of our ancestors, they don't see separation," she said. Hers is one of many tribes fighting for the environment and other causes through the Indigenous Peoples Movement, whose mission is to show how Indigenous issues are everyone's issues. On the IPM website is this quote from Chief Seattle: "Humankind has not woven the web of life. We are but one thread within it. Whatever we do to the web, we do to ourselves. All things are bound together. All things connect."

Right now, Indigenous peoples are fighting for the fate of our planet and for the fate of humans. In Alaska the Tlingit protect the Tongass National Forest from deforestation by the lumber industry. The Sioux tribe and their allies have been protesting the Dakota Access oil pipeline for years on end. Due to their efforts, the project was halted by the Obama administration, but the Trump administration allowed construction of the pipeline to resume. Because of the Sioux's continued resistance, a judge has again ordered the pipeline to be shut down.

This is the way Juliet has decided to live for her ancestors, to stand in for the earth and to show people a different way to relate to nature. The most painful moments of her life have helped her to uncover the secrets of her ancestors. She brings those secrets out from hiding, sharing them generously and with enthusiasm for the future.

During the COVID-19 lockdown, her father finally appeared to her. He told her that he had been trying to get out of drug dealing and do better by her, but it was too late. He said he was hiding from her all those years because he was trying to forgive himself. He wasn't ready to show himself. Juliet cried and cried as she spoke to her father. For the first time, she felt closure, and a huge shadow lifted from her life.

Her father is still buried in Palisades Cemetery next to the projects where she grew up. In December 2020 she ordered him a gravestone.

THE ANCESTRAL ALTAR

Connecting to your ancestors is the first step in your magical practice. It grounds your practice and helps you pay homage to who came before. Prior to setting up an ancestral altar, you'll want to research your ancestry through stories of your family, photos, or archives. If you don't feel a connection to your family—because either you don't know them or you are estranged from them for some reason—research a philosophy that you feel close to and read the works from teachers in that ancestry. Whatever your entry point, it's important that you have an authentic connection to your ancestors, rather than appropriating others' heritage or beliefs.

Gather a few artifacts that represent this ancestry, like books, photos, or heirlooms. At first it's best to limit these artifacts to ancestors you know directly, whether in person or through their works. They should be beings whom you have a good relationship with. Not all ancestors are beneficial, and working with unknown ancestors is high magic best reserved for those with more experience.

Please note: there's a difference between ancestors and guardian spirits. They might overlap, but generally ancestors are blood related or belong to a lineage to which you are initiated or are culturally tied to. Ancestors can be guardian spirits, but not all are. Guardian spirits can take many forms—animal, nature, angelic, godly. Again, don't worry if you don't know who your guardians are. We're here to set up an ancestral altar, and you'll start with what you know.

Ancestral altars are physical spaces in the home that honor the dead, where one can remember and commune with passed loved ones. I find that tending to my altar is an act of service and love for my ancestors. It connects me to them and to the earth and reminds me of what's important. I lovingly move through my house to find beautiful offerings for them, sometimes while singing or recalling a fond memory. Ancestral altars vary depending on the tradition, but there are a few common components of every altar. Follow these steps to begin a simple ancestral altar, and then build upon it intuitively as you develop your own personal practice of ancestral connection.

1. Find a place in your home for your altar, preferably a private and safe space that you will feel comfortable visiting on a daily basis. You might want to clear the energy of your space with a sustainable smoke bundle.

2. Find a table that will fit this space. This can be as small or big as you'd like, preferably made of wood or glass. Clean the table with a solution of Florida water or rose water or a blessing oil.

3. Place a cloth made of natural fibers on your altar. Traditionally the cloth is white, but you may use anything you'd like.

4. Place the ancestral objects that you've gathered on the table, arranging them in a way that feels right to you.

5. If you have a strong relationship with a spirit or deity, you may represent them on the altar. This could take many forms, including small statues, cards, and candles. It's important, especially at first, not to mix too many at once. You should be working with a deity at the time you place them on your altar.

6. Divination tools like tarot cards are common on the altar and provide an organic method for daily interaction with your altar. You might pull a card a day, for instance.

7. Elemental offerings to the ancestors are standard. I like to represent all four—water, fire, earth, and air (and some include a fifth, space). For water, it's common to fill a wine glass of water, and liquor is also customary, though it may be reserved for special occasions. For fire, you might use candles. For earth, I like to offer food or flowers, usually something from my garden. Air and space offerings always make for the most interesting ones, because you must use your imagination. I like to offer things that travel through air and space to reach us, like light from a nice lamp or sound from a small bell.

Refresh your altar on a steady schedule—maybe it's every day or every week. Special offerings and rituals are powerful on new and full moons and on seasonal points like equinoxes and solstices.

TAURUS: THE BUILDER

Taurus is the most sensory-oriented sign of the zodiac, using the resources at hand to create a sustainable and beautiful life. It is the ruler of the second house of astrology, which is associated with possessions and material abundance. Taureans are incredibly self-reliant, and though they appreciate transient connections, they will wait for a love that lasts. While generally perceived as slow moving, Taureans will charge toward what they want. Call on Taurus to work with nature and to generate a long-term connection to what really matters.

ELEMENT: Fixed earth

PLANETARY RULER: Venus

AFFIRMATION: "I have"

FOR YOUR ALTAR: Garden herbs, rose, honey, love deities, the bull, white and green stones, decadent sensory experiences

JOURNAL: Go on a walk and find a raw material like stone or wood. Take it home and sit with it. What is your relationship to the material? Can you mold it? Add to it? What does it want to be?

ALTAR MAGICK

There is so much information out there about how to create your altar, and it varies depending on the tradition. I appreciate the accessibility of the resources that Sen Elias of Crescent City Conjure (@crescentcityconjure, crescentcityconjure.us) posts about ancestral altars and the dressing of candles. Haus of Hoodoo (@hausofhoodoo, hausofhoodoo.com) is run by Vodou mambo Jessyka Winston and offers gorgeous and powerful altar items, as well as highly coveted spiritual consultations and rare insight into ancestral spiritualities. If you're ever in New Orleans, I recommend dropping into their shops in person for an unforgettable experience. Taylor Cordova (@theflower childbruja, theflowerchildbruja.com) has a beautiful online botanica of altar products, curated by a self-described earth magick bruja.

3

THE ANCESTRAL CURSE

For a year in the early 1990s, three generations of my maternal line lived under one roof, our bodies blurring into one, and my grandmother Ninoska would tell me scary stories about her childhood home in Colombia. They were cautionary tales. She mixed in fictional ones as if they were our own, like the tale of La Llorona, which she told me more than once at bedtime.

Hundreds of years ago, near her hometown of Soledad, Colombia, there was an Indigenous woman named Maria, known many villages over for her beauty. Every afternoon she bathed in the river. One day, a Spanish explorer who'd been separated from his convoy brought his horse to rest at the bank across from Maria. They exchanged glances. Passion overtook them. They crossed the river to embrace, and two worlds became one.

They had two children, one brown like her and one white like him. For a while they lived in bliss. Then, as abruptly as he'd arrived, the explorer left to reconnect with his friends, and they moved on to new frontiers. After a few weeks, Maria heard that he'd taken a wife, a White noblewoman approved of by his family, and he was talking about sending for his children.

That night, she carried her babies to the river, one by one, and drowned them along the bank where she'd met her love. For eternity she roams the shores at night, a witch dressed in white wailing for her lost children.

If you're not good, the weeping woman might just come and take you as her own, my grandmother would say. I didn't know at the time that La Llorona transcends borders, appearing in stories across Latin America, or that the meaner of the abuelitas out there alter details to terrorize their grandchildren into obedience.

La Llorona was a myth of the distant past, but every time I heard the story, I felt it in my body. My belly grew warm and hot at the thought of Maria's passion, at the idea that I might one day find a love like hers. Then a whooping feeling, like falling, at the man's betrayal. And at the end of the story, at the river, a cold memory grazed the corners of my consciousness, as I shivered myself to sleep.

Nathalie Farfan came from a long line of seers. Her grandmother's grandmother was born in Peru near the border of Ecuador. There she met the Ecuadorian man who would take her away from her home. Her husband's family disparagingly called her "la India" and secretly cursed her Indigenous roots. She took refuge in her ability to see through their pleasantries. And as much as they tried to erase her genes, she passed her clairvoyance and her looks down the maternal line—through Nathalie's great-grandmother, grandmother, mother—to Nathalie herself.

Nathalie's mother, Anita, suffered from epileptic seizures her whole childhood. Though Nathalie's grandmother Rosy thought this illness was somehow tied to the family's abilities, she took Anita to the neurologist, but modern medicine couldn't help her. In a desperate moment, Rosy visited a bruja, who told them that Anita had a bad spell on her. The bruja performed spirit work on Anita, and she was healed. The seizures stopped for good. The neurologist called it a miracle.

Years later, as Nathalie sat waiting for her mother to die, she wondered if Anita's first visit to the bruja wasn't a blessing but rather the beginning of a curse. Nathalie half listened to the priest reading her mother the last rites, but Anita was already gone.

Anita had Nathalie young, and they lived with Rosy in West New York. Anita was Rosy's favorite child, the central bruja of the house, the one who read everyone's cards and had a ritual for everything. "I've had a presentimiento," Rosy would say, and Anita would dream a dream to explain her mother's abstract premonitions. They sat for meals together and shared their medicine. Above all, they shared the power of story, and as Nathalie grew up in this family of brujas, she observed the gift of storytelling in herself. None of them had formal guides. They developed their abilities in relation to each other and were sustained by the energy of the maternal line.

Curanderismo is a folk healing system with origins in precolonial Mexico. When the Spanish colonized Mexico, the ways of the Aztecs,

Mayans, and Incans mixed with Catholicism and, to some degree, with the African traditions of the people enslaved by the Spanish. In curanderismo nature and spirit are intimately tied, and illness is a result of a supernatural force. A select few, called *curanderas* and *curanderos*, are spiritually chosen to act as healers of the body and spirit. Illness is usually accompanied by strong emotions, and the soul can even become separated from the body. The cure for such an extreme sickness usually requires the participation of the whole family.

This *conocimiento*, or "way of knowing," has traveled across Latin America and is still practiced in communities in tandem with mainstream medicine. Its methods are local and personal, always shifting to meet the needs of its people and the time. It is passed down within families, and communication with family members is a central part of curanderismo. When families migrate, relationships sometimes weaken, and the wisdom of curanderismo can be forgotten.

When Anita was in her thirties, she met a man, fell in love, and decided to have children with him. She was worried about her fertility, and her best friend, America, said she knew places that could help. America was around the same age and wanted to get pregnant, too, so she took Anita to brujos in Queens. Nathalie went with Anita a couple of times and stood in the parlor while her mother was in consultation. Strangers sat chanting and smoking pungent herbs while dead animals hung around, their blank eyes watching the room.

Anita became obsessed, booking consultation after consultation, donating all her money to the brujos. Months passed and still she wasn't pregnant. She went to the gynecologist to get checked out, and the doctor found an ovarian cyst. On further inspection, they discovered she had cancer in her belly, stage four, too far gone. Her doctor estimated she had two months to live.

On her deathbed, Anita's arms were wrapped in chains she'd acquired from her rituals at the house of the brujos. America was nowhere. Anita's sisters shamed her for observing a religion that wasn't her own, and she finally gave in to her mother's pleas to turn to her priest. But they consented to allow a brujo to perform a ritual to properly remove the chains. When the brujo arrived, his presence filled the room like a shadow, and he worked his magic over Anita's body, releasing her. Then came the priest, who performed the last rites of a religion that would have been just as alien to the family centuries ago.

Nathalie was only fifteen, but she thought this changing of the guards was very strange. Why would her mother rely on others' traditions in death when what had sustained their lives were the Indigenous practices of her mother's line? Where were the premonitions and the dreaming? Where was the circle of women holding hands? The magic of their ancestral medicine?

Don't die in shame, Nathalie prayed.

America was not at the funeral, but there was an older lady in attendance, dressed in red from head to toe. After the service, she approached Rosy and asked, "Are you Anita's mother?"

"Si, señora," Rosy said.

The woman in red told Rosy that America had not been by her friend's side because she had gone into labor. The baby was born around the same time that Anita had died.

When Nathalie was grown, her grandmother told her that before the brujo could release Anita from her chains, she needed to confess the rituals she had done on her own in order to become pregnant. She and America had drunk blood, Anita whispered. The brujo told her that the ritual had not been what Anita had thought and that she'd unintentionally transferred her womb to America's. Her friend had betrayed her and taken possession of her life.

"Una vida por otra," he said.

One life for another.

Myths hold all the stories we can't fully tell, and we pass those on and on, hoping that some truth of our suffering is carried within them, that some generational lesson arises for all the sacrifice. In Indigenous Latin American traditions, the folk tale is a way to preserve the pain and wisdom of the ancestors. The folk story transmutes family trauma into a cultural narrative. It helps us link our stories in a flowing tale, however imperfect.

When I see La Llorona, I always see a younger version of my grandmother Ninoska, the way she looked in an old black-and-white photo, one of the only images of her young self. She is a teenager dressed in a white peasant dress, her chin turned up to the sky.

She was born in Soledad, Colombia, to Venezuelan parents. Her mother died when she was a child, and her dad quickly remarried to a lady who kept her and her brothers as servants in their own home. When Ninoska was an adolescent, she was sent away to a convent.

Shortly after, she married a man who kept her constantly pregnant, and while it hurt, she was raised to believe her body was his and not her own. She birthed six children and secretly aborted many more.

We knew she'd had a hard life, but she didn't tell us what had happened to her besides some broad strokes—which sounded a bit like a Disney movie, evil stepmother and all. Unfortunately, there was no happy ending in this tale. She was obviously still living, but she told her stories with a finality to them, like there was no after. It's as if she decided to be one of the cautionary myths like La Llorona. She'd decided to stop living. She gave her life for the life her children could make in a new country.

Ninoska didn't make her sacrifice quietly. She wanted us to know that she suffered, but she didn't tell us about her feelings so much as create monuments to them. Her room was crammed with plastic bags of clothes. Over the years, she collected clothes "for the poor kids in Colombia," but she never sent any of them. Slowly, she piled them in pillowy plastic columns until they reached the ceiling and you couldn't open her door more than a third of the way. You had to walk through a tunnel to her bed, until it too was swallowed. When the room was full, she kept the door closed and slept in the garage downstairs.

The garage was where she really lived. I know a lot of people think about grandmothers in the kitchen, but she was just a decent cook. She was and would always be a cleaning lady. The garage, where the laundry machines were, was where I'd often find her. Removing stains, ironing, switching loads. We were drowning in clothes. The more she collected, the less easy I could breathe. I remember seeing the mass of fabric and wishing we could just simplify, have less.

"But she grew up with nothing, you have to remember," my mother would say. My mother had hoarding tendencies, too, and I wondered if they would worsen as she got older. Or if something would one day trigger the accumulation disease in me.

I associate my grandmother with the mop and the broom, with the chemical lavender smell of Fabuloso floor cleaner. I think maybe it was that cleaning felt like control. I understand that now. After a childhood spent rejecting the notion that women should be the ones to clean, I now find it the only thing to calm myself sometimes. Especially sweeping. The broom feels so much better than the vacuum. I love the sharp angle of it and the feeling of my shoulders working.

While my grandmother spent her days downstairs, my mom's sisters, Linda and Annie, shared a room upstairs for a time, and I'd sit on their bed and watch them dress. I thought them witches, the way they manipulated the air around them, created sparks. They were confident in their nudity, gloriously olive and supple in ways I knew I'd never be, my blood mixed as it was with that of the white and wiry conquistador. They spoke like I wasn't there, not so much looking at me but through me, and I kept their secrets safe.

My parents moved us out of the family house the next year, and sometime after that, the younger aunt, Annie, gave me a note that would link us forever.

When I was around nine years old, she took me and my cousin, Little Annie, to Universal Studios. My aunt's boyfriend, Chris the military guy, drove us in his Jeep. We rode the *Jaws* ride all my friends had been talking about. As we sat looking at the turbulent water, the two-note shark song from the movie got progressively louder, and everyone on the boat squirmed in their seats. The tempo increased and we knew danger was imminent. A massive, bloody shark broke the surface right beside us. Little Annie got quiet and her round face turned a deep purple, and then she let out her trademark shriek.

That shriek persisted the whole drive home to Miami. My aunt lowered all the windows to drown out her daughter's crying. We'd left the hotel in a hurry, a day early. I tried asking why we weren't with Chris, why we'd gotten into a rental car and left without him. The open car wasn't fun like the Jeep had been. My hair turned to whips on my face. Annie squeezed a half-empty Corona between her legs. Her hands were shaking and she was speeding. I looked around the car for something to hold onto, felt a silent beat reaching an impossible tempo. As we approached Miami, she placed a piece of paper on her thigh and scribbled something onto it with her spare hand. She rolled it up into a cylinder.

When we parked in front of my house, she pointed to a Kodak film canister I had tucked into a side pocket of a red lunch bag I was using as a purse. I gave it to her. She dumped the film out and placed the note inside, snapping the top in place. She gave it back to me and put her hands around mine and brought her face close. Her breath was sour from the beer, her freckled face dewy with sweat and tears, and her tawny, curly hair matted to the sides of her face.

"Hide this somewhere," Annie said. "Don't show it to anyone until something happens."

I hid the note in my closet. The next day, I sat in there with the doors pulled closed, staring at the canister in the little red bag that had carried my lunch and my pet rocks and that now held a secret. I knew that whatever the note said, it was something bad, that the thing she suggested might happen was bad, but I was bound to my promise. So I just sat in my closet waiting, and day turned into night.

Then I felt it. A sensation like cold water pouring down my spine and a loud sound that wasn't there. A thread inside me snapped and went slack. I slid the closet door open. I was one of the only kids I knew who had a phone in my room, and it was usually a source of pride, but in that moment, it loomed large in the room, threatening me in its holster. After about a minute, it rang. I waited for my mom to answer, then I picked it up quietly. My grandmother was screaming on the line.

"Se mató, se mató!"

She's killed herself.

I walked down the hall to my parents' room, canister in hand. My mother was getting dressed in a hurry. I held the canister out. She looked at me with confusion and impatience. I just stood there with my arm out. "What is this?" she asked me. I couldn't say. She finished putting her pants on, took the canister, and ripped the top off, almost tearing the note as she unraveled it like a fortune cookie. Her eyes darted left and right. Then her expression turned terrible, and she slapped me.

My mom wouldn't talk about what happened. I don't know if she kept the note or threw it away or gave it to the police, who later questioned me for a half hour at my aunt's house after she'd been taken away, the bed I'd sat on to admire her still soaked in her blood.

The secret of the note passed through me, but I never found out what it said.

I'd later learn that this had all started in the 1980s, when my mom's family met the brother of one of the heads of the Cali Cartel. His name was Lucho, which means "famous in war." My grandmother gave her blessing for him to marry her youngest daughter, Annie, the plucky one with the freckles and the tawny, curly hair. Her daughter Linda had already married a man nicknamed Gordo, who would eventually work for Lucho. Linda and Annie would become inseparable, connected as they were in their fates.

It was the time of the Miami drug war and the Cocaine Cowboys. Nobody in my family was innocent. My parents kept on the sidelines, but they sometimes let Lucho stash at their place. One day, when my mother was pregnant with me, there was a ring at the door. She looked in the peephole and saw an old lady. When she opened the door, two men in masks pushed in, tied her to a chair, and gagged her while they ransacked the place. She screamed and screamed, but since she was muzzled, her screams traveled through her and down to her womb, vibrating in the fluid that held me inside. The next day, a couple was found murdered in the neighboring building. The men in masks never returned, but the terror remained. Such things happened in Miami in those days.

The following years play out like a mob movie. My Uncle Gordo disappeared. My Aunt Linda was told he was shot execution-style and found in a car at the bottom of a lake, but they never showed her the body, only projecting it to her on a screen, citing the bad decomposition. He could have been murdered, or as has been whispered in my family, he could have gone into witness protection for giving Lucho up. Lucho was arrested shortly after. Lucho's brother, Chepe Santacruz, negotiated a lighter sentence for him by giving up information that led to the arrest of Manuel Noriega, the most feared man in Panama. The DEA was on a rampage. Pablo Escobar and the Medellín Cartel went down. Chepe and his partners were killed, and then the Cali Cartel was no more.

This is a family story, and it's a cultural story, and it's a folk story. It's a story that repeats itself inside me, a violence always on my periphery.

My beautiful, wild aunts became ill, one by one. Linda was possessed by chronic migraines and on and off for years locked herself in her dark room, the same room that her sister would later shoot herself in when she could no longer take being followed by the men who threatened her boyfriends and reported her affairs back to Lucho in prison.

My mother woke up screaming in the night. I'd hear her from my room and tiptoe to her door, holding the knob but not daring to go in.

I started to see things that would have made me scream like my mother, if my voice weren't locked up in fear. When my little cousins were grown, they searched for men like their absent fathers and repeated old stories.

I think all the time about what would have become of me if Annie had died. When they got her to the hospital for surgery, they saw that the bullet had gone straight through her chest without hitting her heart. It exited her back and traveled through an internal wall, through the upstairs hallway, finally lodging itself at the family altar in the lower left corner of a painting of a blue-eyed, blond Jesus Christ.

From then on, we called it "the accident." I knew it was more than that, but I couldn't speak about it or of the trespasses of the men or of all the ways we women had become trapped in our suffering.

I couldn't even be mad at Annie for giving me the note, because to everyone else, the note never existed. I recently filed a records request with the Miami-Dade Police Department in hopes of finding it and finally reading its contents, but they could find no such incident on file.

Some family secrets just won't surface.

When my aunt returned from the hospital, she was deeply depressed and on suicide watch. Her siblings decided she was possessed by a demon that was keeping her sad, so they called an exorcist—a brujo, they called him.

They held the exorcism in the sitting room of the family house, with its twenty-foot ceilings, walls of mirrors on all sides, and the trademark pastel furniture of 1990s Miami. The staircase overlooked the room, and the kids who were sent away snuck to the steps to watch from above. The brujo prepared the room. He walked to every participant in turn, the siblings and their spouses, evaluating them. He got to my uncle's wife, who was pregnant, and as he held her belly, he said, "This baby will not be born alive." She turned pale and was noticeably upset, but she held her tongue and stayed. My aunt was laying on a suede chaise lounge, and her family gathered around her. It was nighttime and the lights were off and there were candles everywhere. It was her family's responsibility to energetically hold her while the brujo pulled the demon out and sent it into a mirror he held, where he'd be able to trap it and remove it from the house.

The brujo stood over my aunt and chanted as she fell into a trance. He poured liquids around her, himself dancing in trance. Then he pulled at the air around her, miming a struggle. Every time he pulled, her torso jumped up and she gasped, and the circle of her siblings groaned and yelled around her.

My cousins watched the ceremony in fear. They had seen things like this in the movies and were terrified that ghosts were real. It seemed that the room had started to breathe, and the mirrors were all shaking. Finally, they heard a low guttural scream that seemed to come from nowhere and filled the whole room, and then the brujo raised the mirror in his hands, triumphant. The sad ghost had been drawn out of Annie.

When he left, my aunt's siblings held her, stunned, hoping it had worked.

Annie did get better. But a couple of weeks later, the pregnant aunt went into labor. Her baby was stillborn. I remember the funeral, the little dress, the white shawl over the baby's face, and the whisperings in my mind about the things we sometimes have to sacrifice.

One life for another.

I wondered if the curse continued and which of us was next. After the accident, I was visited by my own ghost. It paralyzed me in terror as it appeared in the corner, a form dressed in white with long, dark hair that made strange choking sounds.

Do all of us women in the family have this shadow in common? I observe this line of tragedy repeating in rapid succession. Their stories are my story. Their bodies are my body. Every happy memory is encased in a shadow. The stories keep circling and multiplying inside me, and they blur into a witch, a weeping ghost.

★ ✶ ★

"This could all be a folk tale," Nathalie tells me after she's finished her story. "But I think there is a truth to these myths."

She's sitting across from me at a long wooden table in her dining room in Maplewood, New Jersey. It's a frigid January day, and she's casual in her white sweatshirt and red beanie, but her body seems to create a gravitational pull, everything in the room, including me, leaning toward her. Maybe it's the weed she keeps passing across the table as we talk, but I get the sense that there are spirits hanging around her, and it's clear to me she has inherited the spiritual gifts of her maternal line.

"Fear is so real," Nathalie says. "I'll still be in a house and lock the door if I'm by myself. I'm still like, where's that murderer? My grandmother saying, 'Ten cuidado. Mira detras de tu espalda, que no esté un hombre allí, un violador.' I lived through anxiety and fear. I was a fifteen-year-old orphan. I went through times when I was like, damn, should I commit suicide?"

Ultimately, Nathalie says, she got through her mother's death by connecting with her female friends. They were the modern-day brujas of their hood, latchkey kids, children of single moms. They mimicked the rituals of the older Latin Americans in the area, but they watched

The Craft and spoke Spanglish and made rituals of their own, a tight group coming together and healing through intuition and cannabis.

She didn't always connect with her Indigenous roots. When she was twenty-one, she got a nose job, trying to erase her grandmother's features. But she couldn't disavow her abilities. After college she lived in Los Angeles with an abusive boyfriend. When she was in her deepest depression, she felt the power of all the generations of women who preceded her, who had suffered and survived through her. They gave her the courage to leave. She decided she would no longer allow herself to be colonized.

She started La Brujas Club as a sisterhood of protection against shame and misogyny. On her website she writes, "A Bruja's power is sacred and authentic. It was born within families, passed down through generations, shared in hallowed circles and felt in corner botanicas. There is power in this history, and while the spirit can be felt by all, the passing down of this craft and legacy needs to start with those who live by it."

La Brujas Club has evolved into a forum for storytelling and healing, especially for Indigenous women and women of color. Members talk about their ancestors and the medicine of their homelands they've been taught to forget. They talk about the bad things that have happened in their families. Nathalie holds a safe space for them all and encourages them to tap into pain, not with the aim at erasing trauma but as a way to build faith that it will evolve into health and wisdom, into power.

"We need these stories," she says. "They're so hard to tell, because they're about our own family members. But we need to tell them."

To Nathalie, being a bruja is inherently political, and telling our

stories is, above all, about decolonization, exposing how we've disconnected from Indigenous wisdom as we've adopted the ways of modern-
day capitalism and patriarchal interpretations of our troubles. But
while she doesn't shy away from the hard stuff, Nathalie departs from
her family's sometimes-grim view of the world, refusing to relinquish
trust in a better future. If you're going to assume this bruja identity,
Nathalie says, you have to own your own story. You have to dedicate
yourself to being honest and healing the collective.

"This is how we break curses," Nathalie says. "Yeah there's bad stuff
out there. We can choose fear and paranoia, or we can heal."

Nathalie is not the only one doing this work. The generational
curse has become a cautionary and inspirational meme in Indigenous,
Caribbean, and Afro-Latinx spiritual communities online. It is generally accepted that trauma repeats itself through family lines until a
descendant awakens to the cycle and decides to break the curse.

Through tags like #generationalcurses and #ancestralhealing,
these communities have proliferated the idea that spirituality is not all
peace and light but rather about facing the hard moments of our lives
and our families' unhealthy responses. This is shadow work. Healing
ourselves is the first step in healing the collective, from the family unit
to larger cultural communities.

This idea has inspired thousands of people, especially women of
color who are coaching each other to reinterpret their hardships as
strength and their disorders as superpowers, giving rise to social media
posts like the following:

"You might be processing what your parent(s) didn't."

"If trauma can be passed down generations, so can healing."

"Your feeling deeply is an ancestral calling to heal."

"The generational trauma stops with me."

We chant these words to ourselves. We repeat and we repeat until we finally believe that we are not fated to our tragic stories.

Before I learned that La Llorona was a common ghost, I thought there was something wrong with me. It was a while before I could interpret this not as a disorder, not as a possession, but as an ability— my sensitivity taking form to tell me that there are deep wounds that need healing. Could it be that the problem was not in me but running through me like a river? This river that crosses borders, that flows from the motherland to my bed.

Ancestral trauma can be transmitted through generations. There are different schools of thought about how this actually happens. Behavioral therapists find that children of trauma survivors are hyperaware of their parents' words, actions, and even silences, and they learn to anticipate their reactions. This often leads to insecure attachment styles in these children, as they repeat the stress response patterns in their adult relationships.

Geneticists have tracked how parents' stress can alter offsprings' RNA strands in a process of accelerated evolution. These impromptu gene changes signal to the next generation: *Be on alert. Something is wrong here.* The descendants of people who have experienced trauma are born with a trigger of sorts. When that trigger is released, survival mode is engaged, inducing the same kind of panic in the descendant that the ancestors experienced, though they might not be exposed to the same dangers or know their ancestors or their family stories. Some even experience memories that aren't theirs.

This has been documented in refugees, especially Holocaust survivors and their children. Their stories suggest there is more to this than biology. The silences of survivors become deafening secrets. Children who generally know that something bad happened, but have never been told exactly what, feel like they are trapped in a story that hasn't finished.

Children of trauma are more likely to repeat the mistakes of their families' pasts, more likely to be violent or become victims of violence themselves. The sensitive ones might be plagued by disturbances like obsessive thoughts of suicide or hallucinations. They might be diagnosed with anxiety disorders or schizophrenia. For many immigrants, Western diagnoses and treatments don't prove helpful. When there is a long line of trauma in a family, it can feel like a family curse.

But as we work through these concepts, the curse dissipates and we realize the ways that generational trauma is systemic and how we might practically change systems to foster healing for future generations. What if what we see as a supernatural illness is the result of colonization and exile—this disconnect from our lands that has weakened our relationships, our stories? What if our sickness is an indication, not that something is wrong with us or our family but that we are actually incredibly strong, finding ourselves in a new world of impossible stress, far removed from the wisdom of our ancient healers?

What if Anita had lived in the land of her mothers when she got sick? Would she have been enveloped by their wisdom? Would they have saved her? Would she at least have been held in the comfort of their embrace in her final moments?

What if my maternal line had been more connected to our ancestral wisdom? What if my grandmother had been able to heal herself? How much suffering might we have avoided if we'd had a healthy line of communication, if we'd had strong healing stories?

One of the ways colonizers have controlled us is to pit us against each other, make us believe the other is evil. In so many of our trauma stories, we demonize other Indigenous ways of knowing. When we are so far removed from our own ancestral wisdom, we are attracted to those who have kept their practices strong—who we've called the brujos, the santeros and santeras, the *houngans* and *mambos*. We fear them as much as we are attracted to them. We ask for their help, but we don't fully trust their magic. Our stories of them have an ominous tone. The chains on the deathbed. The premonition of the stillborn. They give us something, but they always take.

What if the dissonance we experience when we are stuck between alien ways of knowing is a product of the violence of the colonizers, still with us so many centuries later?

Our stories show us just how we have been colonized. If La Llorona had not been swept away by her sadness about losing the Spanish man, maybe she would have remembered the wisdom of her mothers and stayed alive. Maybe she would never have become the witch we fear. We've demonized the victim and projected all our fears onto her, while the colonizer rides away.

THE ANCESTRAL CURSE

✦ ✹ ✦

There is a place called the Canyon de Brujas in Big Bend, Texas, where the Rio Grande separates US land from Boquillas, Mexico, a village so remote that it only recently got electricity, a relic of the past. It is said that witches haunt this land, La Llorona herself, no less, who is sometimes interpreted as an Apache maiden who drowned herself in the Rio to escape being raped by her White captors. The spirit of the maiden is said to wander the canyon in search for home.

It is no mistake that this story of the weeping woman is most powerful at the US-Mexican border, where children of immigrants are being kept in cages as I'm writing this, their mothers crying for them and attempting to breastfeed from the other side of the bars.

La Llorona's wail reverberates generation after generation, transcends borders and cultures, and adapts to the newest trespasses of humanity. She represents new life in America as much as she reminds us of our Indigenous histories. She exists in the liminal spaces of colonization, in the difficult memories that are passed down or kept silent. Her children are the White-passing immigrants who took on the genes of the colonizer and the ones who are still persecuted for their Indigenous features. She embodies the in-betweenness of our American lives and the sacrifices we make to stay alive.

For all this, she continues to pervade oral Latin American traditions and has transitioned to the US mainstream through movies and music. The song of La Llorona was popularized in 1940 by a man, and the lyrics portrayed a man who felt trapped by a woman and guilty about hurting or leaving her. But recent songs written by contemporary Mexican artists like Natalia Lafourcade, although varying only slightly in the lyrics, seem to empathize with the sad woman's perspective, revealing a mortal saint, a pain that can be any one of ours—a pain that is just a step away from wisdom.

The weeping woman contains multitudes. She is the Aztec goddess Cihuacōātl, the "Serpent Woman," who was associated with midwifery; she was terrible in appearance but also the protector of babies and women who died in childbirth. She is Kali, the fierce Hindu goddess who destroys man for his greed and betrayal. She is Lilith, the one who chose exile rather than remain confined in paradise to the will of man. She is the powerful river orisha, Oshun. She is Santa Muerte, the personification of death and hope. The weeping woman is the goddess that embodies the power of the feminine will, in all its forms.

Such feminist reinterpretations of La Llorona abound, resisting the notion of the spiteful or incurably mentally ill woman. Is La Llorona a bogeyman thirsty for more casualties, just a scary bedtime story to keep us in line? Or can she be reimagined as an Indigenous protectress of the land and the womb against colonization, as she did not allow the White man to claim what was hers?

To me, La Llorona is the original bruja. She was sensitive. She was open to love. She was caged. She was raped. She was abandoned. She was suicidal. She was grieving. She was a mother who wouldn't let her children be stolen away. She is the complicated story that is hard to tell. She is a cautionary tale. She is a lesson we mustn't forget.

What she has taught me is that my body holds curses and blessings in equal measure. Can I simultaneously face trauma and embrace healing? Can I be reborn in the same river that carries my family's sad stories? Anoint myself in their pain and emerge stronger for all my tears, like La Llorona?

Sometimes I catch myself humming her haunting song, and the words transform from lamentation to prayer.

Take me to the river, Llorona.

Cover me with your shawl, Llorona.

SPEAKING TO THE SPIRITS

One of the most important things an ancestral altar affords is a medium through which we can speak with our ancestors. We might have never met some of the ancestors we honor at our altars, or maybe we couldn't speak with them freely while they were alive. Maybe there is a deep family hurt that we are working through, and the altar gives us the space and time to acknowledge this pain and work toward clearing it.

The altar has allowed me to voice what was previously silent, to break the silence for a whole line of our family. It allows me to create stories that make sense of pain. To speak those stories aloud is a powerful act. Writing and speaking your past and your truth is hard. It is also clearing, and an important step to healing. It's like confession, but without the priest.

If we go back ten generations, we have one thousand ancestors running through our blood. That's a lot of memory. That's a lot of stories. You can be the one in your family that starts to tell these stories, even if you have to fill some of it in with your imagination or with your questions or with other stories. In this way, you can be the documentarian of your family.

The best time to communicate with ancestors is on powerful full moons, eclipses, equinoxes, solstices, or the Day of the Dead if you observe it. Here are a few guidelines for how to get started, but as you practice speaking with your ancestors, you'll find your own way of communing and telling your stories.

1. Write. I like to keep a journal for my questions, bits of story, research into my ancestry, and memories. Over time a story begins to emerge, part historical, part fictional. I write it as it comes.

2. When you are ready to share with your ancestors, approach your altar. You may perform your usual rituals, like lighting candles or making offerings. Breathe deeply and slowly. Ground down in front of the altar. Feel the energy field below your feet. Pull the energy up through your body and up into your crown.

3. Imagine a line of bodies stretching ahead and a line of bodies stretching behind you.

4. Begin to speak. Maybe you start with something from your journal

and go from there. Let your intuition guide you. Don't worry about the way it sounds. Let what comes come. It can be mundane details about your life, or it can be a pressing question you didn't get to ask when your ancestor was alive.

5. Use a divination technique if it's part of your practice. Maybe you are practicing mediumship and will receive messages through different sensory avenues, like hearing a voice. Or you could use tarot to receive messages.

6. Express gratitude and close the space. You might snuff your candles or leave a written affirmation on the table or say a prayer as a closing ritual. Whatever you do, it's important to honor the moment and the space before walking away. You might sit in meditation for a while before closing.

GEMINI: THE MESSENGER

In all the zodiac, there's no sweeter talker than the Gemini. It rules the third house of community and communication, student and teacher relationships, and siblings. Gemini will help you any time you're at a loss for words or intellectual clarity or need to absorb a lot of information at once. Geminis seem flighty because of all their interests, but they care deeply for their work and their people. Gemini helps us to see how seemingly unrelated things are connected and how we might transmute information into wisdom for our communities.

ELEMENT: Mutable air

PLANETARY RULER: Mercury

AFFIRMATION: "I speak"

FOR YOUR ALTAR: Nervine herbs, flowering weeds, messenger or androgynous deities, the magpie, yellow and green stones, shiny new things

JOURNAL: Think of an old family memory or myth that has never been recorded. Or alternately, think of a story you've always wanted to tell, biographical or fictional. Which sense or feeling is most crucial to expressing your story? What form will your story take? Is it a silent film? A song? A sculpture?

ANCESTRAL WISDOM

Most ancestral traditions pass wisdom orally through generations, and sometimes it can be hard to learn about them if you're not an initiate. Ancestral Voices (@ancestral_voices, ancestralvoices.co.uk) offers a wealth of learning resources, including e-courses created by scholars and practitioners. And Ancestors in Training (@ancestorsintraining, ancestorsintraining.org) is a new educational praxis project that supports inquiry-based learning and fosters a community looking to the future of ancestral spiritualities.

Mujeres de Maiz (@mujeresdemaiz, mujeresdemaiz.com) is a grassroots multimedia women's activist organization in East Los Angeles, California. They support community collaborations between educators, organizers, and artists to empower women of color.

4

GUARDIAN SPIRITS

Marie des Vallées was a peasant in Normandy in the 1600s. Her father died when she was a child, and the man her mother remarried abused her until she was forced to leave home. She was highly eccentric for the time, alone as she was in the world, without the company of a husband. One day, she refused an advance by a man. Sources are inconsistent about whether it was an attempted rape or a marriage proposal. After that, she became possessed by a demon she believed was sent to her by a witch that the man consulted after his rejection.

Marie was taken to the local archbishop for an exorcism. The process lasted days and bordered on torture. She was ordered to carry a flaming burner of sulfur and rue and inhale the smoke and chug bottles and bottles of holy water. When her possession persisted, she was imprisoned for months, where she was matroned, or tested for virginity, since witches were believed to have sex with demons. She passed the test. She was not a witch but a victim, the archbishop concluded. She was released, but her symptoms worsened.

Marie was eventually taken in by French Roman Catholic priest Saint Jean Eudes, who had established a refuge for women in trouble, orphans and sex workers and outcasts of all sorts. Eudes faithfully documented Marie's disturbing visions. She remained possessed her entire life, professing herself a sacrifice on behalf of all the women who were persecuted for witchcraft at the time. She said that she descended into hell to experience the torture that had been inflicted upon them. In that place, wherever it was, she was burned and hanged and raped, over and over. Confronted with such constant terror, she tried to kill herself, but she said God stayed her arm. Though she was never canonized, she is considered a saint by some for all her suffering.

Suffering was the fate of women of that time who chose to live outside the norm. Some women were called *witch* because of their divergent sexualities or unconventional social roles or natural abilities. Not all witches were burned. Some, like Marie, were indoctrinated, covered by sainthood, both a protection and a cage. If women couldn't offer their bodies and wombs in the traditional service to man and country, their ailments would be attributed to demonic possession, their reproductive organs would be inspected, and they would become locked in service to the White God. Witch hunts spread across the world in the 1500s and 1600s, and as often as women were killed, they were also taken up and hidden by the church through missionary convents like that of Saint Jean Eudes.

In the 1800s Saint Mary Euphrasia Pelletier expanded Eudes's mission into an international order called the Congregation of Our Lady of Charity of the Good Shepherd, eventually overseeing 110 convents in 35 countries. The mission of the convents was to provide protection for women who were in danger. Most of the time, the protection went hand in hand with correction. Europe wasn't just colonizing the world through their governments and markets but through religion and facilities aimed at detaining people, especially women. While the original intentions might have been good, convents like these ultimately served to disappear and subjugate women.

The redeeming part of Marie's story is that somebody saw her and took her in and documented her personal visions, and she is remembered more than most people ever are. I'm trying to feel in the dark for all the people who did not get their redemption. The ones who were thrown into cages and forgotten, or who never made it to a cage. All the ones with unmarked graves. But it's hard to feel anything for a faceless mass. That's why we have saints, I suppose. We put statues of them on our altars, and their stories stand for countless others we'll never know.

My grandmother Ninoska only ever told us a few things about her childhood, and one that she repeated to many of us was that her parents had sent her to a convent in her town in Colombia. She said that the convent was much like a jail, with evil nuns and a priest who would try to lift up her skirts. I always thought it was another one of her exaggerations, like one of her myths. I never heard more about it until October 2020, when she died, and I went to Miami for her wake and funeral.

My mother said she wasn't lucid when she died. She was lucky to have died at home surrounded by her children, instead of at the hospital where the family would have surely been kept from the room because of precautions to prevent the spread of COVID-19. My mom believes my grandmother could still hear them, since hearing is the last thing to go. The siblings stood together and watched her take her last breath. It was more like a gasp, they say, and her eyes opened very wide for one moment, and then she was still. My mom and her sister Linda said they saw a golden light. My aunt Annie saw a dark hand pull her soul out. At the moment of her death, each of Ninoska's six children stood intent, with their various emotions and perceptions and memories. The descendants' incongruencies existed without contradiction in that room, in their final minutes with their mother.

I think when someone close to us dies what we see or feel is mostly about ourselves, our own relationship to death.

It took Ninoska's death to finally unlock the stories in us all, like a curse lifting. The night before the wake, I talked with my mother, aunts, and uncles, and I could barely keep up with the stories. A dam of secrets had broken. I took furious notes. I started to piece together bits of stories I'd heard. A timeline started to form. It stretched back for generations.

Ninoska had been calling for her grandmother Cancianila in her last moments. She'd seen and talked with Cancianila all her life, but her guardian was absent in her final days. "Tata, porque no vienes?" she was heard saying. *Why won't you come?*

It was my first time hearing about Cancianila, my great-great-grandmother. My family says she was a spiritualist, an eccentric. She had worked in a circus in Barquisimeto, Venezuela. They think she might have been a trapeze artist, because they have memories of

Ninoska mentioning the tightrope. It must have been the late 1800s. There is no record of her I could find, but I've created an image of her in my mind, this strange woman who defied norms at the turn of a difficult and exciting century for women, whose line leads to me.

When Cancianila got too old, she was forced to leave the circus. I wonder if that's why she decided to marry the blond man higher than her social class, or if she was really in love. Ninoska might have been able to answer that—if I'd known to ask the question while she was alive. Cancianila had one child, Ermelinda Paz. The man left before Ermelinda could make any memories of him.

Ermelinda had a more traditional upbringing in Venezuela and married Antonio Escobar, a soldier of the Colombian army who was stationed in her hometown. She moved to Colombia, where she adopted two girls from Antonio's previous marriage, Teresa and Rosita, and gave birth to children of her own, my grandmother Ninoska and Jairo. The girls didn't know they were adopted, and Ninoska considered them all her siblings. When Ninoska was just a few years old, Rosita died of tetanus at fourteen, and Ermelinda mourned her passing as if she were her own.

Antonio's brother was gay, and when the army found out, they discharged Antonio. Antonio blamed his brother, who ended up killing himself in shame. Antonio became mean and anxious, and Cancianila rescued him from ruin. She had won the lottery—not once, but twice— but since she was a woman without a husband, she could not claim the prize money. Antonio claimed it for her and kept her in the large quinta he built on two acres. Antonio had little love for his mother-in-law, but he tolerated her, using her money to start many businesses, including a fleet of buses, restaurants, and bars.

When Ninoska was eight years old, her mother, Ermelinda, died giving birth to her last child, Hermes. Everyone called him Catire, which means "fair skinned," as he was lighter than all his siblings, taking after Ermelinda's absent father. Ermelinda was not much older than a child herself when she died. Cancianila was overwhelmed with grief at the loss of her only daughter. In a fit of rage, she told Teresa that she was not really Ermelinda's daughter, and Teresa left and eventually made her way to the United States alone.

Antonio hated Catire for killing Ermelinda, and he withdrew from his children. He sent them to stay in the carriage house where the servants lived. He kicked Cancianila out of his home, and she later died alone of tuberculosis. Antonio took many mistresses, all of whom he would call "the seamstress" when the children asked about them. In short order he married one of them, a woman from a good family who was said to have worked as a madame in a brothel.

Gladys Millon Acosta matched Antonio's meanness. She had two sons with him, Orlando and Antonio Jr., but they were regarded no better than the other kids. Ninoska dropped out of grade school and took them under her wing. Now, it was just her and four younger boys to look after around the quinta. She did everything, cooked and cleaned for them all, like a servant in her own home. Gladys often sent the kids out on personal errands. According to Ninoska and Jairo, she would spit on the floor and say that if they weren't back by the time the spit dried up, they would get a beating. Gladys had a pet monkey that terrorized all the kids, but especially Ninoska, who the monkey would try to mount. Ninoska hit it with a ladle once when it wouldn't let go. She was terrified of it. The monkey was the unease she constantly felt under her evil stepmother's watch.

At puberty Ninoska started showing signs that she was in love. One of the Martinez boys kept coming around the quinta. He belonged to a lower social stratum. When it looked like they might run off together, Antonio and Gladys sent Ninoska to a convent called El Buen Pastor just a few miles away.

When I heard "El Buen Pastor," little alarm bells went off in my ears. I searched it on Google Maps in my grandmother's hometown, and it showed up only as "Carcel de Mujeres." *Women's Jail.*

I searched for archival records of the jail, and it led me back to a convent that began in Europe in the 1600s, called the Congregation of Our Lady of Charity of the Good Shepherd. In 1890 a chapter was established in Bogotá, Colombia, in response to wealthy families who had been calling for a local institution to deal with "female corruption." They wanted somewhere to send their daughters who were not so much in conflict with the law as with their family's social expectations. The facility became known as "El Buen Pastor" for short, a translation of the Good Shepherd.

Over the century following the flagship facility in Bogotá, El Buen Pastor expanded throughout the country. In the 1920s a chapter was built in Barranquilla. That's the one where Ninoska was sent. The convents began as places of "reeducation" for young women from well-to-do families, but over time, they also served as prisons, mixing women with children and the seasoned criminal with the teenage rebel. The average captive became poorer and poorer, and today the majority of the population of El Buen Pastor are of the lowest castes, reflecting the poorest of Colombia's "strata" of residents. (These strata still exist today. Labeled one to six, they seem not unlike the districts in *The Hunger Games* to me.) Today El Buen Pastor is the most famous women's prison in Colombia, having detained many high-profile women. A disproportionate number of prisoners in El Pastor are of Indigenous origin.

I suddenly understood why my grandmother had been so obsessed with telenovelas, her daily soap operas. Her life had been just as dramatic, and she saw herself in the stories. I cried once at the funeral, and it was when I imagined her watching the little television above the stove in the kitchen and seeing herself in characters we laughed at, in story lines we, with our privileged upbringings, found ridiculous. I wish I would have seen her clearly sooner.

There are stories like these in every family if you look deep enough, hidden time lines that don't surface until after a death, if ever. I tell this one now to stand in for all those we will never know. It is full of mundane details and relationships that are hard to track, like a Gabriel García Márquez novel. I document Ninoska's story here for posterity, so that over time I might find the magic in it, that my witness might turn a suffering woman into a saint.

Ninoska quickly found that the convent was nothing more than a glorified jail. The nuns used corporal punishment, and the priest was a pedophile. She was scared and worried about her brothers. She tried to go over the walls and was captured and temporarily thrown in a cell with rats. She hated to be confined, and she spent her days crying.

Over time she started to care for the other children in the jail, too, sweeping and cleaning their clothes and pulling lice off their hair. Routinely she would self-harm, burning or cutting herself, to try to be sent to the clinic, from where she hoped she'd be able to call home. At one point, her older sister Teresa returned home and got her out, but then quickly abandoned her, and she was sent back. After months and months of this, the Martinez boy, Edmundo, would finally be able to release her by offering her marriage. She was barely fourteen.

This is not a princess-saved-by-the-knight-happily-ever-after story. The Martinez family was very poor. Edmundo took Ninoska to a small dirty room in their home, and she started to have children. Eventually Antonio provided them a better place to live. There, Ninoska raised six children and had countless miscarriages and home abortions. Edmundo took other women and left her, and she moved all of her children to the United States alone.

By the time Ninoska died, she had thirty-three living kids, grandkids, and great-grandkids, and none of us tried hard enough. She was a difficult woman. I tried talking to her about her life a few times, but there was this giant wall. If there was ever a moment I thought I'd finally broken through to her, she would harden just as quickly, and she could be so mean as to repel you from the room. She was always sweeping, always sweeping, and she would sweep you away, too, if you got in the way.

A MAGICAL ANCESTRY

Griselda and Miguelina Rodriguez occupy a space that in the times of Marie des Vallées could have gotten them killed or thrown in a cage, that is still today a tightrope walk.

They are Afro-Dominican brujas with PhDs.

Otherwise known as the Brujas of Brooklyn, Gri and Migue, as they refer to each other, are twin sisters who openly practice and teach the magic of their Indigenous ancestry. In one of their earliest memories, they're three or four years old, and they're standing in front of a two-tiered street altar in the Dominican Republic. It was giant to them, both strange and familiar. Their mother is Catholic, and there was a lot of shame associated with Afro-Indigenous spirituality in their family, so they tucked the memory away. If they practiced anything related to their African roots, it was covered in the veil of Catholicism. They often had parties for Saint Michael, whom Miguelina was named after.

Through their academic work, they dug into their ancestry and developed their identities as brujas. It didn't happen overnight. They had to go through "the dark night of the soul," as we say. Delving into the past, whether it's your family or cultural ancestry, you're bound to rub up against some difficult truths or sad stories. The way the Brujas talk about those years, how they held each other and got each other through the hardships, maybe they wouldn't have done it alone. But together they pulled back the veil of Catholicism and found a spirituality that they both felt destined to.

They each engaged with Dominican communities in different

ways. Griselda, who describes herself as "mama Bruja," traveled to the Dominican Republic to conduct her fieldwork, where she interviewed Afro-Dominican women and saw for herself what she had suspected, just how their labor is devalued and exploited in national and global economies. The Afro-Dominican woman is at the center of everything, of the family, of industry. She keeps everything going. But she does not reap the benefits of her own labor. Her story is rarely documented, and she is not glorified upon her death.

Miguelina studied Washington Heights, where the biggest population of Dominicans in the United States lives. Since the 1970s, funding has been slashed in the neighborhood, and at one point it was considered the murder capital of the city. Nobody wanted to live there, until it started to become gentrified. Miguelina quotes Spike Lee, noting that White people are experiencing "Columbus syndrome," thinking they discovered the neighborhood. They took advantage of the home prices and rents that had remained lower than the average market in New York because it had been undesirable for so long, because it had belonged to Dominicans who kept it going despite the lack of public support.

In a capitalist system, White people and rich people benefit from the labor and lives of the ones they deem "minorities." This is what the Brujas have seen.

When you conduct critical ethnographies as they've done, you become embedded in communities, and if you remain sensitive, you also investigate your place within it all. Gri and Migue were a part of the communities they were studying, but they were also apart. They were US residents, and they had the social capital that comes with a higher education. With that comes great responsibility.

We've been taught to think that economics and spirituality are two different things, but they feed each other. Spirituality is a currency that runs through the Caribbean and Caribbean neighborhoods in the United States, that offers a source of resilience to people who work for little pay or recognition. Spirituality creates a network of mutual aid that fills the gaps where markets and governments fail. Spirituality is the source of the peoples' power. The Brujas saw this in their studies. As they walked the thin line of academia and borrowed their disciplines' language to explain their experiences in their papers and their dissertations, they felt there was something missing. Even when you're researching marginalized communities, you have to frame your work in homage to the White institutions that have taught that native ways are irrational or nonacademic. It's a catch-22, to try to reveal a system of oppression through another system of oppression.

After all, many of our universities were built on land that was taken from Indigenous peoples. Native wisdom was literally paved over. In 1862 the Morrill Act gave thousands of acres of federal land that belonged to Indigenous peoples to states so they could build what have become known as the "land-grant universities." The universities became another arm of colonization, feeding labor into agriculture and mechanics in response to the industrial revolution. This legacy of universities as pipelines to the market endures today, with the myopic focus on STEM education at the expense of the social sciences and liberal arts programs, which are experiencing massive cuts throughout the country. What's more, universities are increasingly depending on temporary, low-wage contract positions, held mostly by women, to run the heart of the business as administrator salaries become more and more bloated.

Descartes's separation of mind and body became the benchmark for reason across the Western world, propagated through the university, and until very recently, the woman was excluded, her body only reasonable as a vehicle for reproduction. The subjugation of women and the genocide that occurred to Indigenous civilizations—especially matrilineal ones—throughout the Caribbean and the Americas happened under the guise of progress, of rooting out witchcraft and evil and spreading "knowledge." The Indigenous leaders who held the ancient secrets of the world, who lived as one with their environment, who embodied many genders and sexualities, who healed and taught and birthed and fought for their people, were exterminated or went into hiding. Now we consume indigeneity through voyeuristic academic studies and spiritual tourism.

For those with Indigenous ancestry, the way back to wisdom is usually blocked. Over time wisdom is replaced by fear and that fear is passed on and on through generational silences. Descendants might identify superficially with their struggles as a sort of badge of honor, and they will consider themselves lucky to have been born on lands of reason and progress, and the colonizer will become the savior. They might even shun their roots. But in their genes, the truth remains, memory waiting to be released.

For the Brujas of Brooklyn, the process of reclaiming this identity and spirituality was gradual. While they were in their PhD programs, trying to balance all the demands that came with that, the research and teaching and writing, they were also each going through huge life changes. They went through hard breakups. Their thyroids got sick. Migue developed thyroid cancer. It was a wake-up call to them both, as they saw how their own bodies were falling victim to the cycle of production to which academia is not immune.

In those hard moments, they held each other, and they remembered their childhood selves, the ones who stood before the giant altar in their home country. It was calling to them, this ancient way of healing and knowing. They reached for the resources at their disposal, what they tapped into through their yoga and doula communities. They started to get up early in the morning and do Kundalini practices. They opened up to their spiritual power. They healed, together.

They awoke to the power of their Afro-Indigenous roots. Their ancestral spiritual system is called the 21 Divisions, also known as Dominican Vudú. They believe it's the path that they chose to walk before they came to earth. It was their destiny to remember their past and bring this spirituality into their everyday lives for healing.

After the sisters completed their degrees, they became educators within the academic system and healers in their communities in New York. Over the last few years, they've been attracting more and more attention for their work, appearing in NPR and *Oprah Magazine*.

"Healing is hard shadow work," Griselda says. "You can't take Bruja 101. You have to go within, and you have to do it yourself."

Now that the Brujas have been teaching younger women for a

while, they're concerned that witchcraft has become a fad for many people, something to post on their social media. This happens in a capitalist system, they say. Periodically, something will become marketable and a lot of people jump on the bandwagon. They don't realize that it's not about image or money. They don't realize that they're dabbling with sacred magic. They want to fly before they can crawl. They want to feel enlightenment without the hard work.

"They're going to weekend retreats, and they're calling themselves healers and charging a lot of money to do things like Reiki and lay hands on people," says Griselda. "You have to live aligned with your work. If you're selling a lifestyle of healing, you should be living it."

The Brujas are happy when young people become interested in the sacred path of healing. They believe that every person has the ability to tap into their intuition and heal themselves, whether they call themselves bruja or not.

Gri and Migue have been connected to womb work their whole lives. Their mother had them at forty and had a hysterectomy in her early fifties, so they were exposed to womb imbalances at an early age. Then at twenty-two, Miguelina found out she had HPV. While she was driving to interview for her doctoral program, she was told she needed a LEEP surgery. From that moment, womb healers started to enter the sisters' lives.

Griselda went on to train to be a doula, and this ushered the Brujas into yoni and womb work. They believe womb wellness is the seat of power, and not just for those with wombs, but for everyone. Womb health is everyone's work, because the womb unites us all, as we each come from a womb. We can each tap into the sacral chakra energy of creation and healing. While they practice their ancestral religion privately, in their communities they spread their knowledge through the practices of Kundalini yoga, which are based in Eastern traditions that center energy work through mantras and *kriyas*.

Though it might seem that yoga is an external influence in Caribbean lives, in fact, there were a lot of practitioners of Eastern religions across the islands. Half a million East Indians were brought to the Caribbean through the indentured labor trade in the 1800s. Their ancestral religions were suppressed the way African traditions were, but they were also syncretized into the culture.

The Brujas of Brooklyn embrace their in-betweenness. Whether they're teaching in the CUNY system or at yoga studios, they mix all these influences, and they're not precious about it. They'll play trap and reggaeton. They don't always wrap their hair or wear all white. They are themselves. They teach Black, Latinx, and Asian students. Their aim is to make any space they inhabit inclusive and welcoming, because they know how intimidating it can be to enter a botanica or yoga studio or college classroom.

They also offer services connected to the reproductive justice movement, which has always centered people of color, people with disabilities, and LGBTQ+ rights. They challenge the mainstream narrative of who can birth and how we birth in our society, as the birth industry is largely bound by regulations and systems that don't honor all bodies. While some people have been banned from terminating births, others have been forcefully sterilized. At the heart of this hypocrisy is the control of marginalized bodies to support a patriarchal, capitalist society.

"People of color have been at the mercy of people trying to control our bodies since this nation was founded," Griselda says. "We have to start creating our own thing."

On the full moon in Leo in January 2021, the Brujas went on Instagram Live with intuitive healer Hasani Reyes for a conversation they called "Healing the Mother Wound." They talked about the power of forgiving parents who hurt them because of their own generational traumas. While abuse is not excusable, forgiveness is healing, and we owe it to ourselves to let go of anger and resentment toward parents who couldn't or didn't do better.

The Brujas talked about how their mother sent them to live in the Dominican Republic when it became too difficult to raise them alone as an undocumented immigrant. While they felt her absence, they are grateful that she knew her girls would be better off with other family members, where they could have a community of support. This time spent in the Dominican Republic shaped them into who they would ultimately become.

To heal the mother wound, Reyes and the Brujas say, we need to reframe hardships as opportunities. If you are questioning your parents, if you've been hurt by your family, then you're being called to end the pattern of generational trauma of which you're becoming aware. This awareness is a privilege in itself. Most immigrant parents simply didn't have access to the kinds of mental health resources we have now through social media, and maybe they could have seen their patterns sooner if they'd had that access.

The Brujas ask: Can you accept that your mother has hurt you, while in turn seeing how she was hurt? To heal the separation between you, can you focus on how she did show you love, however small?

I thought of my own relationship with my mother. I was anxiously attached to her as a baby. I would cry incessantly unless she held me. When I went to school, she started working and was never home. We didn't do what mothers and daughters do. There were no beauty rituals, no coffee dates, no shopping sprees. She wasn't there, and I learned to place my attachment elsewhere.

Now, as an adult, I know she was suffering. Her mother had always struggled with mental illness, and they never did those mother-daughter things either. My mom and dad fought all the time, and she took refuge in her work. I felt partly responsible for her wanting to be away, because I often took my father's side, not realizing that I was instigating trouble. When I was a few years old, she left us home alone while my dad was out, and she returned later with her purse full of things. I told my dad about it, and they fought. I remember sitting on the floor of my room, trying not to hear, the lace on the bedspread scratching at my back. That was the first time I learned of my mom's compulsive shoplifting, and I think our mutual betrayal drove a wedge between us.

Listening to the Brujas of Brooklyn's talks about motherhood over the years has led me to reframe these memories in terms of love instead of trauma. I think my mother stole because she was trying to gain control over something in her life. It was the way the accumulation disease of my grandmother took hold of her. She was unhappy in her marriage to my father. So she took what she could, and she often gave me her spoils. Now I see it as her love language. Now that I've had my own unhappy relationships, I know how devastating it can be to feel trapped like that. The accumulation disease tries to take root in me, shows itself in my attachment to people and things. I hold on tight when I'm scared to lose.

My mom didn't abandon me. She was trying to show me how to fight, how to get free.

There's a woman called "La Cachetona" who was recently interviewed at El Buen Pastor in Bogotá. She was nearly sixty years old at the time and on her third stint in prison. She wrote her life story in notebooks that nobody will ever read. She used to want to kill herself, but now she's used to being locked up. She said to the reporter that the life of an imprisoned woman revolves around one thing: abandonment. The fear of being forgotten.

Our impulse toward freedom and connection, however irrationally or immorally it might show up, is our legacy. My mother says that in her final days, Ninoska kept mixing up her children and grandchildren as she called for them all in turn. I'd like to think that whoever we were to her in the end, that we were safe, that we were loved, that we were some part of her that broke free.

Poderada. That's the word my mother used to describe her, in the end. Powerful.

PROTECTION TIPS

At this point you've learned how to initiate a relationship with your ancestors, how to build an ancestral altar, and how to begin ancestral communication. The next step is to learn how to protect your spiritual spaces. Protection might feel like a defensive word, but first and foremost, protection means preservation. In other words, we want to do what we can to keep our altar and the channel to the ancestors clear. Protection is done out of love, not fear.

Tending to an ancestral altar is an act of remembering. We often approach our ancestors because we need help or seek empowerment. But it's not one-sided. The altar is a window into a relationship, and as much as we ask, we must also offer. Remember. Honor. Protect. When I keep my altar, I am preserving the lives of the ones who came before me. I am keeping them alive.

When I bring my ancestors food and tell about my day and ask a question, I am calling back to life those who have left the earth. I am calling the old ways to appear in the present. Ritual is a physical form of devotion. In my service to my altar, I'm lending movement and object to that which is unnameable, to faith.

Anybody who has practiced for any amount of time has struggled to keep up their space. We get busy and we let our altar go, and it collects dust and the food offerings start to turn and our water might have a dead fly in it. It happens! Setting up a regular, sustainable schedule and being disciplined and consistent about rituals and offerings will help keep the altar, and the lines to our ancestors, fresh.

Besides tending regularly to the altar, reinitiating protection measures through methods like spellwork, sigil magick, and boundary rituals will ensure a strong and protected space. Without these measures, at best, your connection will be weak, and your intentions and spells might go unanswered. At worst, you might mistakenly set the wrong intentions or invite unwanted spirits into the home. Don't panic!

Here are some general tips to keep yourself and your ancestors protected:

✳ Keep altars clean and offerings fresh. I like to renew the water as a daily morning practice, and every week I clean the altar of dust. Every month I'll remove all the altar items and clean them with diluted Florida water and oils. I have a separate cabinet for my altar items, and every month I'll put some things away and bring other things out, depending on the occasion. I usually do this leading up to new moons, when I'm cleaning my whole house. That way, my altar is fresh for the next day's intention setting.

✳ The broom is a great clearing instrument that has been used throughout Indigenous cultures to sweep away negative energy. On new moons I "sweep" the energy around the altar by holding the broom a few inches from the ground and moving in small circular motions.

✳ Occasionally burn incense to clear the air. It's important to open windows and doors when you're doing this, so trapped energies have somewhere to escape (and so you can breathe)! I like to use sustainably sourced products.

✳ Create protection boundaries. I use salt to create boundaries around the altar. This keeps the ancestors and spirits from traveling all over your home or keeping you awake at night. This is especially important if your altar is in your room (which I don't recommend, but sometimes it's inevitable, especially if you have roommates). The boundary will also keep others from infringing on your sacred space. This is crucial if your altar is in a more public space. The boundary creates an energetic shield. If you can leave the salt down, do. I usually sweep it up after a couple days, and refresh occasionally, maybe seasonally, maybe before you have visitors. (I also use this salt boundary along my thresholds, especially the main entrance to my house.)

✳ Experiment with spells and sigils. Spellwork and sigil magick lend themselves nicely to protection rituals. I like to use these during full moons in tandem with releasing rituals. It's a vulnerable time, when the moon is fully lit and exposing things that are usually kept hidden. Is there a prayer or a symbol you connect with that makes you feel safe? You can speak this out loud as a spell. It can be simple, like, "Guardians, please keep this space protected." You might draw the symbol on a piece of paper and leave it on the altar or draw it in the air with smoke. I like to keep them hidden behind mirrors or under tablecloths, because hidden sigils are the most potent.

CANCER: THE MOTHER

Cancer is the maternal archetype of the zodiac, ruling the fourth house of home and family. Cancer is the great protectress. It is the only sign ruled by the Moon, representing the divine feminine. Cancerians feel deeply and prioritize the needs of their loved ones. Less obvious to most is their unusually creative spirit. They can be undercover eccentrics. Turn to Cancer when you need a guide to inspired connection with the cosmos, or to practice syncing with natural cycles and self-care routines.

ELEMENT: Cardinal water

PLANETARY RULER: The Moon

AFFIRMATION: "I protect"

FOR YOUR ALTAR: Lilies and lotus flowers, watery fruit, water and mother deities, the crab, blue and silver and white stones, nurturing offerings like food

JOURNAL: What would you protect with your life?

DISRUPTING THE PATRIARCHY

Decolonization scholarship and healing practices addressing generational trauma have proliferated in recent years as more people seek to reclaim their ancestral spiritualities. Dr. Rosales Meza (@dr.rosalesmeza, drrosalesmeza.com) has a PhD in counseling psychology, but she sees the field of psychology as a system of colonization that disproportionately pathologizes women of color. She believes therapy is an Indigenous practice, and she offers classes called "Decolonizing Minds" and "Sacred Boundaries," along with many other resources for healing generational trauma.

Pānquetzani is the creator of Indigemama (@indigemama), providing Indigenous birthing services, herbal medicine, and classes through her account @indigescuela (indigescuela.com). Indigenous Women Rising (@indigenouswomenrising) is working to make sexual health and reproductive justice accessible to Native families.

II

SPIRITUAL ACTIVISM

"Every moment is an organizing opportunity, every person a potential activist, every minute a chance to change the world."

—Dolores Huerta

5

JOY AS RESISTANCE

The DUMBO Archway is a dramatic place to hold a party. It's forty-five feet high, and when you walk up to it, you feel like you're stepping into an old stone cathedral rather than the underside of a bridge. It was built in 1909 as a support for the Manhattan Bridge. Back then, this part of Brooklyn was primarily industrial, littered with broken down cars and oil barrels and waste of all kinds. In the 1980s the archway was used for storage, creating a block where Water Street used to run unimpeded to the waterfront. Residents dubbed the area DUMBO (Down Under the Manhattan Bridge Overpass) as a way to deter developers. But by 2008 the area had become gentrified, and the archway was cleared and transformed into a public community and event space.

A decade later, the golden stone of the archway glows with the annual Brooklyn Brujería festival. Off to the side of the main action, Chiquita Brujita is rarely the center of attention, but the way she dances without getting tired, I'd swear her movement generates the energy that keeps the heart of the festival beating. Hundreds of people congregate for the occasion. *Cantadoras* chant, tarot readers pull cards, the *bembé* circle pulses with drums and dancing, and magical people meet at the market, some for the first time since finding each other on social media.

When Chiquita Brujita twirls, her yellow skirt spreads out like the petals of a flower. Every time she turns, she transforms. Self-proclaimed Nuyorican, the daughter of an Afro–Puerto Rican mom and a half-Black, half-Jewish dad, she is Chelsea, carrying the rhythm of her home in Spanish Harlem with a wide smile and open laugh. Then she is Oshun, the river goddess draped in gold, representing joy and fertility and sweetness, calling for her children to join her. Then she turns again and there is the creative force once more, Chiquita Brujita, who brings her friends together.

This is what Chiquita Brujita does. She throws parties. But they're never just parties. In the fall of 2017 she was in the middle of planning an event when Hurricane Maria devastated Puerto Rico. Unexpectedly, in the midst of one of her greatest creative endeavors, she felt the pain coming from the land of her people. The Category 5 hurricane completely destroyed the island's power grid, leaving millions of people without electricity.

How do I level these two things: joy and chaos? Chiquita asked herself.

With the help of DJ Geko Jones, she turned the focus of the party to raising awareness about the devastation in Puerto Rico. It took place in the beautiful atrium of the Brooklyn Museum, but Chiquita found it hard to summon her usual ebullience when she felt so furious at the government's pitiful response to the disaster. Federal aid was slow to reach the island, especially in comparison to aid that had been sent to Texas and Florida for previous disasters.

When Donald Trump met with officials in Puerto Rico that fall, he downplayed the number of deaths, which at that time was officially in the dozens, suggesting it was nothing compared to the thousands who had died in Hurricane Katrina. At a relief center in a local church, he threw paper towels at the crowd as if they were T-shirts at a baseball game. Later he tweeted that it had been a great day in Puerto Rico.

Nobody knew it at the time—though San Juan mayor Carmen Yulín Cruz saw it coming and publicly reproached the president—but the devastation would lead to the death of thousands over the following months, mostly from diabetes and sepsis due to lack of electricity and clean water. Chiquita felt herself battling a rare feeling of hopelessness. What could she do when what she would raise would only be a drop in the bucket of the billions of dollars in aid Puerto Rico needed immediately?

Though her resources and reach were limited on short notice, the party in the Brooklyn Museum was the seed for what would become the next iteration of her community work, the annual Brooklyn Brujería festival and "joy raiser." The festival first took place in September 2018, on the one-year anniversary of the hurricane, under the DUMBO Archway. Magical artists of all kinds gathered to honor Puerto Rico's culture and resilience in the face of natural disasters and the federal government's neglect.

As she planned the second annual Brooklyn Brujería festival, Chiquita took on another problem that resonated with New Yorkers: the atrocities affecting immigrants and asylum seekers. Donald Trump had ended the DACA program, which protected immigrants who were brought to the country as children, and given the US Immigration and Customs Enforcement (ICE) authority to reopen hundreds of deportation cases. Undocumented people who had begun to make their lives in this country were suddenly very vulnerable. They feared getting in trouble in any way, as the smallest infraction could call attention to them and accelerate their deportation cases.

ICE was also separating children from their parents at the Mexico-US border and locking them up in detention facilities. In 2017 a pilot program in El Paso, Texas, allowed officials to detain and criminally charge adults who crossed the border without permission. It didn't matter if they had small children with them. The children were taken from them, and parents were not given any way of tracking where they were taken. There was no system in place to reunite families. By mid-2018 the practice of separation was made official. The Department of Justice implemented a "zero tolerance" policy. Migrants who crossed the border without documents, whether they were asylum seekers or not, were prosecuted and imprisoned, and children, hundreds as young as infants and toddlers, were transferred to the US Department of Health and Human Services. They were taken to one of a hundred shelters, often in rural areas far from any possible contact with family or proper medical care. Under mounting media pressure, the Trump administration revoked the zero tolerance policy and admitted that more than twenty-five hundred children were still separated from their parents. There was not yet a process in place to reunite them. In October 2018, while reunification efforts were still underway, Amnesty International reported that the number of families affected by the separations earlier that year were actually around six thousand, more than double what the Trump administration had reported.

In 2019 we began to understand the scope of the violence taking place at the border. The *New York Times* reported that the federal government had received more than forty-five hundred complaints about sexual abuse of children held in detention over the previous few years. The Human Rights Watch presented testimony before the US House Committee on Oversight and Reform. Their investigation found that thousands of children were being held in custody for weeks without adult supervision or access to proper hygiene. Many were sick and went untreated. Older kids were looking out for younger kids in the absence of institutional care. Besides the fact that these child immigrants have almost no rights to begin with, detention centers are mostly located in rural areas, far from access to the usual social safety nets and oversight. Though President Biden promised a more humane approach once in office, his administration has reverted to the extended detention of children while reunification efforts resume.

There are cages like this everywhere, at the borders of our civilization. Detention centers for immigrants we don't want. High security prisons for citizens we can't deport. We put them in the rural places of the country, what we call the "wilderness" beyond our highways, so we don't have to think about them.

To Chiquita Brujita, this hits close to home. She is a child of immigrants, and if her circumstances were just a little different, she and her family might be labeled illegal. Don't we all deserve to be safe? Shouldn't we all have the right to seek asylum? She thought of all the young immigrants who made up her beautiful community, and she felt a maternal impulse to protect them.

Chiquita Brujita is not yet crowned, but she comes from a line of priestesses of Santería. She is the youngest bruja of her family, and Oshun has been identified as the orisha of her head, the guardian orisha who is revealed upon preparation for initiation. Oshun is present anywhere people come together in celebration. She is present at the borders of human movement, where people most need her protection. She is especially present near rivers. At the archway leading to the East River separating Manhattan and Brooklyn, her golden glow falls on everyone attending the second annual Brooklyn Brujería festival. Her power pulses through the beats of the drums and the songs of the cantadoras. Her wisdom flickers in the cards drawn by the tarot readers. Her colors are reflected in the banners that read JOY AS RESISTANCE and in the big Brooklyn Brujería letters hanging in the middle of the archway. Chiquita honors Oshun by dancing all night, raising the energy, fiercely protecting her own, and inspiring everyone to keep the vibrations strong. She dances for those who can't show up because they are held against their will.

Taking up and holding space for others the way Chiquita does is a radical act in a country that refuses to acknowledge the full lives that immigrants carry from their homelands. Chiquita dances on the razor's edge of joy and sorrow. She dances, because she feels both emotions at the same time. They burn through her body as she transmutes them into something else, a feeling in the air that inspires and nourishes.

Chiquita Brujita is a spiritual activist. But it's not the fundraiser events that make her so. You don't have to have a big following or be an organizer or even protest on the streets to be a spiritual activist. As Gloria Anzaldúa writes, "Our spirituality does not come from outside ourselves. It emerges when we listen to the 'small still voice' within us which can empower us to create actual change in the world."

We associate activism with the loudspeaker, with the street march, with the showdowns with police. But activism starts with the heart, open and raw and vulnerable. Attend any protest and you will hear it beating under the surface. It lives in places of mass human activity, at the borders, at the banks of rivers, under bridges. We build these structures to control our movement, to keep some out and others in, but over the decades the energy of our movement imprints on a place, and if you're sensitive you can feel it, even see it sometimes, like the streaks of light in a long-exposure photograph.

When I was a teenager, I recklessly experimented with energy. One night, I packed three of my friends into my car and drove west on the infamous Tamiami Trail, which took us from our suburban homes toward the Everglades. It was a weekend in 2002, and we were up to no good. The horizon was aglow in dusky orange, like we were headed toward a huge bonfire in the distance. We were rolling joints and turning up the radio: Missy Elliot and Nelly and Eminem. The beats were fast. The landscape looked like the remains of an ancient ocean bed. The petrified melaleuca trees morphed into the fossilized bones of giant rib cages as we sped by.

We made a left onto Krome Avenue, at the time a two-lane highway known for its fatal wrecks. The sun had set, and darkness wrapped around our headlights. After a few minutes, we came to concrete barricades surrounded by thick foliage. This was it, according to my friend, who'd been there before. This was the entrance. I pulled over and we got out of the car. There was nothing and nobody around, and it was a dark, starless night. The air was full with alligator groans and the shrill of millions of cicadas.

We climbed the barriers and forced our way through the brush, our clothes catching. We came to a chain-linked fence that had been cut to let us through. One of us held it open while the others slid by. We were all nervously laughing. There was a long tarmac path that stretched into the darkness. We walked in silence, huddled close together. The path split off to the left, and as there was nothing but brush in the other direction, we turned. Soon, we saw the white facade of the facility materialize like a fish surfacing from deep waters.

We called it the "Insane Asylum," because that's what everyone called it.

It was a large concrete building covered in graffiti. There were no doors and windows, and we faced a long open corridor as we walked up. This is where we decided we would stay for the following couple hours, at the mouth of a building we knew nothing about. We sat in a circle and called on the spirits, unsure of ourselves, half joking. "Show yourselves!" we yelled into the night. I had been teaching myself how to open my body to the spirits. I grounded down into the earth and simultaneously opened the crown of my head, as if there were magnets pulling me in opposite directions. I imagined light pouring in and making its way down to my seat. When I practiced this in my room, spirits came like moths to a flame, and I got scared and shut it down, shaking my arms as if trying to get spiders off.

Out in the darkness, we were quickly distracted by our nervous laughter, and we turned on the boombox and passed a flask and dared each other to walk the long hallway with only the one flashlight we brought. We heard rumors that the ghosts of the inmates still walked the halls, but I was more worried about squatters as I took my turn.

I went first because I liked my friends to think me brave. I turned the flashlight into every small room I passed, holding my breath until I saw it was clear, then releasing it in a hiss as I kept walking. My heart was beating in my ears, but it was not the only beat. The place pulsed with energy. It was full and alive. A heartbeat was knocking at me from below the floor, asking to be let in. I clenched up. I moved my light over the next small room. Another corner of graffiti. The beat intensified. I felt something opening in my belly.

Suddenly, I was in my body more than I'd ever been. A surge of energy passed through me, and everything was cold and clear behind my eyes. I was very awake. It was too much. Like stepping into a current. Whatever it was, it wanted to escape. It wanted to go with me. I froze at that moment and let it enter me. Then I shook my arms out and turned and ran back to the entrance. My friends laughed at me for being scared, and I didn't know how to make them believe that it wasn't fear, exactly, that had driven me out. It was also awe, elation. I had felt a presence, and it had tried to hitch a ride. It succeeded a little, and I felt how big it was in there, how there was a whole universe inside me.

I tried to explain, but it's hard to put a whole universe into a few words. My friends laughed at me, saying it was just adrenaline. We spent a couple hours laughing and dancing and screaming. We felt the joy you can only feel when you're sixteen and do something you're not supposed to do, when you expose yourself to the bare elements and set yourself free.

It was so easy to feel full of power then, when I was young and unaware of the privilege of moving through space without consequence. My personal boundaries were so porous, and I ignored others' boundaries, physical and energetic alike. I didn't know that to be borderless was as much a risk as it was an ability. I indiscriminately let others in, floating from person to person, absorbing their energy. I hadn't yet learned about consent and why it's so important.

I had just broken up with my first boyfriend. We had been best friends for two years. We were romantics, soul mates. We'd once kissed at night in the middle of a field in a rainstorm. We listened to music and wrote each other notes and watched *Buffy* together. His was the first penis I touched, and I was terrified. I didn't know if I wanted to. I wanted to have what Willow and Tara from *Buffy* had. He and I felt like that—almost, but not quite. I didn't know how to tell him. We were Cubans in Miami, and it wasn't OK to be gay. I asked him to wait, that I'd be ready soon.

A year later, I was sixteen. I still wasn't ready, and I felt constantly anxious about it. I spent the night at a girlfriend's house. We slept in a room with two full beds, me on one, her on another. The door was cracked. I heard someone come in. It was her twenty-year-old brother. He got in the bed with me. I froze. He had sex with me while I tried not to move. I felt trapped, felt his energy entering me against my will. It hurt. I closed my eyes and thought that maybe this was how it was. Part of me was curious about the new experience and excited to get it over with. This could be good. I could make this a good thing. Shortly after I told my boyfriend about it, we broke up. I thought, OK, this is how this goes.

It was the same kind of feeling that night out at the Insane Asylum. The energy was hungry, violent in a way a drowning person can be when they use your body to get up for air.

We think of magic as the opposite of science, but magic observes natural law. Energy is not created out of nowhere. The trained witch knows that when you channel, you're inviting energies with long histories. I was so excited to explore the unknown that I didn't think of the possibility of harm. Maybe if I'd had a guide, I would have learned that channeling is not the exerting of power but the relinquishing of control. I was a naive medium glowing bright, exposed to strange energies, unprotected.

In 2015 I read that the Insane Asylum was being demolished in order to widen the street. I wondered if we had been wrong to call it that. I found that it had actually been a missile launch facility that the US Army built in 1965 as a response to the Cuban Missile Crisis. The site was decommissioned in the late '70s, and in the '80s the location was used as a temporary refugee camp for immigrants, which became known as the Krome Camp.

The Everglades wasn't just this place that I'd imagined since childhood. It was a brutally real place where people lived on the margins, among them the Miccosukee who had hidden in the swamps in rebellion until they could emerge and declare themselves sovereign, and the migrant workers in temporary camps who are trapped in the kind of indentured servitude that is our food labor system. The Krome Camp arose among them, and it evolved into a permanent detention center nearby.

A short while after that night with my friends, I was driving home from school on the Rickenbacker Causeway in Key Biscayne. Suddenly, there were hundreds of Black people on the bridge, running in the streets, hailing cars. A few ran to my car as I stalled in traffic. They threw their bodies against my windows. I saw my reflection in their pupils. I was scared, and suddenly I found my boundaries. I locked all the doors before they could try to open them. I looked ahead and inched my way out of there. In my rearview, I watched as officials rounded the people up.

When it actually counted for something, I was not brave at all.

I learned later that they were Haitian. Their boat had run aground, and they were making a run for it. Unlike most Cubans, Haitians can't stay if they make it to land. Most of the Haitians who were on the causeway that day were sent to places like Krome for detention and, ultimately, deportation.

The camp was known for its many abuses of its detainees, who were beaten and raped by the guards. Layers and layers of a violent history imprinted the energy of fear and containment and desperation onto the place.

✦ ✖ ✦

At the Brooklyn Brujería festival, circles formed and dissipated around the music in the Archway throughout the day, as Batalá New York and Bombazo Dance Company performed percussion-forward folkloric music. The acoustics under the bridge were wonderful. Just outside the Archway, tables and tables of brujas were selling their art and services: CBD potions, sustainable smoke bundles, magical talismans, and self-care beauty products. I weaved in and out of the crowd and caught snippets of conversation at the tables, which turned into impromptu knowledge shares. Many market goers asked questions about how to avoid culturally appropriating products in their daily health and beauty routines. Makers talked about collaborating on future projects.

I sat on a bench to watch everything, the way people converged and flowed and redefined personal boundaries. At the tarot tables, emotional intimacy was accelerated. On the dance floor, strangers pushed against one another. Next to me, people started to yell above the music. The crowd parted, and I saw a person being consoled by a circle of friends. Chiquita Brujita appeared to talk them down. From the little I heard, I gathered that a man had yelled a transphobic obscenity in a threatening way. Transgressions like these punctuated a night largely marked by joy, as people let down their guards.

Day turned to night, and the market was broken down and more people danced and talked. Bulla en el Barrio took the stage. They ended the formal festivities with ancestral music, the *costeño* music of my childhood. It's a take on traditional *bullerengue*, a *cumbia*-based, Afro-Colombian style that usually revolves around cantadoras, women who chant folk stories and perform call-and-response lines with the audience.

Chiquita Brujita is inspired by traditional *cantos* such as these by performers like Celia Cruz and Petrona Martínez. Cantadoras take private family folk stories and healing ancestral music and showcase them in public spaces. They channel the power of the past into an ecstatic present moment. They don't just take the stage. They hold space for people to connect to their roots and share their gifts for protection and healing. The music is more than words and notes. *Cantadora* means keeper of the stories. Every land has its own brand of folk music, with its own stories and lessons. The danza. The pasillo. The choro. They all have one thing in common. They keep the healing wisdom of the ancestors alive through the joyful expression of the body. This is powerful medicine one can call on in times when protection is needed.

The train barreled overhead, mixing with the drums, and suddenly the whole place was a portal, a chakra, a concentrated energy center. Some places are like this at certain times when people get together. When we say we feel a presence somewhere, I think we're feeling this energy mixing with the energy centers of our own bodies. To perceive this, to channel this, we have to be entirely present in our shared experience. And to be collectively present on such a large scale is magical, like that transcendence you sometimes feel at a music festival or a political rally.

The body ritual is used in Indigenous and Afro-Carribean religions to express both joy and suffering, whether in dance, trance, spirit communication, or exorcism. Sometimes the body opens to the spirit world for a few moments. It moves with chaos, releases into the current of life and death, and creates an expression of spirit. This state is sometimes labeled "ecstatic."

In ecstasy, joy is not the opposite of grief. It is its sister state. Joy is wide awake, taking everything in. Joy is honest pain, pain transmuted. I chanted the words of the bullerengue, and the line between joy and grief faded, and I felt the transgenerational ties of my family that stretch behind me and in front of me into infinity.

I remembered the cumbia of my childhood parties. My aunts always hosted, and for a while, it seemed like they held a party every weekend. I didn't make many friends in grade school, because I had so many cousins. There were dozens of us, and we were best friends. There was always a birthday or anniversary or holiday to celebrate. We were loud, and because of that, the music was always turned up. Horns and flutes and accordions and drums. The grown-ups yelled to each other above the music. It was not in an angry way, usually, but there was an innate aggressiveness to it all, this arms race of sound.

It was a lot for a sensitive teen. I retreated to a corner and listened to the far-fetched stories the uncles told. I had an ear for gossip and liked to know what was going on with everyone. Every now and then, one of my uncles sauntered up to me and asked me to dance and tugged at my hands before I had a chance to say no. I yanked my hands away and ran off. They joked that maybe I didn't like men.

It was true, mostly. Their presence set me on edge. I just wanted to be with my female cousins and aunts. I never wanted to dance with the men, whose hands controlled the movement. The few times I had, my wrists hurt from trying to go another way. I felt caged in and exposed at the same time, everyone looking, making comments about how my body was changing. I was rail thin with a disproportionately round butt that solicited honks and catcalls from strangers when I walked home. I was just starting to become conscious about how parts of me were desirable to men—my hips, my blonde hair—while others—my bony nose, my small breasts—weren't. "Don't worry," my aunts and grandmother would say. "We can have those fixed for you later."

Toward the middle of the night, when everyone was good and drunk, my *tía* Linda emerged in her pollera, a long, white traditional skirt from Colombia, ruffled at the ends. She had a long necklace with a half shell tucked in her breasts and a bottle of aguardiente in one hand. Everyone agreed she was the ideal female form. When she was younger, she had been a finalist in a Miss Colombia pageant. Long, thick hair to her hips. Tall, and unapologetically taller in heels. Big breasts, small waist, thick bottom. As the first part of her show, she walked around flirtatiously, filled her half shell with a shot, and no matter your age, she made you take it right there from her breasts. She was the matriarch, and we were all her kids.

Then came the cumbia.

Cumbia is the folk music of Colombia. It's named after the word *cumbé*, a Guinean dance. It was born in times of slavery, a mixture of African drums, Indigenous Colombian flute, and Spanish dress and choreography. The dance is most popular on the Caribbean coast in the upper valley of the Magdalena River, where my family is from.

I loved watching my aunt dance cumbia. When she'd gotten everyone's attention, she put down the bottle and started to move. She held the ends of her skirt in her hands and made a figure eight with it as she slowly covered the perimeter of the circle that had formed around her. Her movements were deliberate, almost subdued, but her hips told another story. They swung rapidly from side to side to the beat of the *tambora*.

Cumbia is many dances and many stories in one. To watch my aunt dance cumbia was to see the layers of who we were. The Spanish dress represented assimilation. The steps were written, and we followed. But under all that fabric, the naked body moved to the beat of the drums, improvising toward the opportunities of the moment. The drums were the part of us that can't be caged in. And above it all was the flute, the *gaita*, the sound of the first people which pulled the heart up to a greater truth and told a story as old as time.

It's said that cumbia is a courtship dance. But the man and the woman barely touch. My aunt was the center, and the uncles stepped into her path and took their steps and retreated. The woman was in control, and consent was required to approach her. She held her boundaries even as she was open. She had the choice and the power. She was also the sacrifice, the beautiful form we offered to the party gods. She took all the attention off others, so we could dance freely, in our own way, satellites to her reigning movement, all screaming *huepa*!

At DUMBO, as the train passed overhead and drowned everything out, I let loose a single "huepa." I moved to the drums and let memories flood through me. Dance taps into the same sacral energy involved in sex. My relationship with my boyfriend at the time was beginning to unravel, and I was starting to feel the old cycle of insecure attachment. For a decade I had been a light for soul searchers, addicts, and people in transition. I became codependent, drawing worth from my ability to fix others or make them feel good. I had forgotten what it was like to dance alone. I let others lead. I melded to each partner. I didn't know how to establish boundaries, and I lost myself in others' emotions and timelines. I always got hurt, and then I became resentful. I wanted to break this cycle, but I didn't know how.

Chiquita Brujita said the event was a *limpia*, a "collective cleansing," and now I know what she means by "joy as resistance." The path of the spiritual warrior is to remain open to both the dark and light in ourselves. Destruction and creation are ends of the same soul process. We cannot open to the magic and wonder of the universe and then close ourselves to the suffering.

Chiquita inherited her grandmother's Obatala when she passed. He is the father of all the other orishas, and to honor him you walk a path of sobriety and responsibility for others. This is what got Chiquita started on her path of philanthropy. A deep love of humanity is at the center of every celebration. Chiquita creates a space in which people may share freely, and this, as Audre Lorde writes, "forms a bridge between the sharers which can be the basis for understanding much of what is not shared between them, and lessens the threat of their difference."

All spiritual activists are mediums in the sense that they open to the shadows. They filter suffering and transform it into healing. To turn pain into joy is the greatest gift we can give. This might be hard to do when we've grown up witnessing a lot of pain. Trauma can have a way of tinging everything with fear. Mix this with the activist's awareness of the ills of the world, and feeling joy might seem impossible at times. This is why spiritual activism is an act of bravery. We commit to living the best lives we can even as we keep opening to the way our freedoms have been violated. We willingly step into the unknown with no armor, with our tender hearts beating in our hands.

If we are able to experience and spread joy, we must try. It is both a privilege and a responsibility to put that energy into the world and create connections of love wherever we can. If the first tenet of being a bruja is connection with the ancestors, then the second is the service that we can offer to collective evolution. It can be a small contribution. It can start with ourselves, by learning how to love and take care of ourselves, and if we have the energy, extending that care to those closest to us. Our personal joy is an act of resistance to a structure that would oppress the many for the benefit of the few.

Being a bruja is inherently political.

"Recognize that pleasure is a measure of freedom," writes adrienne maree brown in her book *Pleasure Activism*. "Part of the reason so few of us have a healthy relationship with pleasure is because a small minority of our species hoards the excess of resources, creating a false scarcity and then trying to sell us joy, sell us back to ourselves."

Pleasure has been a difficult thing for me to embrace. Over the years, I've gone from long relationships with men to promiscuous sprees and back to long relationships, everything in hyper speed. I thought I was searching for love, but after each failed relationship, I felt inexplicable shame. I had never told anybody but my boyfriend at the time about my first full sexual experience, until recently. I was cavalier about it, joking. The friend I told was concerned, asked me if I'd ever talked to a therapist, said that it was rape. I had never thought of it that way.

I didn't even think about it that way when all the women started coming out with their #MeToo stories in 2006. I hadn't said no, hadn't struggled. I had just frozen. All the posts made me angry for some reason I didn't understand at the time. Now, I see it was triggering me to face a dissonance between what I thought and what I felt.

It didn't fully hit me until I read Evan Rachel Wood's February 2021 testimony against Marilyn Manson. She said that he horrifically abused her, and that for a long time she believed it was her fault, because she had frozen instead of fought. She said, "Sometimes we are held down, not just by our attackers, but by what we know about our place in the world. She may freeze because she is terrified but also because she knows, deep down, there is nowhere for her to go."

Wood did research on this freeze response, and she found it is called "tonic immobility." During her testimony, she cited the 1977 issue of *The Psychological Record* stating that freezing is a common trauma response among animals, who sometimes perceive "playing dead" as the best option for survival.

Marilyn Manson was my childhood idol. He had unlocked some

understanding in me about my attraction to all genders and to androgyny, and he made me feel so normal when the rest of the world made me feel like a freak. Suddenly, Wood's testimony threw everything I thought I knew about him into question, and like a domino effect, it also disrupted everything I thought I knew about every relationship I'd ever had. Had I been unconsciously responding to that first sex experience? How had it changed my natural inclinations? It takes a long time to process some things, which is one reason why many people don't come out about abuse until years later. This is why personal testimony is so important. It can save lives.

Some things take years and years to see. You have to peel back the layers and layers of history, and it's really hard to put the truth into words, to show any evidence of cause and effect. But the truth lives in our bodies, if we have the courage to open to it.

Under the bridge, surrounded by strangers, I felt myself whole, unfolding from the inside. Music flowed through me and I fell into a trance. Something else took hold. This is it. This is what our ancestors lived and died for. They didn't just want us to survive. They wanted us to find connection, to thrive. They wanted us to have movement, not for us to be contained. And this is what we have to fight for everyone to access. Our bodies aren't objects to be consumed or locked up. They are mediums for the spirit within this great collective ritual called living. Under the bridge, I felt the universe opening inside, the terrifying and empowering freedom of all that space.

This joy is the future, the part of us that is limitless, not yet written.

GODDEX MEDITATION

The Goddex is a deity who contains both divine feminine and masculine energies. In many myths the male and female are joined as one, whether in androgynous or hermaphroditic form, or through sexual union. They represent both the warrior and the protector, creation and destruction, earthly form and energetic transcendence. Who is your favorite deity of any gender? In times of powerlessness, I often call to Ardhanarishvara of Hindu mythology, the union of the male Shiva and female Shakti. They remind me that I am whole, even without a partner, and that I am not alone.

If you have an established meditation practice, you might try incorporating a short deity visualization at the beginning or end of your practice. If you're new to meditation, here are some basics to get you started:

1. Find a comfortable seat. It doesn't have to be cross-legged on the floor. You can also sit in a chair, or if you're feeling tired, you can lie on your back or practice this in the bath. Whatever you choose, you want to be relaxed and in a space where you'll be uninterrupted for at least a few minutes.

2. Let your eyes close and call attention to your natural breath. Slowly

begin to deepen your breath. Expand your belly on the inhales and release your exhales slowly. Do this for a couple of minutes. When you notice yourself running with a thought, simply return focus to the breath.

3. When you feel ready, call your deity to you. Visualize them in front of you. See the details of their face and clothes. See the color of their aura. See their light expanding to encompass you. Don't worry if they don't appear right away. They could come to you through any of the senses. If you know a mantra associated with them, you can chant or sing it and open to what arises. At first it might just be a feeling. Pay attention to where you feel sensations.

4. Close your meditation by thanking the deity and returning focus to your breath. You might also take some time to journal after your meditation. How did you feel? What did you see? Did your deity transmit a message? It might be a good moment to write about what it is you would like to protect in your life. Is there a cause you care about that you might petition your deity about during your next meditation? They are more likely to appear the more consistent your relationship to them.

LEO: THE RULER

Leo is the queen of the zodiac, the only sign ruled by the Sun. It rules the fifth house of romance, joy, sex, creativity, and children. The Leo archetype is loyal, proud, and loves attention. Leos have big hearts and great hair or a penchant for wearing crowns. Though they love the spotlight, they require more alone time than you'd think. Connect with Leo if you need a jolt of confidence or a reminder of your self-worth. Leo will also help if you need to establish healthy boundaries to preserve your own agency.

ELEMENT: Fixed fire

PLANETARY RULER: The Sun

AFFIRMATION: "I will"

FOR YOUR ALTAR: Bitter herbs, sunflower, citrus, sun deities or royals, felines, gold and yellow stones, anything that raises the energy or that calls in light

JOURNAL: What makes you feel powerful? If your energy feels off, ask yourself where you are directing your attention. Are you giving more than you're receiving, or are you depending too much on another's gifts? How can you reclaim or nurture your power?

PLEASURE AND POWER RITUALS

Sometimes self-care looks like giving conscious self-improvement a rest and just enjoying yourself. There are few better guides in the bruja community for learning how to give and receive pleasure than Gabriela Herstik (@gabyherstik, gabrielaherstik.com), an ally beloved in the bruja community who offers fire self-love and self-lust affirmations to awaken your inner goddess. She has helped me reclaim the erotic as a source of pleasure and freedom, instead of pain and containment.

Also check out Yvette Montoya (@yvetteactually, brattybrujita. com), a bruja and journalist who specializes in sexual energy and spiritual hygiene, and James Ocelotl (@odinsbrujx), a two-spirit practitioner who makes custom harnesses and kink wear.

You can't have pleasure when you're exhausted. The Nap Ministry (@thenapministry; napministry.com), run by "Nap Bishop" Tricia Hersey, advocates for rest as a form of resistance and reparations for people of color. She said on the podcast *Undistracted*, "I refuse to let capitalism own my body when they still owe a debt to my ancestors." Rest and resistance to grind culture is one of the greatest ways to honor your ancestry and protect your ancestral birthright.

These topics are triggering for some, especially for those who have experienced abuse. It's important to have support from a therapist or counselor while facing traumas and opening to pleasure.

6

ABUELITA MEDICINE

Home is dark wood floors and soft dawn light, slow mornings with coffee, herbs hanging, the feeling of being tucked into a secret forest thick with fairylike bugs. I've made this place from memories of childhood dreams, where I'd go in my mind when my parents were fighting. I'm nostalgic for a home that's never existed. There's a Portuguese word for it: *saudade*.

Now I live in a house that nobody else wanted. That in itself is a point of pride. It's a tiny bungalow built in the 1920s—super cottagecore vibes. The electrical wiring is old, and very few outlets have a ground. I think a high-tech media system would set the whole place on fire. It smelled feral when I moved in. Cats pooped in the crawl space under it, and nature was making quick work of reclaiming it. I bet that's why it sat on the market for so long before I came along. It was just about the only house in Tampa Bay I could afford alone on my freelance income that was in good enough condition to qualify for a loan. The bank nearly turned me down each step of the way. I got lucky, and I had the privilege of access to first-time homebuyer resources. I call it the little witch cottage, and it's the best thing in my life.

Capitalism rarely centers care. We see this so clearly in real estate, especially in gentrifying neighborhoods. Investors buy houses they don't need. They push out renters who have been there a long time. They beat out low-income families, because they have cash or they can bid more. They do the minimal work to make the houses look nicer, and they flip them, maybe double the price in a matter of months because the neighborhood is on fire, and then they sell to people who can easily afford the mortgage. Developers tear down old houses that could have made lovely homes, homes that have stood there for a hundred years, and they build new construction with cheap materials that won't last half the time. Housing becomes unaffordable for many, especially for people of color.

This is a nationwide trend in urban areas in the United States. In the mid-twentieth century, White people moved to the suburbs, and laws and policies created de jure segregation, relegating immigrants and people of color to urban centers. Highways were built through their neighborhoods, isolating them, and poorly managed housing projects rose up to meet the demand for homes. With their properties worth so little, it was difficult for homeowners in these neighborhoods to build wealth, and prospective homeowners were often the target of predatory loans, if they could get loans at all.

When the housing market collapsed in 2008, lending tightened up, particularly for Black buyers. White buyers were much better positioned to take advantage of the lower home prices, and they increasingly returned to the urban centers they had once rejected. By the time the market stabilized and Black residents could qualify for loans, they found they could no longer afford homes in their own neighborhoods, as older houses were replaced by new development. These are some of the ways the market has kept Black and Brown people from building generational wealth.

I am somewhere in the middle of all this, caught up in the great current of markets through which we unconsciously move. I moved to Tampa when the recession hit, and first I lived in the suburbs, because that's what I always knew. As much as I hated it, there I was again, among the big-box stores and the gated communities. I was in my mid-twenties, and I had followed a guy I thought I was in love with, but really, he was like the suburbs: safe and familiar. Or so I thought.

He was my godfather's son, and we had grown up visiting each other's families between Miami and Tampa. Something about us felt fated, simultaneously idealistic and comfortable. With my move to Tampa, we thought we could finally start our lives together, but it was hard to afford rent, which hadn't adjusted to reflect the recession. We shared a three-bedroom apartment with two other roommates. We took the jobs we could find. I took night classes for my master's degree while working full time between a Cracker Barrel and a call center. A couple years into this, that's when things started to fall apart.

He started to become upset if I didn't cook dinner right. I had never learned to cook and was crash-coursing my way through it, and every meal caused me great anxiety. He resented my education, my increasingly liberal views. He got into conspiracy theory rabbit holes and frequently cited Alex Jones rants: *Lizard people control our government. The Illuminati has a plan to take our guns. 9/11 was an inside job. Something big is coming, and we have to get ready.* On the weekends, his parents called family meetings to prepare for what they saw as the pending apocalypse. I tried arguing, but it only prolonged the meetings, which I was always eager to see finished, so we could just eat and hang out.

One day I helped the family bury barrels of food in a rural property they owned near Dade City, north of Tampa. We were to meet there when shit went down. When we were done, my boyfriend and I went walking around a pond on the property. There was an alligator in the middle of the pond. My boyfriend pulled out his Glock, which he always carried on him. He took aim and fired, shooting the alligator on the snout.

The alligator writhed. She turned vertical and jumped up so her tail was swishing on the surface of the water, defying gravity. I fell to my knees. I felt a terrible rattling inside of me, like some reptilian survival response had been activated. I couldn't believe what he'd done. When I looked up, he was smiling.

I didn't remain the little flower he'd thought I was. One night he dragged me to our room by my arm and threw me on the bed and held his hand over my mouth as I tried to scream. I struggled under his weight, but I couldn't break free. I tried screaming for our roommate, who had seen him dragging me, but he didn't come. Then a hand came down on my temple, and everything went dark.

I was in a dream then, walking on the heads of alligators still as stone. I was nine years old, pressing my ear to the hot pavement. I was on the roof looking out over the strawberries. I was someone older, from the future, in a house with wooden floors and yellow stained-glass windows.

In my moment of darkness, something inside me reset. It was only a moment, but it was enough. He got up and left me there, gasping through sobs. I felt just how unsustainable it all was, trying to make a life with someone who didn't even know me, who resented me for the little he did know about me. I barely even knew myself. If I stayed, I would never know myself. I would be absorbed by him, become what he wanted, in this life he wanted, that I never wanted. I would die.

It took months for me to be able to afford to leave. The recession had stripped me of everything, including savings and a good job. I couldn't even afford a moving truck. In those months, the abuse continued. The verbal abuse was almost worse. He said I was worthless and that nobody would want me, and I believed him even as I fought him. On a night out on New Year's Eve, he threw his drink in my face as the crowd counted down, and as everyone cheered, I ran out into the city I barely knew, the fireworks shooting off in the sky overhead.

I refused to sleep with him after that, so he started to cheat on me. One time, he slept with one of our roommates' guests who was crashing in the room next to ours. I heard them through the wall. I was too ashamed to tell anybody or to ask for help. When I finally had enough to leave, I barely said a word to him. I just packed my things and within a day, I had a whole new life.

I couldn't afford to live alone long, so over the following years while I started my PhD, I moved closer to downtown Tampa, where the rent was cheaper. I moved from roommate to boyfriend to roommate to boyfriend. I didn't really know if I was with them because of money or because I was scared to be alone, or both. Life was a series of reactions to crises. A boyfriend told me he was in love with one of my friends. My heart broke, and I immediately looked to fill the loneliness with others. I said yes to the first person who asked me to marry him, hoping it would save me from this pattern of dead ends. But it was part of the same pattern, of course.

He was an alcoholic. On the night before our elopement, he pushed me to the floor. Again I was too embarrassed to tell anybody, so I blocked it out and signed the marriage papers. The violence escalated. He threw things across the room. He told me I was worthless. He hid handles of vodka in the bushes. Sometimes he leaned over me in bed, pinning me down and whispering obscenities in my ear. One day he almost drank himself to death. We lived with roommates, and one of them called the ambulance. That's how I started to snap out of it. I felt ashamed that I hadn't learned my lesson. While he was in rehab, I filed for divorce. And then I got right into another relationship.

We can get caught up in currents like this. We're told that things are a certain way, and we internalize and act upon those beliefs. I was told that this land presents opportunities that were not available to my parents. I adopted a colonizer mentality. I wanted everything, all at once: the house, the car, the marriage, the children, the big career. I borrowed money I didn't have the means to pay back and entered relationships with people who weren't right for me. I became indebted. I built a cage around myself.

Amid all of this, I had a moment of clarity in which I imagined myself as an old lady. What would grandma me say? *Get yourself a place of your own.*

By the time I settled into the little witch cottage, I felt a security I had not felt in my whole life. My mortgage was low enough to afford even in the worst of times, and I didn't have to depend on anyone to pay the bills. I had small streams of income that were somehow enough. I spent most days in the yard, bare feet in the ground, getting to know the place. I remembered how much I'd loved dirt as a kid. It filled the places where I was empty, cooling the hot rivers flowing inside me. It called for me to stay low to the ground instead of flying away in the tornados that would occasionally spring from my thoughts. The earth held me and took my anxiety so I could breathe. It wanted me to touch it, to turn it and add to it. I was its medicine, and it was mine.

I slowly unclenched the places inside that were locked up to keep the past at bay. I opened up to let them all flow: The hard memories of childhood. The feelings of grief and fear. The heartbreak of so many failed relationships. The constant striving to have something and be someone. I let it all do what it would. It swirled and swirled around in me. When I couldn't stand it, I dug my hands into the dirt and gave it to the earth. What felt like poison to me was its nourishment, just as oxygen is a plant's excretion and a necessary intake for us. I turned the dirt, because it helped me feel better, and life sprung up from our touching. Plants and bugs I'd never seen before emerged.

There's a patch of Spanish needles I let grow wild in the back of my yard. Spanish needles is considered a weed, because it's aggressive and produces prickly seeds that cling to your pants. This is what makes a weed a weed: its inconvenience and its persistence to grow where it's not wanted. I've always thought it beautiful, how it springs up in collective force after a heavy rain, dotting the yard with specks of yellow. The first year I lived in my little house, I noticed hundreds of bees in its flowers. It wasn't a weed to them; it was sustenance. That's when I decided to give my yard to the bees. To have this kind of control, to let things be. To call this mine, this healing bubble in the middle of Tampa, next to Waters Avenue with the speeding cars, surrounded by neighbors blasting salsa music, dogs barking in their yards. It's a lifeline.

★ ✹ ★

"Some of us have survived many apocalypses," Loba said.

In April 2020 we had been in lockdown for a month, so I was eager to take La Loba Loca's Zoom workshop, "DIY Plant and Garden Tending for the Apocalypse." The quarantine in response to COVID-19 did feel like the end of a way of life, and the world outside seemed threatening. People were starting to look up from their lives of striving and accumulation, some for the first time. They were waking up to their environmental footprint, to economic imbalance, to the racism that is deeply embedded in this country. The ones who didn't fight or ignore all the ways they were hurting, those who opened to vulnerability, began to see their role in it all, how they had bought into systems that separated them from the realities of other people and the environment.

La Loba Loca, Loba for short, saw this time of isolation and uncertainty as an opportunity to share how to tend to the earth. They are a queer Brown herbalist and feminist activist in Los Angeles, which they refer to as "Tongva land." Loba is from southern coastal Peru. They share what they call "abuelita medicine" through low-resource gardening, the way their abuelitas lived in Arequipa.

To Loba, gardening is a process of healing generational trauma, and it's a practice of resistance. It is not a beautification project. It is not landscaping. It's not done to "fix up" real estate to sell higher. To Loba, land ownership is settler colonialism. Because it is based on a market, it is inherently extractivist. In other words, owners of property tend to be inclined toward what they can get from the land, whether directly or through its sale.

In contrast, Loba's gardening is a way to offer help to all life-forms, not just to ourselves. We are giving back to the earth, feeding the soil. We tend and serve plants and soil for all the generations, whether we own the land or not. The aim is to build multispecies communities on the land to which we tend. Loba says this kind of land is a *chakrita,* an Andean word that means "my endearing piece of soil." It is an energy center, an altar to nature and spirit.

To garden like an abuelita, we feed the soil, not the crop. Our aim is to heal the soil, not to produce. Every soil is different. You have to get to know it and what it needs, says Loba, making *pagos a la tierra,* "payments to the earth," through material things like composting, but also through energetic offerings like the love and gratitude you feel for the earth.

Loba's abuelita medicine is a technology rooted in both spirit and nature. We call it permaculture now, a term that was coined relatively recently to describe the holistic gardening that observes natural processes. Loba doesn't like the word *permaculture*. To them, it's a way that White people take credit for what Indigenous peoples have been doing for centuries, whether it's reusing materials, keeping scraps of food for the soil, or saving seeds.

Our agricultural history in the United States has been based on the opposite of sustainability. It was created through the labor of enslaved people, and it depleted the land. Cotton, for example, uses so much water to grow that it causes erosion and degradation, and it requires more pesticides than almost any other crop, but it was considered a "cash crop," the opposite of a weed.

Loba shared the story of George Washington Carver, a Black agricultural scientist who was born into slavery. He invented methods to prevent soil depletion from repeated plantings of cotton, tapping into ancestral and Indigenous wisdom and helping poor people grow food and live healthier lives. It's very hard to be this kind of medium, to balance such different ways of knowing with such different aims, to direct it all toward the common good.

This is what it means to decolonize gardening and herbalism to Loba. In recent years, there has been a growing interest in backyard gardening, beekeeping, and homesteading in general, and that interest has skyrocketed during times of COVID-19. This market for sustainability is a paradox, as it takes time and money and land to be able to achieve self-sufficiency within capitalism. If you don't have resources, if your ancestral land has been stolen or poisoned, if you rent an apartment, if you have to work long shifts at multiple jobs to provide for your family, living off the land is easier said than done. It is a privilege to be able to build a sustainable garden in your backyard during a recession worse than the one that began back in 2008.

For Loba, true sustainability means access for everyone, and we can start pushing the needle in the right direction through mutual aid networks. Mutual aid is a form of political participation that challenges the tenets of capitalism and the free market. It is based on the voluntary exchange of resources for the benefit of the collective. Through mutual aid, we can take care of each other during hard times and meet the needs of the people as we work toward more sweeping structural and political change.

The term *mutual aid* was coined in the late 1800s by scientist and activist Peter Kropotkin. In contrast to charitable donations, mutual aid is characterized by self-organization, egalitarianism, direct action, and the aim of social transformation. Mutual aid networks are grassroots efforts without a single leader. The COVID-19 pandemic has triggered a rise in mutual aid organizations and knowledge sharing to meet emergency crises, such as homelessness, starvation, and domestic violence, that are not being addressed quickly enough by local and federal governments. For example, Indigenous Mutual Aid was established as a hub for Indigenous relief organizing. They have compiled a directory of mutual aid organizations and an exhaustive list of resources about pandemic organizing.

Mutual aid networks function as stopgaps to tide communities over in times of crisis, but in the long run, the goal is to influence government intervention and systemic change. This won't happen through the type of armchair activism that has arisen during the pandemic. Are we turning our backyards into gardens to battle problems like bee colony collapse and local food insecurity? Are we committing to the hard work of embodying anti-racism at our personal risk? Or are we just temporarily mitigating personal crises and virtue signaling to our followers on social media? Are we biding our time until we can return to "normal"?

The progress of mutual aid networks is further challenged by the kind of apocalyptic mindset that propels individuals to buy up all the toilet paper on the shelves in a panic. Apocalyptic thinking is based in fear and self-preservation rather than compassion and humanitarianism. We use the earth and animals, and even other humans, as resources instead of fostering mutually beneficial, long-term relationships with each other. What would our abuelitas say if they heard us calling this the apocalypse, after what they've seen? It betrays our privilege and our ignorance of the oppression some communities have endured for generations.

This fear response to emergencies is not new. I saw it growing up in Miami, the way people would shove each other out of the way at stores and fight at gas stations when a hurricane was on its way. I saw it among my ex-boyfriend's family members a decade ago, as they hurried to bury their barrels of food. If we could only create long-term structures and policies of preparedness that anticipated spikes in resource demands, we could work together in a more loving way and all have what we need. We wouldn't resort to violence or hoarding when we are threatened.

Though Loba used the term *apocalypse* in a tongue-in-cheek way, spiritual communities have fallen prey to conspiracy theories heralding the end of the world that are eerily similar to the ones I heard my ex regurgitating from Alex Jones. While preaching love and light, many spiritual and wellness influencers peddle misinformation about vaccines and shadow governments, mirroring the theories of the alt-right. This "conspirituality" is becoming a runaway train, and it's harder and harder to tell which spiritual influencers are the real deal, and which are full of their own compost.

Practitioners like Loba are grounding (literally, in Loba's case) sources of wisdom. Loba uses the subscription service Patreon to spread their knowledge about various forms of abuelita knowledge and mutual aid. They write about everything from seed libraries to heirloom corn. They also write about queer health and bruja feminism. These might seem like unrelated topics, but Loba shows us how they connect. Sustainability is not just about resources, it's about the acceptance of all forms of life. Capitalism thrives on categorizing people and controlling what one does with one's body and who can join together. To be a weed instead of a cash crop, to resist the White heteronormative cisgender standard and grow as you will, is to strain a system that doesn't have the health of all in mind. Gender wildness is the natural order of things, and as mutual aid grows, so will systems that don't divide people based on identity or orientation. Those who are attached to the old structures will say it's the end-time. But life will go on. We don't have to dismantle oppressive systems so much as divest and reorganize and radically spring up together.

Loba is constantly evolving. In April 2021 they announced that they are changing all their social media handles from "La Loba Loca" to "Flora Pacha," in honor of their ancestry and their love of plants. "Plants are the best teachers when it comes to destroying borders," Loba says. When we grow wildly, those who would benefit from dominating us will prickle at our presence. They will call us dangerous, and they will try to tear us apart. We must grow over them, because we are the majority.

Speaking of literal plants, Loba says there's no such thing as *una mala mano*, "a bad hand for gardening." It's all about learning and access to learning. If you can't grow something, it's not necessarily because you're cursed. It takes a lot of trial and error and just the right conditions to make things work.

"Planta lo que te crece," Loba says. *Plant what grows for you.*

With practice, my green thumb gradually emerged. I started to cook again, and to shed the shame I felt about it, the memories of being told I was no good at it. I started to take care of myself as a parent would take care of a child. I started to heal the part of myself that thought she didn't deserve care. I started to learn that self-care is the foundation for any sustainable life.

In the book of Revelation, the apocalypse is the destruction of the world, but it's also a time when things that were hidden reveal themselves. When things aren't working, the period of breakdown can be the start of something better.

Some call this period we're experiencing "late-stage" capitalism. The market is failing many people, and we are starting to form new networks of support. To Loba, "gardening for the apocalypse" is not about the end of the world, but about creating a new world based on an ancient way of being, about getting back to basics and improving access to the land for everyone. It's about the well-being of the soil, the plants, the animals, and the humans for many generations to come.

On Indigenous Peoples' Day, my honeybees were robbed by other honeybees. The summer rains had created big cracks in their hive, and the other bees smelled the honey and had a lot of ways to get in. There was a multiday battle, and I watched it, powerless.

It never takes long to find parallels between the bees and the problems in our world. I sit with them, and their buzzing soothes me, and little questions arise, like, who gets to own anything? I try to practice what I preach with them. I try to help them instead of doing it for the honey. But I can't hide that I feel a great pride that they're "mine." And then they get robbed, and I can't help but feel that I'm getting robbed.

I am in between in this story. I am from a family that has been dispossessed and disconnected from their land, and I am a settler. For as hard as it was for me to get here, I enjoy the great and increasingly rare privilege of "owning" a piece of land.

I stand on land stolen from the Tocobaga. We would've called the land wild, the way it looked when they were its steward. I don't know what the Tocobaga called the river that runs through my neighborhood. The Timucua called it the Mocoso River, and the Seminole called it Lockcha-Popka-Chiska. We call it Hillsborough now, for the favor of an English earl the White settlers of Tampa had hoped to attract. In the 1500s, Hernando de Soto came across the river and enslaved the Tocobaga people, exposed them to disease, and murdered them. In the eighteenth century, the land around the river was a forest of centuries-old bald cypress and longleaf pine and live oak. Don Francisco Maria Celi of the Spanish Royal Navy cut most of it down to build his ships, and he is commemorated for this with a plaque in Riverhills Park.

The banks of the river are now lined with houses, but it retains its wildness in that it betrays those who try to tame it. People without homes bathe in its springs, and residents drop sacrificial offerings that appall and offend the people whose shores they wash up on—headless chickens and carved coconuts. I saw someone post about it on the neighborhood Facebook page, and someone else explained that the offerings are for the orishas. One poster responded, "Orishas are demons . . ., priests of Satan sent to lead the gullible and unsuspecting away from the singular deity of Christ." These are the same people who post about the best lawn pesticide or how to kill the possums in their backyards. They don't allow the many to flourish. They want to let live only what is convenient to them. Their religions have lost the connection to nature.

When we tend properly to land, with love, acknowledging and honoring those who tended the same land before, they become ancestors of sorts. We share a lineage through our connection with the land. We can commune with them, those ancestors who turned the earth and put their struggle and pain and joy into the underground network, through our service to the land. Their lives and lessons are stored there, and the earth is ready to share it, when we are ready to accept what emerges. Sometimes it's the hard truth that we are also settlers, and that we owe it to the land to pay back what we've taken.

Decolonizing is not a metaphor. There are practical and real ways that the federal government and property owners can give back to Indigenous organizations. There is a growing "land back" movement that focuses on returning land and resources to Native people. The Indigenous organization NDN Collective has launched their LANDBACK campaign to help coordinate these efforts. Their cornerstone mission is the closure of Mount Rushmore, as it is a symbol of White supremacy. In July 2020 Trump gave a speech at Mount Rushmore in which he said, "Our nation is witnessing a merciless campaign to wipe out our history, defame our heroes, erase our values, and indoctrinate our children. Angry mobs are trying to tear down statues of our Founders, deface our most sacred memorials, and unleash a wave of violent crime in our cities." Throughout his speech, he refers to the ancestors again and again, but he does not mention Indigenous peoples. To him, the ancestors began with the founding fathers of the United States, and those who would fight against this revisionist history are traitors.

The NDN Collective calls for the return of Mount Rushmore to the public lands of the sacred Black Hills of South Dakota, for starters.

They are calling for White people to unsettle lands that have rightfully belonged to Indigenous peoples. In many cases this has been agreed upon by the federal government through treaties, and those treaties have been broken.

Indigenous organizations are at the helm of progressive politics in this country. They are not just calling for land back for themselves but for the freedom of all people and for the health of our earth. They are calling for the abolition of the prison industrial complex. They are increasing awareness about the climate crisis and human trafficking and the unfair stigmatization of sex workers. They are advocating for pregnant people's right to choose. Within spiritual communities, they are standing against spiritual tourism and the appropriation of Indigenous wisdom for profit, especially when it comes to plant medicine. Even the spiritual market creates an extractivist mentality that hurts Indigenous communities. We see this with the rise in demand for sage, which is being overharvested. We see this in the Amazon, the earth's medicine cabinet, which is on fire due to overlogging. Ultimately, nobody will benefit from this medicine if we don't protect it.

We call these kinds of politics radical, but tending to the earth is also highly practical. It ensures survival, not through temporary extraction of one life for another, but through pagos a la tierra that rewild and enrich the soil for future generations and multiple species, creating generational wealth and interspecies relationships. This is abuelita medicine—the path to securing what we need for survival and the path to healing is one and the same.

141

The little witch cottage has withstood nearly a century of storms. I wonder who lived here before me and if the Tocobaga lived on this very plot of land. In 2017 when Hurricane Irma barely missed Tampa, a rumor went around that the city had been spared so many times because the Tocobaga blessed its burial mounds around Tampa Bay. Blessed is the closest word to describe how I feel to be here. I wish for everyone to feel safe and nourished by the land, the way I feel at home.

Because of the great privilege I have to claim ownership here, I have decided to pay an annual tax to local environmental and Indigenous organizations, like Florida Indigenous Rights and Environmental Equality (FIREE), which organizes protests around the Tampa Bay area and is responsible for the Tampa Bay Divestment Coalition, aimed at divesting local funds from fossil fuels.

Abuelita medicine is a spiritual activism, because it's a sustainable means of decolonizing and unsettling. It encourages each of us to be a steward of the environment, giving as much as we're taking. We renourish the soil for future generations. We pay homage and reparations to Indigenous peoples whose land we're on. We resist practices of gentrification that exclude the people who need help the most. We heal the violence we have experienced and the violence we have inflicted on others. We welcome all into refuge. We nourish ourselves through nature. Through mutual aid, we purify this chakrita we call home.

LIBATION RITUAL FOR THE LAND

A libation is a liquid offering to the earth that is common in African traditions. It is often offered to ancestors, and it can also be offered to ancestors of the land. Before you offer libation, you will want to research the ancestral lands that you occupy. Who were the original settlers of the land? In tandem with your ritual offering, you might consider making a periodic financial offering to an existing Indigenous or Black organization or mutual aid network in your area, patronizing local Native and Black businesses, and/or volunteering your time to an Indigenous or human rights movement. In some places, there are existing reparations programs in place. For example, non-Indigenous people in the San Francisco Bay Area can pay the Shuumi Land Tax, which supports the work of the Sogorea Te' Land Trust. In Seattle, settlers can pay rent to the Duwamish tribe through a program called Real Rent.

Once you know the ancestral history of your land, honor the original stewards with these simple steps:

1. Stand barefoot on the ground and face east, preferably close to dawn.

2. Pour a clear liquid into a ceremonial glass. Water or clear liquor is traditional.

3. Pour out the liquid onto the earth while saying a prayer of your choice. Maybe you can find a prayer associated with the people who you are honoring.

4. Close with an om, ashé, amen, or however you like to close prayers.

If you can take a little more time, hold a tea ceremony before the ritual to prepare the libation, maybe brewing a mixture of herbs. Or you can partake of the libation yourself after the ceremony.

VIRGO: THE HEALER

Virgo rules the sixth house of health, service, and daily routines. They often get a rap for being nitpicky or perfectionistic, but Virgos are quite flexible, as they adapt to the needs of the moment in their lifelong quest of serving others. While the Virgo archetype is the maiden or the virgin, Virgos are in tune with sex and pleasure, knowing that physical connection is part of a balanced routine. Virgo will help you connect to the earth and align with practices of wellbeing. Tap into Virgo energy when you feel overwhelmed by the corruption of the world; it will help you see how you can show up for yourself and others.

ELEMENT: Mutable earth

PLANETARY RULER: Mercury

AFFIRMATION: "I serve"

FOR YOUR ALTAR: Healing tonics, nuts and berries, flower crowns, mentor spirits or healers, white and pastel stones, earthy palettes, anything purifying

JOURNAL: Write out your ideal daily and/or weekly routine. You might include categories like meals, exercise, social activity, rest periods, chores and errands, hobbies, spiritual rituals, volunteer service, and employment. Adjust this list depending on your own priorities. Note that each day does not have to be perfectly balanced; some items might be daily tasks, while others are weekly or even monthly or seasonal. Over the course of a week, track how closely you keep to your routine. At the end of the week, adjust your routine so you have the best shot at sustaining it. Maybe you simplify if your plan is too ambitious, or maybe you set stricter boundaries on priority tasks to stick to the most important goals.

INDIGENOUS PROTECTORS

Black and Indigenous people and organizations are increasingly reclaiming their roles as stewards of the land. Seeding Sovereignty (@seedingsovereignty, seedingsovereignty.org) is an Indigenous-led collective that promotes decolonization through land, body, and food sovereignty initiatives. They offer resources and educational materials to help you connect to mutual aid networks and pay reparations. Indigenous Women Hike (@indigenouswomenhike) is another great resource for land back information and book recommendations. Seeds to Forest Defense (@seedstoforestdefense) is a community account raising awareness to protect Chumash land.

Alexis Nikole (@blackforager) is more of an environmental scientist enthusiast than a mystic, but many witches of color follow her for her genius videos on food foraging. While her videos are lighthearted, there is a political foundation to her work. She says that foraging for wild food was always part of the Black experience on this land. When slavery was abolished, laws prohibited foraging and gathering on public lands, just one of the many ways Black people were bound to the plantations even after abolition. For Alexis, foraging is an act of rebellion to restore this forgotten knowledge. She says people of color have labored to feed the world for centuries, and it's time they reclaimed these skills for themselves.

QUEER MAGICK

Edgar Fabián Frías is borderless.

I stumbled onto their Instagram account through the #brujx hashtag, and it instantly made me feel happy. Their feed is full of far-out imagery and bright colors and affirmations that remind us that things are not black and white. "This post is a spell," Edgar often writes in the captions of graphics proclaiming:

I AM

VAST I

AM LIGHT

I AM

DARK

I AM

VOID

SPIRITUAL ACTIVISM

I AM ALLOWED

TO MUTATE

WHENEVER

FOREVER

THERE IS LOVE

WAITING FOR US

BEYOND THE

GENDER BINARY

I've semi-intentionally curated my Instagram feed for a strong daily dose of spiritual affirmations. Sometimes it's too much, and I become sick with it all, the way you can feel when you've taken vitamins on an empty stomach, like trying to shortcut nutrition. These sentences set against beautiful backdrops telling me to be powerful and to cut out negativity often have the opposite effect. I feel exhausted with all there is to worry about. I can't just rush my unhappiness away.

Edgar's art doesn't make me feel this way. It makes me feel like I'm eating a food I've never tried, and it's so fun and good I forget about what's bothering me. It reminds me that life, as severe as it can feel sometimes, can also be free and full of possibility. That's not to say Edgar ignores life's problems or the shadow side of the world. In fact, their feed is full of references to the ills of capitalism and the threats of fascism and the violence that has been committed against transgender people. But for all that realism, Edgar is forgiving and inviting rather than judgmental.

Edgar's art reminds me that we can take on these problems and also allow ourselves to be imperfect, flowing with uncertainty instead of becoming rigid. I sometimes have trouble flowing, or "being in the present," as we say. I can be so hard on myself. I get caught up in producing and achieving instead of remembering the creative imperative behind my work. I sometimes get paralyzed by the fear of failure.

With the pandemic bringing so many things to a freeze, I saw I wasn't alone in this fear. So many of us were scared to stop, as if we would find ourselves worthless if we didn't produce. We were trying to soothe ourselves through the collective paralysis. "It's okay to rest," we say. "Really! Don't feel guilty about watching TV and ordering pizza and sleeping ten hours." But it's hard not to feel guilty. It's hard to shake the conditioning of our childhoods, all those voices telling us we have to make a mark on this world before we die.

Edgar reminds me that I can just be, and that is enough. Edgar self-describes as nonbinary and queer. They hold a master of arts and a license in marriage and family therapy. They're an artist, curator, and educator. They are so many things. I can be so many things too. I am infinite! As Edgar writes in their Instagram description, this is their "Queer Mutant Magic," acknowledging all the entities inside. When we get quiet, we can hear them all.

A professor of Indigenous studies, Sarah Biscarra Dilley, saw the multitudes Edgar contained right away. "You've just been trying to quiet the voices you hear," she said. Edgar says it was a moment of a witch seeing a witch.

The witch as a figure is so queer. In the 1800s the word *queer* meant "to spoil, to ruin." The witch dissolves the boundaries of what we think we know, shapeshifts and challenges our perceptions—for instance, the idea that there are just two genders. It's unsettling to see what we have held as truth turn to cosmic chaos in the hands of the witch. So we've blamed it for everything that goes wrong. "Burn the witch!" we've said, before it's had the chance to show us too many truths about ourselves.

Queer was just as much a slur as *witch* was, and it too is being reclaimed. Like all words in transition, it still offends some. It is an uncomfortable word. Like a spell, saying it aloud creates an opening into uncertain territory. We don't like uncertainty. I think many of us struggle because we are so scared of what we don't know that we stick with what is expected even if it doesn't fit. But a sadness starts to creep in, about the chances we haven't taken, all the paths that could have been.

This is where Queer Mutant Magic comes in to save the day. I relate it to Aleister Crowley's *magick*, a word he used to distinguish occult and ritual magic from stage magic. Magick is the art of willing change into existence. It is a constant openness in relation to the world. Magick resists the human tendency to harden concepts into static objects. Magick is in the process of becoming. The mutant embodies this magick. It is a symbol of a progressive, unbounded future.

When I was a kid, Walter Mercado was magickal like this. He was the most famous astrologer in Latin America, and my grandmother would watch him every day and hush us when he came to the horoscope for Cancer, her sign. He was neither male nor female, and I loved this. He wore capes and giant rings. I couldn't believe that my grandmother loved him so much because she was generally a homophobe. It was like he created this rainbow bridge between our generations. Most of us weren't exposed to nonbinary people back then. He planted a seed of possibility in our minds.

"Nonbinary means forever emergent, forever fluid, forever whole," Edgar posted on their Instagram on Transgender Awareness Week in November 2020. "Thank you Goddexx for helping us build & deepen our connections to one another and to our beloved past present & future Trancestors and Queer Ancestors!"

A recent Pew Research Center survey found that queer adults are twice as likely as other adults to identify as a member of a non-Christian group. Many discovered witchcraft in childhood as they learned how to express their otherness while coming out to their families and communities. The witch breaks the boundaries of gender and sexuality and empowers those on the margins who have historically been oppressed by mainstream religions.

The witch kept me safe when I didn't have any other way to express my queerness.

Edgar grew up in East L.A., and their family members were Jehovah's Witnesses. Edgar always dreamed about crystals and was fascinated by geomancy, a form of divination that employs markings and patterns of the earth. To them, the earth is full of color and creativity. The ancestors whisper from the rocks and the soil. One day in conversation with their father, they found out their ancestors are Indigenous. Their grandfather had apparently worked with crystals. Something clicked for Edgar then. Their imaginative world wasn't a sci-fi fantasy. It was ancient wisdom. Their ideas weren't new. They were very, very old. They asked their father why he had never said anything before. Their father said, "I didn't think you'd be interested."

Edgar's people are indigenous to Central Mexico. They are known as the Wixárika, or the Huichol to outsiders, but both these terms actually refer to their language. They call themselves the Wixáritari, which means "the people." They have preserved many pre-Columbian practices of ancestor worship and the use of the *hikuri* cactus (peyote) in rituals. Each year, they embark on a pilgrimage to their ancestral lands in Wirikúta to harvest the cactus. They go on foot, and they assume the roles of gods as they pass incredible natural landmarks, ancient springs and steppes, the things of dreams.

The pilgrimage takes about forty days, from the ocean to the valley of Wirikúta, where they believe their ancestors originated. The final leg of their journey takes them to the summit of Mount Cerro Quemado, where in their mythology the sun was born and Grandfather Fire reigns.

If you look up images of Huichol gods, you'll see art in electric colors and images of gods mixed with animal spirits. The art the Wixáritari make about their creation myths looks alien-like and futuristic. What does it say about us that these ancient ideas and stories call to mind sci-fi and the imaginary? These boundary-busting possibilities are so removed from our colonized lives that we can't even imagine they could be real. But here are the Wixáritari, still living in the ancient dream world of their gods.

The Wixáritari are rare in that they have successfully fought against the colonizing forces of the Spanish. Though they have been stripped of their lands, like most Indigenous societies, they have fervently rejected Catholicism. They refused to be boxed into a concept that robs them of their ancestral magic.

Binary gender is another concept that is largely rejected in many Indigenous populations. There are a wide variety of genders across Indigenous groups, all with varying mythologies and traditional roles. You may have heard of the two-spirit people, a relatively new term coined to describe Native individuals who don't identify as either male or female, or who identify as both, as a "third gender," or even as multiple genders. Two-spirit folks often fulfill the role of healer within their communities.

Imagine a world led by these people, in which boundaries are opened and new possibilities arise. Imagine returning the land to them. What would that look like? Edgar imagines a trans future, and not just in the sense that we accept a reality outside of the gender binary. Edgar imagines a trans future in which all borders are lifted, any of us can be anything, and all is possible—a world in which we are like our gods, and magick reigns again. Trans people show us a way to this world.

That is why, as Edgar says, trans people are sacred.

I don't know where the feeling of loneliness comes from, but it's a more frequent visitor as I get older. I was a kind of monk when I was a child. On the weekends, I would wake up at dawn, crawl out my window before my parents woke up, and stay out until midnight, without games to entertain myself with or even food. I never felt lonely. I was enraptured by the smallest things, by the veins of leaves and tadpole tails. They were electric. I sat under a willow tree for hours in what I can only call meditation, using the tree trunk to get up into the air with the birds and down into the earth with the worms. My parents would eventually find me sitting alone there, and they'd take me home and force me to eat.

It seems surreal to me now: sitting for hours with my breath, making small altars in the park with twigs and rocks, singing and loving all that arose, knowing that I was connected to everything, not wanting for anything. What came so naturally to me then has become so difficult to conjure now.

Violence has a way of making you hide. Every time my heart broke, I created walls. My heart broke so many times that the walls caused separation, and I no longer felt connected to everything as a default. For as open as I used to be, I found myself isolated in my experience, except for the few moments I felt safe enough to let my guards down around my close friends and lovers. Sometimes the childhood shadow bled to fill the whole room, and I couldn't find the corners to peel it back.

I learned to reach for spiritual remedies for my anxiety, and I usually kept it from progressing to depression. Yoga and Reiki were preventative medicines. But while I was in my PhD program, I realized I needed a more intensive therapy to confront the lifelong shadow. Like many graduate students, I was chronically stressed, and my energy was scattered. I was exhausted much of the time because I had to hold down multiple jobs to pay the bills while I worked on my dissertation. This triggered old traumas. I was seeing the shadow more and more at night, along with other intrusive apparitions. It was causing panic attacks like the ones I'd had in childhood.

I tried on-campus therapy, but it felt superficial. I filled out checklists that suggested I might have a generalized anxiety disorder. Therapy wasn't an option while I was growing up, so I hadn't learned to trust it. If it was even accessible, there was a big stigma around it in my family. I personally didn't like that it usually didn't take spirituality into account. So I diagnosed myself many times over the years: demonic possession; sleep paralysis; PTSD; spontaneous spiritual awakening; a lurking depression that runs in my family, waiting to be triggered in my genes. None of the explanations ever led to feeling better.

I wasn't so interested in what was wrong with me so much as how I could get well. One day I noticed that behind my house, separated by just an alleyway, was a bungalow with a sign for a shamanic practitioner. I made an appointment. This is how I met Anna, who would become a years-long teacher and counselor. She was the spiritual guide I had looked for growing up, and her practice was both mystical and practical. There was no separation between spiritual and mental health. With her I did not have to split myself the way I did in my PhD program or in spiritual circles or in other therapists' rooms. I could be rational and scientific and academic and also believe in worlds beyond what I could see.

In shamanic cosmology, there is a middle world, an upper world, and a lower world. Anna showed me how to access them. She asked me to think about a portal to these worlds from my life, and instantly I was back at my childhood tree. I realized as I learned about these worlds, that I had already accessed them many times before. This was a wisdom I knew in my bones.

Training with Anna was more of a remembering. I remembered how to travel to call on spirits for help. The lower world was a place of natural forces, elemental helpers that provided balancing medicine. The upper world was full of angels and guardians and ancestors. The middle world was the place closest to our waking reality, separated by a sheer veil, where lost souls walk. This, Anna said, was where my great-grandmother likely operated, but to channel middle world spirits like her would take much more training. It was the trickiest place, filled with the darkest souls. I thought about the last time my great-grandmother channeled, how the spirit had tossed her around, how it must have been so terrible to make her quit her practice.

As I learned, I started to reframe what I thought of as sickness as an ability. The shadow wasn't a problem but an opportunity, the reminder of an inherited sensitivity that I might one day explore. I realized anxiety and depression were not failings but logical reactions to a culture that values productivity more than health.

In many shamanistic communities, deep emotions are not seen as a disorder but as a gift shared by medicine people. If I had been born to one of them, maybe I'd be a medium in training. Depression is a difficult state, but it is also an ancient power, a key to secret passageways in the universe.

Imagination is the ability to form concepts not available to the senses. We think of it as separate from reality, but it is itself a way to connect to an alternate reality. Through this kind of imaginative process, Anna taught me to access worlds that have been shared by communities throughout the world, throughout ages. I found that what I have seen and experienced are not individual hallucinations but ancient collective experience.

I learned that the shadow is a common vision. Sometimes called the "old hag," many people have seen it at some point of their lives, usually in the corners of their room. It is often accompanied by paralysis and acute fear, and the old hag sometimes sits on your chest, making you feel like you can't breathe. Neurologists call it a sleep disorder, but how can something so common be a disorder? Maybe it's the opposite. Maybe the shadow is an ability. I discovered during times of paralysis that I could willfully untether myself from my sleeping body, move toward the shadow in my room, and walk through it into a realm of lucid dreams.

Scientists have begun to study how to communicate with people while they're in these states between sleep and wakefulness. For so long I'd thought there was something wrong with me. Could it be that what I've been experiencing is not a pathology, but the border between the occult and science, a new frontier of communication?

Following my sessions with Anna, my anxiety improved. Having experienced loneliness and isolation, I was more empathetic to those around me who were troubled. I helped build a local spiritual community over the years that followed. But Anna warned me that the spiritual path was not a straight line. If I was to commit myself to growth,

the path would meander, and I would eventually encounter more dif-
ficulties. If I kept telling the spirit world I was ready, it would deliver
obstacles for me to keep confronting and clearing.

Nobody I know was unscathed by 2020. If you were well emotion-
ally, you might have suffered financially. If you weren't sick yourself, you
were impacted by collective grief over what we lost. The virus sparked
a time of great transition, and we are each still navigating our place in it
all. That year showed me depths of grief I had no idea existed, as I dealt
with a tragic death and the biggest breakup of my life. I found myself
alone at the end of year, and I was sitting with old wounds I hadn't ever
fully processed. For the first time, I could see the pattern of my relationships as though outside of it. I had been engaged in trauma bond
after trauma bond. I was tired of hurting.

In the deepest dark of my depression, I found myself wishing for
movement, any movement—or better yet, a pilgrimage, some community ritual, a prescribed route to ease heartache and connect with a
higher power against this depression. But I didn't live in an electric
world of medicine people and gods. Over the years, the lessons of my
time with Anna had faded.

So I called on her again, on the last month of the most terrible year.

This time we met on Zoom. I was barely mobile. I looked at my
mirror image on the screen and couldn't recognize myself. Anna
immediately saw how bad it was, and she cradled me somehow. I've
always found it comforting to speak with a woman a little older than
me, who has experienced a similar kind of heartbreak, who has learned
to live alone and love herself. It shows me it is possible to be OK.

Our virtual sessions are much like traditional talk therapy. I vent and she listens and reflects what I say and provides helpful perspectives. The talk part is always highly practical. She asks me what I'm doing to support myself in terms of food, medicine, and self-care practices. The shamanistic part comes after we get off the call. She instructs me to do something calming while she journeys to other worlds for me. After our last call, a friend dropped off an herbal bath she'd gotten from Haus of Hoodoo in New Orleans. I decided to take the bath while Anna did her thing. I pressed the herbs to my skin, and I became nauseated.

Later Anna called back to tell me what she'd found. She said that the angels, guardians, and other spirits she'd called on had bathed me in herbs, rubbing them on my skin, and that I might feel a purging. My mind boggled. There was no way she could have known about the herb bath. As she spoke and gave me instructions for rituals, I felt the work they had already begun. When I got off the call, I became ill. For days, I purged. I was so weak I could barely get out of bed. I was scared I had COVID, but I also knew that as physical as my sickness was, it was also spiritual. A strange spell had been cast. I felt the way I usually feel when I take mushrooms or some other hallucinogen, both completely connected and strangely detached from my experience. But I was sober.

Days later, once I'd recovered (and after a negative COVID test), the darkness I'd been feeling started to feel less like emptiness and more like a pregnant possibility, like a universe ready to spark galaxies into being.

I still felt sad about everything I had lost, but there was hope again. I remembered that love is always there and that I can connect to it. It is really hard to find sometimes, but love is there. I felt immensely grateful for the beautiful friendships in my life, so many people on call to support me. Maybe sexual relationships aren't as central as we've made them out to be. We can connect through so many entry points if we can see the electric life in every being.

I think a lot of people could use this mutant magick right now.

Following my session with Anna, I was able to overcome the stigma I had internalized about medical diagnoses and treatment, and I finally went to a doctor for help, who prescribed an antidepressant. It helped me loosen my identification with trauma. I remembered before my first sexual experience to all the moments in my childhood I had connected with magic to express my feelings about my female friends. The way I'd turn their names to sigils and draw them in the wall of my closet and hide them behind posters. Or how we would cup our hands together under our desks to feel the heat in the center of our palms. How we sat in circles and chanted spells that spoke of things in our hearts we couldn't put into words. How I loved them.

I had the alligator dream again on the last day of 2020. I was still crossing that vast swamp, and the alligators had their mouths open, ready to swallow me. But I was lucid this time. I let myself fall into a gaping mouth, and when I opened my eyes, I was in a world full of beings of light, ancestors and angels and guardian spirits wrapping me in their arms.

★ ✸ ★

Edgar's images might seem far out, but they channel an ancient imagination. Imagine a world in which individuals wouldn't be labeled crazy or criminal for feeding this imagination. Strict borders and prescriptions for where and how we should exist create sickness and violence. Gloria Anzaldúa writes about this in *Borderlands/La Frontera*, calling the US-Mexican border an open wound and the forbidden sorts its inhabitants: "the squint-eyed, the perverse, the queer, the troublesome, the mongrel, the mulatto, the half-breed, the half dead."

The sickness that we create with our borders can be healed through borderlessness, through an opening to each other, an acceptance of all the infinite ways we can manifest on this earth as humans.

To Edgar, school is rebellion. They were raised in a family that didn't necessarily expect them to get a higher education. Rather than go into manufacturing as assumed, Edgar studied art and therapy. Though these might seem like two very different degrees to us, in Edgar's ancestry, the artist-healer is very much a traditional role. But Edgar found that they were at opposing ends in the academic institution. The cognitive-behavioral model that reigns in the world of therapy often ignores energy and art and spirituality. We need all of these. Though we are seeing a revolution in mental health, the paradigm of diagnosis and pharmacological treatment still reigns, and it's built on little boxes to tick off. It plugs into the larger system of capitalism to which we are supposed to conform. If we can't handle our jobs, if we can't produce, there is something wrong with us.

What if we were taught that our illness is not a detriment but a sign that we have so much more to offer? What if we are not sick but are in fact responding to a sick system that is no longer designed to care for the majority? What if we lived in a world where we don't have to rush to identify ourselves as one thing? I don't know what that world would look like, but I do know that it would strain, or even break, the capitalist colonial system that has only valued us by our production or consumption.

"Capitalism is creating a world that is not made for who you really are," Edgar says. "Art is where you can do the things that don't fit." Through art, Edgar creates bridges.

I wish for more teachers like them, for artist-healers. Edgar embodies the age of Aquarius. A lot of astrologers believe that the 2020 winter solstice, with the great conjunction of Jupiter and Saturn in Aquarius, was the beginning of a new age of revolution and radical imagination, a renaissance after a dark age. I do like to think that we are in a transition from late-stage capitalism and dogmatic Christianity toward something new, something that feels more like a network than a hierarchy. I imagine that in this new world, we can each be ourselves. But I think we are only at the beginning of the breakdown, and it will take many decades to see another renaissance.

My generation has come of age during multiple recessions. Living in this time of insecurity, it's hard to create and imagine better things. For as confident as Edgar seems in their work now, it was not always like this for them. They spent their early twenties feeling isolated, thinking nobody would ever understand their art. It's not easy to make your way as an artist in a system that makes everyone peg themselves to career aspirations. But over time as Edgar kept honoring what they loved and opening to the world, the world began to support them. Today, Edgar is an accomplished multidisciplinary artist. They've done everything from digital art to big installations, and they're guided by Indigenous epistemologies, feminist praxis, and queer aesthetics.

I imagine a world without insecurity, where everyone has what they need, where each person is a creative force. We've relegated creativity to artists of specific mediums, as if there were no creativity in treating a patient or conducting lab research. Or as if our day jobs were all that defined us. What if we were all taught that we each have something unique to create for this world? If we all turned our minds to creativity rather than consumption?

I've suggested that capitalism is not working and should be dismantled, but what if we don't need a destructive revolution? What if we just keep opening to each other and making more room for one another? What if our consistent and radical care for others in this world can transform what we call capitalism into a new, healthy network, like a forest growing back in where everything's been paved over?

What if revolution is not a fight? What if it's an opening to more and more love?

SELF-LOVE SPELL

Let's be honest: a lot of us are in it for the love magic. I don't personally do any spells that seek to manipulate or remove free will from another, and I believe the more powerful spells are those that we perform with clear intentions for ourselves. Self-love is one of the most difficult and important things we can cultivate in our lives. When your love is centered on yourself, you won't ever have a shortage of love in your life, and you'll have a strong foundation for addressing mental health issues like depression. You will radiate love, and you'll find that it will be easier to find others to share this love with, whether platonically or romantically, because you won't need to "get" love from them. I like to do this simple self-love spell to call all forms of love into my life. For this spell, you will need a pink or green taper candle, a carving tool, rose oil, a lighter, and a mirror.

1. With your carving tool, carve your name into the candle, then douse the candle in rose oil.

2. Stand in front of a mirror and light your candle.

3. While you hold your candle at your heart center, look into your eyes and say "I call in love and abundance into my life. I embody love

in all its forms. I do not want for anything." You may use another mantra or affirmation if it speaks to you more. Feel the vibration of the words in your heart center. Do not break eye contact, and continue to repeat until your candle burns all the way down.

4. When you are done, anoint yourself with a dab of rose oil or take a diluted rose water bath.

Always use fire safety when dressing and lighting candles. You may substitute the oil for another if you have an allergy, of course. Other oils good for love spells include vanilla, jasmine, ylang-ylang, and sandalwood. Or, you can skip this step if you have a sensitivity to fragrance. If you want to go further, when you are done with your spell, take some time to write in your journal. After such a long period of literal self-reflection, you might have something to say to yourself. What kind of love do you wish for in your life, in all forms—whether it's partner love, friendships, or passion projects? Allow yourself to imagine your wildest dreams, things that might not even seem possible. What small thing can you do every day to call this love into your life and reactivate the love spell between official rituals? What boundaries do you need others to honor in relationship with you? Is there anything or anyone you need to cut out of your life to make space for the love that you deserve? Do you need help doing this? Is there a friend or a therapist to whom you can turn?

LIBRA: THE LOVER

Libra is the zodiac's cool-headed lover, ruling the seventh house of love and partnerships, including business collaborations. Librans have a refreshing perspective and are prone to indulging in the finer things. They can be surprisingly eccentric, often pushing the boundaries of what is considered beautiful. To them, beauty and justice are inextricable. Libra can be called upon when you need to take a step back and balance the different areas of your life in order to make way for love and beauty and the best things the world has to offer. Look to Libra to transform your passion into long-term partnerships.

ELEMENT: Cardinal air

PLANETARY RULER: Venus

AFFIRMATION: "I balance"

FOR YOUR ALTAR: Roses, apples, opal, brass, heirloom jewels, love deities or muses, herbal scales, pinks or greens or florals, anything that sets the mood for love

JOURNAL: What does self-care mean to you?

SPIRITUAL SELF-CARE

The self-care industry has boomed during the pandemic, and spiritual self-care offerings abound on social media, ranging from retail products to trauma-informed therapies. The Brooklyn Bruja (@thebrooklynbruja, thebrooklynbruja.com) is a mental health advocate whose digital art openly addresses trans health and mental health issues, including borderline personality disorder, posttraumatic stress disorder, and anxiety.

Trauma Aware Care (@traumaawarecare, trauma-aware-care .mykajabi.com) offers courses, resources, and tools to support your healing journeys. If you're looking to become a trauma-informed spiritual practitioner, this is an important resource.

The right product can make your self-care routine truly magical. It's important to source sustainably, as products such as smoke bundles, crystals, and essential oils can put strain on the environment and Indigenous communities. Check out Brujita Skincare (@brujitaskincare, brujitaskincare.com), Moon Mother Apothecary (@moonmotherapothecary, moonmotherapothecary.com), Bread xButta (@breadxbutta, breadxbutta.com), Chakra Zulu Crystals (@chakrazulucrystals, chakrazulucrystals.com), Bossy Bruja (@bossybruja, bossybruja.com), and Bruja de Crystals (@bruja.de.crystals) for healing goodies.

8

WHITE WITCHES

"Me llamo Ismael," said the driver, as he picked me up from the José Martí International Airport in Havana.

I got in the backseat, releasing the breath I'd been holding. Hundreds of people packed the terminal, waiting for family members to arrive. I gave Ismael the address on the Avenida de los Presidentes in Vedado. He seemed young, in his early thirties like me. But his face was lined, and his eyes were fixed ahead, like he'd already seen all he wanted to see. We were in what my guidebook called an *almendrón*, a 1950s car converted into a taxi. It sounded to me like the Spanish word for almonds. This almond was bright red and had a little American flag glued to the dash.

Ismael said he would take me the scenic route so I could see the Malecón, the famous esplanade and seawall. It whirled on our periphery like a crumbling white snake, dividing pavement from blue gulf. We passed a mural with the words: "Patria o Muerte!" *Fatherland or Death.*

As soon as I'd walked into the airport terminal, I was detained. I was interrogated for an hour by customs officials who didn't yet know how to handle a US-born Cuban traveler. If circumstances were different, they might have tried to keep me from returning to my home, a fact that was not lost on me as I stood before them, trying to convince them I wasn't there for nefarious purposes. They were close to my face, unblinking, downright threatening, and as the minutes went by, I wondered if I'd made a terrible mistake.

Everyone in the United States was barred from going to Cuba, of course, until President Obama announced loosened travel restrictions to the island in late 2014. I immediately booked my ticket to Havana. It wasn't quite my homeland. All the Monteaguts were in the Oriente Province on the southeast corner of the island. I couldn't go there, because I didn't know any of my family, and none of the other twelve preapproved travel visa categories applied. But the Havana Biennial was taking place in May 2015, and another US-born cousin, Agnes Chavez, had already been invited as a participating artist in a collective exhibit; I qualified to travel for the event through the educational institution that funded her installation, an immersive and interactive experience called *Origination Point*, about the in-betweenness of being a Cuban American.

I said nothing, just nodded my head when they let me leave the airport on the condition that I not travel outside the sanctioned tourist areas. As soon as I stepped outside, it felt like I was in another time completely. The air was like a gel that slowed my movements. I took a deep, damp breath and hailed the taxi.

Ismael pointed to a spot along the seawall. "There. That's where my brother launched the boat he made." I asked him if his brother survived, but he didn't answer. He let me off on a corner of the Avenida near the Hotel Presidente.

I met Fidela at the Airbnb down the street, a dreamy, seafoam-green colonial house that was home to a Spanish couple who traveled on and off the island as they pleased. Fidela was the caretaker of the place, and she was stuck in Cuba forever. She lived in Guanabacoa, a colonial township nearby known for Santería. She invited me to go home with her, which I knew would break the conditions of my visa.

My curiosity won out in the end.

Fidela instructed me to wear jean shorts and flip flops and to carry only the pesos of the natives. "No CUCs," she said. She pronounced the official currency as "cooks."

"And don't talk to anyone," she said. "Or they'll know you're American."

We took a crowded bus from the house to a square in Old Havana. We piled into a shared car. We were the only women in the car, and I tried not to say more than a polite hello to anyone, though the men were chatty. The taxi dropped us in the outskirts of Old Havana at Central Station, near the birthplace of José Martí, the famous exile who found a second home in Florida, like so many of us. I wondered what he would think of me, a second-generation Cuban "returning" to the place that had ejected us.

We boarded another bus. Fidela helped me pay, and we took our seats for the twenty-minute ride to Guanabacoa. I looked out the window and froze as we passed security stations occupied by military police with rifles in hand. They didn't stop us.

Guanabacoa was hilly in comparison to the city. Everything was haphazardly paved and dusty, and there were few trees. We got off the bus at a high point from which I could see the whole town, and I imagined that we could be anywhere in Latin America, that maybe my mother grew up in a place like this, in a dusty town in Colombia. We made our way down to Fidela's small house, sandwiched between others like it.

Fidela invited me into a small rectangular living space with sparsely decorated walls and simple tile floors. The central decoration was a three-foot statue to San Lazaro, the saint of dogs and the sick. He wore purple robes, and his exposed skin was covered in lacerations. Two dogs stood at his feet. As Fidela passed him, she dropped a few cents into a bowl she'd placed in front of him. She said she periodically donated the money to a clinic for people with skin problems.

"Do you know the saints?" she asked.

I told her I did, that I grew up Catholic and that my family had altars upon which they placed offerings to the Virgin Mary and the archangels. Her eyes lit up as I said it, and she motioned for me to follow her to the back. Tucked off the kitchen was a little room, empty except for a tiny table covered in a white sheet: a mesa blanca.

"Here's where the *real* saints are," she said.

On the table were various small objects—glasses filled with water, a mortar and pestle, incense holders, a pamphlet with cracked, yellowed pages, and a deck of tarot cards. My eyes weren't yet trained to see the symbols and images and colors of the orishas in the room.

"I'm happy I can show you this," Fidela said. "I don't bring it up to most people."

I understood why she kept it secret. It's still taboo, even now. I had been taught that Santería was the work of the devil. My family had stories of santeros doing bad things to people. I wondered what it would have been like to have a grandmother like Fidela, who showed me secret things in secret rooms. I don't think she would ever call herself a bruja, but what Fidela did was subversive and magical to me. It felt like I was finally being exposed to a piece of my inheritance, what my great-grandmother had kept from me.

Fidela's kitchen was the cheeriest room in the house, with orange walls and an assortment of gadgets and spices. She made me a meal of ground beef, rice, and beans. While we ate, she told me about the daughter who left for Texas on a rare work visa to play the violin in concerts. She didn't know when she would see her again.

Her face got very still.

"Child, why did you come here? Don't you see that we are all on hold? There's nothing for you here. Go. Go home and don't come back."

Fidela is the female version of Fidel, a popular name in Cuba. It means "keeper of the faith." It means to carry on, even when there's no work and little opportunity, even when you're separated from your family by walls of laws, even when you feel stuck, with no way out. Cubans love to play with words, and among the many dualities inherent in daily Cuban life—the dual currency, the symbiotic existence of communism and capitalism—is the doublespeak one must learn in the event that the government is listening.

For instance, the word *fe* means "faith" in Spanish. But when some-one asks you, "Do you have faith?" they are really asking if you have "FE," or *familia extranjero*, relatives in exile in other countries. Cubans with FE can afford a little more than those who don't, as they receive money from their relatives abroad.

Fidel was my father's middle name. When he became an adult, he had it reduced to an *F*. And when he was older, he had it removed alto-gether, as though it never existed. If you ask him about it, he'll say that he didn't want to share a name with Castro, whom he saw as the enemy of freedom. Understandable, but I always felt that it was also a kind of disavowal of his roots. That he'd lost faith in his home country after his family's exile and his mother's untimely death.

Elsie's death is a deep family hurt I was born with. I think I went "back" to Cuba to try to heal it, but I didn't learn anything more about my family. How could I return somewhere I'd never been? One night I sat in a jazz club on the top floor of a rundown building, listening to a Cuban woman singing, the Malecón buzzing with people below, and beyond, the Florida Straits that formed the formidable barrier between my home and this place I'd once thought was my home.

I guess the jazz singer saw I was walking around with little *fe*. She stopped singing, pointed at me, and said, "You. You are NOT Cuban."

That really unsettled me. I had to sit with those feelings a while. I wasn't like Ismael. I wasn't like Fidela. I hadn't lost brothers and daugh-ters. I wasn't trapped on an island. I had so much more opportunity. I felt guilt about this for the first time. While I've never felt like I fully belonged anywhere—I'm too White in my family and my family's homelands, and not White enough in some professional and academic circles—there is privilege in the ability to occupy an in-between space and embody different realities of my choosing. I have the privilege of movement, of assuming different identities. Over the course of my "reclaiming" and "returning" to my parents' homelands, could I possibly be hurting people? Did my white skin place me squarely on the side of the colonizer, no matter my culture or upbringing? How much was I appropriating cultural traditions that weren't mine in my exploration of my burgeoning bruja identity?

Was I being a basic White witch?

I confronted these feelings again at the twentieth annual Allied Media Conference in 2018 held in Detroit. The conference is founded on media-based organizing that seeks to dismantle White supremacist systems and cultivate spaces of joy and care for QTBIPOC (queer, trans, Black, Indigenous, and people of color). I came across it because I was looking for a "bruja conference" and saw their new track of sessions called "Magic as Resistance," focusing on brujx feminism, Afrofuturism, and trans magick. I had never seen anything on these topics on such a large scale and was blown away by the number of people at the conference, thousands of people from all over the country who were interested in magic and organizing.

The sessions in the new magic track were packed. I had to arrive twenty minutes early to each session to get a seat. One afternoon I was settling into one of the sessions about Latinx healing spiritualities, which was just as full as the rest. There was a good mix of White and Brown Latinx people, people of Indigenous origin who didn't necessarily ascribe to the term *Latinx*, and Caucasian folks. After introductions we started to talk about colorism in Latinx communities and what it meant to be White passing, or if that was even really a thing. "You either have white skin or you don't, right?" some were saying. "And White Latinx undeniably enjoy more privilege than their Brown family members." The discussion was picking up when we heard a commotion outside the door. Someone was screaming at top volume. Other quieter voices were trying to calm the big voice down. "I'M HERE TO DISRUPT THIS, THEN," the voice called out. Then the door flew open and a Black trans woman entered.

She addressed all of us at once. She was told she wasn't allowed in because the session was packed. Then she walked around the room and pointed at each White person in turn and told them to give up their seat. "This is not for you!" She screamed and pointed in each face. "These sessions were created for us, not YOU!" She pointed at my face. I saw the Cuban singer pointing. *You're not Cuban.* "You're taking up space that should be for us."

I quickly gathered my things and left the room. From just outside, I observed as the people took their leave. A White person, I couldn't tell if they were Latinx, stood their ground to defend their right to be in the room. There was a screaming match, faces close. I got hot faced just watching it. The session was canceled. I had never felt so many conflicting emotions. I didn't know what to think or how to feel. Everything was just swirling and swirling inside, fear and guilt and anger and empathy and, above all, a desire to explain myself. I couldn't stand it anymore and had to go outside for air.

It was the most educational session of them all. I couldn't put it into words, but the feeling was it, why I was there. It was why we were all there, this complex navigation of identity and purpose that every organizer faces after a time. It was easy to know what we were all against. What was harder to understand was where we each belonged within the system of organizing. Where were we White-passing people supposed to stand, and what was our responsibility?

Since then I've come to learn that there is no White passing, not really. I am technically White, a White Latinx. My brother with the browner skin might be able to say he's not totally White, but my reality is that I have white skin, and I do not just pass in White spaces, I thrive within them.

My great-grandmother did too. Elvira was White, but her guardian spirits were Afro-Cuban. This was common among the espiritistas of Cordon, as they believed that Black spirits had become trapped in limbo through the slave trade, their wisdom given voice through the medium's body. They were the first ones Elvira called on when she channeled spirits, and they were the ones who closed each ceremony. African guardians were common, a mark of authenticity, and her relationship with them was probably more utilitarian than indicative of her respect for African tradition.

I feel guilty about this, about the way she, and other espiritistas in Cuba and the United States, must have appropriated so much from African religions while not respecting or serving its people. Espiritismo offered many White people a chance to benefit from the African influence on the island without the risks and stigma involved with practicing Santería.

What makes the African traditions so powerful is that they have acted as a resistance to colonization in lands with long histories of hardship for Indigenous and Black people. When used for commercial gain, spirit guardians call back their power. When taken far from their land, they retreat, unless they are properly honored. They were colonized in life, but they will not be colonized in death. Try, and they will leave you for good. They return to the occult places, far from reach.

I wonder if that's what happened to Elvira and her guardians. Her disconnect from tradition and the land, her grief over the sudden loss of her daughter—did it weaken her connection to her spirits? Maybe she didn't give up her practice. Maybe her spirits left her. Maybe this is what it means to lose the faith.

That's the complicated legacy that was handed down to me, why I encounter this friction in the in-between spaces I inhabit. So maybe it's my responsibility to observe and respect when someone tells me to get the fuck out.

⋆ ✯ ★

Lacey Conine, a.k.a. the Hype Priestess, is a White Mexican. She is the self-described creatrix of Witch Walk, a monthly event and market for witches, brujxs, and occultists of all kinds that started in Santa Ana, California, but has since transitioned to a completely virtual platform during the coronavirus lockdown.

She was born in Ashland, Oregon, "hippy central," surrounded by crystals and tarot cards and divination, instead of her native Mexican traditions. Now, she realizes that a lot of that stuff *is* indigenous.

She grew up in Washington State, and she always considered herself Mexican growing up, because her mother was Mexican. She didn't speak Spanish, and she didn't really have any Mexican traditions, but when people asked her "what she was," she always said Mexican. In Washington, where the majority of people are White, she stood out. She never questioned her place in the Mexican culture. Until she moved to California.

Being among so many Mexican people for the first time was a complicated feeling. On the one hand, she was excited to finally be surrounded by her native food and traditions. On the other hand, she didn't know what she was allowed to explore. Could she just start celebrating El Día de los Muertos, for instance? Who was the authority on this?

Lacey recently discovered that both of her maternal great-grandparents were from the Coahuiltecan people of modern-day Texas, where her family originated. Her mother moved away from Texas before she was born, so she is not completely comfortable claiming indigeneity because of where she was born and raised. She is also Slavic and French and "just White" on her Dad's side.

What am I allowed to embrace? And what am I allowed to celebrate? she asks herself.

According to demographers, the United States will be made up of a majority of mixed-race people in my lifetime. What we call ourselves will be increasingly complicated. At the moment, it feels more natural to those of us who inhabit the in-between to ask more questions than we answer.

Lacey focuses on what connects her rather than what separates her.

For fifteen years she worked for an action-sports retail company, and she'd become very depressed. She developed plantar fasciitis and could only work for three hours standing up. But she was great at her job, and she was making great money; her company wanted to promote her, so she would be making even more money. *Do I quit, or do I push my body through this and take the promotion?*

She took the promotion.

One day a couple of years later, she just couldn't do it anymore. She called up her manager and said she couldn't go back. Just like that, she was done.

From then on, everything started clicking with her online presence, Hype Priestess. As her following grew, she realized this was her new path. She launched Witch Walk, and it was successful off the bat. To be part of Witch Walk, you have to submit an application and indicate whether you're a BIPOC business. For the most part, if you had an established business that was in the realm of magic or wellness, you passed the vetting process and were accepted. The last thing Lacey wanted to be was a gatekeeper.

But wherever there's a gate, there's usually drama. A company run by a couple of White Wiccans was denied entry into Witch Walk as a vendor, because Lacey found that they weren't being inclusive and were appropriating from other cultures. She thought they would be taking up the space of people of color with similar businesses that are more connected to ancestral traditions. The Wiccans went to the city to file a discrimination complaint.

"Some Wiccans are the Karens of the spiritual markets," Lacey said. "No offense to Wiccans out there."

She really struggled with her inevitable role as a gatekeeper of Witch Walk after that. She agonized about how to perform as an organizer in the most inclusive way possible, how to use her privilege and her platform to support the QTBIPOC community without discriminating against anyone. But after a while, she relaxed into it, realizing that it's all about listening to people.

She still feels strange calling herself an "influencer." Sometimes she gets anxiety about the things she would post. Sometimes it's paralyzing to be out there publicly in any way. But when she shakes the imposter syndrome off, the hype really is real. There is magic in her following and in the community that she has nurtured.

The only regret she has is not connecting to her ancestors before she started to monetize her hobbies, as so many millennials are wont to do these days.

"Not everything has to be in the spirit of capitalism," she says.

This is something she learned from a mentor, Marisa de la Peña, who counseled her on how to be an ally. It's all about connection and getting down to your roots, whatever they are. When you know yours and feel comfortable with your own place, it's easier to provide space for others to explore their own ancestry and to operate from their truth. Ultimately, it is about love and light and inclusiveness—but not at the expense of people who have a real right to the space. You have to stay in your lane.

"Everyone is working it out," Lacey says. "As we have more and more access to this wisdom, the line of political correctness keeps moving."

★ ✖ ★

When I was a teenager, I attended classes for my Catholic confirmation every Wednesday. I loved the history of religion, and I saw a lot of similarities across different religions, especially the Abrahamic ones. I asked questions about the major themes in these religions and the pagan myths I studied on my own time. The pastors did not appreciate this. We were supposed to memorize prayers and accept the Bible's words without questioning. It didn't matter that I was the most interested person in the class. The pastors told my parents that I was "difficult."

I couldn't just go around talking to my family members about my new interest in the bruja or things like astrology or tarot. Even though they sometimes enlisted help from practitioners of brujería, they did so in secret, like getting drugs from a dealer. If I tried to openly talk about it, they would denounce it as devil worship. In our houses we had pagan altars and rituals, but they were all for Jesus and the Virgin Mary, so these practices were "Catholic."

Now that brujería is more understood and accepted, it's a tricky business to go about "reclaiming the occult," especially for those of us with more colonizer blood, who look White and whose ancestors have contributed to the reason ancestral traditions had to be occulted in the first place. What's more, there are spiritual pantheons that are not for us even if we identify as a bruja. To this day, many spiritualists have the wrong view of African spiritualities as demonic.

So we'll build our own magic, we say. We'll piece together knowledge from here and there, cherry-pick what works for us. Well, "magic" is a tricky word too. And words matter. They are spells, so we better know what we mean by them. Words like "witchcraft" and "brujería" have been used to dehumanize and discount Indigenous and African people during times of slavery. They've been used by those who erroneously believe that the African connection to nature and ancestors is somehow more "supernatural" than, say, the Catholic belief in saints. If we use those words without knowing better, we cast bad spells, strengthen centuries-old oppression and exploitation.

My great-grandmother Elvira and her family had the privilege to leave Cuba after the revolution. As the zeitgeist of Spiritism died down, she discarded vestiges of resistance to the establishment and became a secular sort of Christian. We followed suit. We passed as White. We plugged into capitalism, and we carried the blood of the Spanish colonizers wherever we went. We did not talk about the past.

Ability is not necessarily a license, and even if I had the power to become a medium, does it give me the right to channel African powers that aren't for me? What if a reclamation of the occult looks like an apology for all the harm my ancestors might have done, for the harm I have done, even unconsciously?

Though we were forced to leave our homelands, we are not truly the dispossessed, not like the Black Cubans who managed to leave, only to have all their cultural institutions erased, while White Cubans gradually built generational wealth. The truly dispossessed are the people who didn't even have the chance to leave the island, who have had little choice for hundreds of years, the descendants of the Taíno and the enslaved Africans who preserved great religions in the face of great violence.

For some, reclamation is about becoming initiated into the ways of our grandparents. But maybe for others, it's about unsettling neat histories that make us heroes and others villains. Maybe it is about really diving into the occult—not the romantic vision of family rituals, but literally, the secrets of our pasts. Maybe it's about confronting the ones that don't make us feel interesting or good, like how we used to call Voodoo the devil's work without knowing anything about it, or, even worse, how we tried to capitalize on African traditions when they became popular.

For Lacey, reclamation is about using her platform to amplify the magic of spiritual workers of color. During the pandemic, the Witch Walk has moved virtual, and Lacey says it's even more popular than it was before, as it's expanded into new markets. She hopes that in the future we'll see Witch Walk in cities in Florida and New York, and especially in New Orleans.

But ever-increasing expansion is not Lacey's goal. During the pandemic, Lacey took the time to slow down and care for her health. She has been living with anxiety and depression her whole life, and being productive had been a coping mechanism, a way to prove to herself she was worthy even when she felt bad. The pandemic and the Black Lives Matter protests of 2020 opened her eyes to the toll the work had been taking on her health. The expectation to constantly create content was especially exhausting. For all her criticism of capitalism, Lacey still felt that she measured her worth by how much she was putting out in the world.

In the summer of 2020, she started opening up about her childhood and her lifelong mental health challenges. She said she started to recently become aware of how disconnected from her body she has felt her whole life, how she has been wired to feel like the worst-case scenario is bound to happen. Lacey sees this as a generational curse to break. She started taking a neuroplasticity course that is designed to retrain her brain to have different responses to triggers. She is learning to accept her thoughts and feelings while redirecting them to actions that foster self-love and self-care. Her last post of 2020 was in September, when she posted that she was taking months off to focus on the course, and she edited her bio to include "TRYNA HEAL," and "Healing myself to heal the collective."

Following her journey and reading her healing story has encouraged me to do the same. When I began writing about my ancestral spirituality years ago, I thought my aim was to train myself how to be a spiritual healer, as my great-grandmother had been. Now I see that my first goal is closer to home. There is still so much I must do to make peace with my own anxiety and depression. Before I can heal others, I have to heal myself. And then I have to pay my dues and my share of reparations before setting up shop in the spiritual market. These are the prerequisites for any sustainable type of spiritual activism.

The night of the Allied Media Conference, adrienne maree brown was scheduled to give a talk in a room far too small, and attendees fought among themselves for seats. When she entered and saw the commotion, adrienne assured everyone there was enough room, and we followed her to a large auditorium. Recently, she shared on her Instagram account:

"what if radical movements erred on the side of inclusion rather than exclusion. wouldn't that be wild. what if we replaced gatekeepers with ushers and helped people find where they belong."

When I find myself feeling anxious about my place in the bruja community, I remember that it is made of people who are constantly moving between borders and identities. I take a deep breath when I feel that I will be rejected, and I remember what I have to offer.

I belong here.

TAKE ACTION AS AN ALLY

We all have roles to play as spiritual activists. If you are White, it's your responsibility to inform yourself and figure out how to organize without burdening people of color to explain how. Black Lives Matter has posted resources for POC and non-POC organizers, including a healing action toolkit to ensure actions are centered on healing justice. The toolkit outlines steps for supporting wellness in the midst of action and organizing, and it encourages a visionary mindset focused on the good that might come of our action, rather than our wounds. The toolkit includes grounding exercises like breathwork and chanting, sharing vision with other organizers, building altars, and providing food and hydration and other support resources. The toolkit can be found at blacklivesmatter.com/resources.

At the beginning of our journey as spiritual activists, we learn to center our personal joy and protection, honor the land upon which we stand, and engage in self-love and self-care practices based on healthy boundaries. These efforts create a sustainable foundation from which we can pull energy to act for others. When you feel grounded in these practices, the next step is to take action for a cause. I have offered Black Lives Matter, because it is a great example of a movement that has provided detailed resources for action and care, but there are many organizations with similar toolkits.

Here is a nonexhaustive list of ways you might choose to take action:

✳ Volunteer: Take time to serve the organization or cause of your choice. It's best to do this on a consistent schedule rather than a one-off event, even if it's just an hour a month. You might offer your help in person: you can help the organization promote their brand and events, or you could offer support services to members.

✳ Donate: Set up a regular monetary donation to your organization, and encourage others to do the same.

✳ Show Up: Align your life with your cause. Attend events, boycott incongruent products or organizations, talk to your friends and family, and cut out anything that is toxic to the highest self you're striving for.

✳ Educate: Educate yourself and stay abreast of current events. This is especially true if you are White. It's up to you to educate yourselves and other White people so that people of color don't spend their energies catching everyone else up on what they've been experiencing for a lifetime.

✳ Take Care: Remember to return to your self-care rituals to replenish your energy. Rest often. Recenter joy. Connect to the land. You are no good to the cause if you are exhausted or sick.

SCORPIO: THE SHADOW WORKER

Scorpio is the witch of the zodiac, and arguably the sign that stirs the most emotion, good or bad, among witches and brujas. It represents death and rebirth and the alchemical process by which we transform one thing into another. Scorpio breaks down the material into the cosmic soup, and it creates art from chaos. For as solitary as Scorpios tend to be, they usually have a hand in the affairs of others. Call on Scorpio when you need to remember the magic of the universe or recharge in the mystery of it all.

ELEMENT: Fixed water

PLANETARY RULER: Pluto

AFFIRMATION: "I transform"

FOR YOUR ALTAR: Nettle, roots, dark stones, sages or mystics, potions, poisons, snakes or arachnids, anything black, protection sigils or attraction amulets

JOURNAL: What wounds or secrets am I harboring? How can I turn what hurts into a lesson?

DECOLONIZING RESOURCES

Latina Rebels (@latinarebels) is dedicated to revealing the complexities of Latinidad. For example, not all Latinx speak Spanish! To downplay someone's Latinx identity because they don't speak a colonizers' language betrays the internalized colonizer in all of us.

The Great Unlearn (@thegreatunlearn), curated by public academic Rachel Cargle, imagines the world we can create when we unlearn the concepts and conditioning that hold us back.

Hood Herbalism (@hoodherbalism, hoodherbalism.com) offers herbal classes and scholarships for BIPOC communities. The Living Altar (@thelivingaltar, livingaltar.com) is a collection of resources for magical resistance.

III

BRUJA LIFE

"I'm a witch."

—Erykah Badu

9

BRUJX FEMINISM

The women meet at dawn. They are naked. They gather in circles, around stone or fire or water. They hold hands. They chant. The horizon changes. A current runs through their arms, magnetizing them together. They are brown. They are red. They are yellow. They are white. They are queer. They are trans. They are multiplicity and fluidity. Together, they pull energy up from the earth. The earth runs through each of their bodies, up to the crowns of their heads and into the sky. They are the matriarchs of this world, and they are greeting the elements before turning to their work.

This is the world of Poeta Goddess, brainchild of Kimberly Rodriguez. Her artwork is set against backgrounds of skin tones, earthy colors, pastels. She draws feminine bodies communing with nature and the spirit world. A line of her poetry graces most of her images. They are bits of prayer, affirmations. They paint a world free of patriarchy, where ancestral maternal connection reigns. She channels her art. It's a kind of mediumship. She opens herself. The visions come to her. They are both ancient and aspirational.

Kimberly grew up in a creative household. Her parents were born in Mexico, and they were poor. They created and built what they needed with their hands and the resources they had. They grew their own food. They sewed clothes themselves.

They migrated to California, where Kimberly was born. They were undocumented. Kimberly and her siblings inherited the craftiness of their parents. Especially Kimberly. She was always drawing, creating. Her parents encouraged her. They didn't pressure her to study to be a doctor or a lawyer. In her home, she was accepted for who she already was.

Over time Kimberly came to express herself through what she wore. She went to the Academy of Art University in San Francisco where she studied merchandising in the fashion industry. The inclusivity she felt at home evaporated, and she was suddenly the minority. It was uncomfortable to no longer be around those who looked like her, but she persisted through the program. She knew what a privilege it was to be at college, all the work her parents had done to get her there.

After graduation Kimberly worked on fashion branding and digital marketing campaigns. She soon realized the system was not built for bigger bodies, Brown bodies, bodies that looked like hers. Rather than representation, there was one ideal that everyone sought to emulate. These companies were making profit off convincing people their bodies were imperfect.

She did this for two years until she was over it. She left her job and took a chance on herself. She had focused on clothes for so long, and now she found herself drawing naked bodies, full and relaxed, not bound by fabric. In the process, she dropped her barriers, what had kept her separate from her ancestral roots.

Though mainstream images of women are shifting to include bigger, browner, and queerer bodies, anything that departs from the thin White woman created for male consumption still feels "other." The other woman is a response to the idealized female form of Hollywood. Kimberly is working to erase the notion that there is an ideal form at all—to integrate the other woman, the shadow woman in all her forms, into the center of our collective consciousness.

Now that I subscribe to Poeta Goddess's Patreon, I look forward to her monthly print mailings. They come in a cute brown envelope with a couple goodies thrown in, like stickers or fairy dust. But the print and the accompanying affirmation is the real treasure. In the December 2020 print, a naked woman holds a lit candle at her center, the wax dripping down her fingers. There is a sensuality to it that has nothing to do with the male gaze. Behind her are big butterfly wings. The outline of the wings are stone, and inside the wings are images of landscapes, day on one side, and night on the other. She wears a crown of roses. On her upturned face is a look of peace. Around the image, this line:

I honor my voyage and trust that I am always guided.

In so many of our popular mythologies, there are two women: the dark and the light, Lilith and Eve, Kali and Durga, Persephone of the underworld and Persephone of the spring. The woman makes sense only as a split form in order to serve the story of the male. From the perspective of the male, only one side of the woman is desirable. The other is feared or desired obsessively, to the point of subjugation.

Take Lilith. Lilith's role in the expulsion from Eden has occupied the minds of artists and writers for centuries, and most of the images are dark; the poet and painter Dante Gabriel Rossetti describes Lilith as a reptilian form. A plaque discovered in Syria in the 1930s that is believed to be a pregnancy amulet against Lilith from the seventh or eighth century BC reads: "O you who fly in (the) darkened room(s), / Be off with you this instant, this instant, Lilith. / Thief, breaker of bones."

The only actual mention of Lilith in the Bible is found in Isaiah 34, which suggests that she is a flying demon. The Revised Standard Version of the Bible calls her "the night hag," and other translations depict her as a terror that comes in the night to curse pregnant women and children. Some translators have linked "Lilith" to *lylh*, the Hebrew word for "night."

Lilith, the spirit of the night.

The first time I read about Lilith, I felt a spinal chill. I finally had a name for the shadow in the corner of my room that paralyzed me in fear. Naming her made her more real and also less scary. It gave me hope that she was not (just) a monster. In recent critical treatments of Lilith, she has been reimagined as the ultimate feminist, the strong female who saves Eve from a life of subservience to Adam. She shows Eve that there is another way. She does not shy away from the dark. She is resourceful, making her own path outside institutions that would oppress her.

I play a revisionist history of Lilith and Eve in which they were lovers, loving the earth together. Lilith was tall and wiry and she draped herself on the branches of the tree in Eden, stirring in Eve a wild creativity. Their creations were their children, the crowns of flowers and the stone circles of prayer they made with their resourceful hands. They wanted without needing. Lilith lay her head on Eve's pillowy stomach and pointed long fingers at the stars.

Until Adam came round. He told Eve she could not exist without him. Suddenly, there was debt and need. Eve went both ways. For a while Lilith and Adam shared her company, eyeing each other from across paradise. Lilith filled her and Adam drank from her. Lilith grew tired of this. She saw that they might have been a nourishing circuit if Adam would only have given of the energy he hoarded. But he would not.

Lilith would not come second or third. She would always come first to herself.

Before she left Eve, she offered her fruit under the tree in the middle of paradise. If Eve would be with Adam forever after, Eve should at least know what she was missing. When Eve ate the fruit, she felt the energy centers turn inside her. Juice spilled down her face and seeped down into the roots of the tree. She saw everything she could potentially be and make with Lilith. The magnitude of the truth was almost too much to bear. The energy turned inside her, the universe expanding to fill her body so that her skin became as thin as paper. Just another breath and she would dissolve into nothing and everything.

How powerful they were together.

Lilith transformed into a snake to leave Eden without Adam noticing. In her absence, Adam could feel her influence remained. Eve was insatiable. She buried treasures in the ground for Lilith and watered the mounds of dirt with her tears and coaxed new stems of trees up with her laughter and loved herself until she shuddered onto the ground. Adam did not like that Eve felt pleasure or longing that she didn't share with him. He petitioned God to take her away from the source of her rapture, so that she would have to turn her attention to him. Thus humanity began, springing from the man's desires.

From then on, love would always be an unequal affair. The tree of Eden was abandoned, its secrets forgotten. It's said that to eat the fruit from the tree is to remember wholeness. If you sit by the tree long enough, you'll feel a coiled energy stirring, moving from the ground to the sky.

In Jungian psychology, the shadow is our unconscious, the parts of ourselves that are hidden and unintegrated. The appearance of "shadow work" in the mainstream spiritual lexicon is a response to the underlying toxic positivity of some communities. The admonition to stay away from negativity on the spiritual path might seem reasonable, but often "love and light" spiritualities amount to spiritual bypassing, the tendency to use practices like yoga or meditation to avoid facing unresolved problems. It's possible to engage in these practices superficially to feel good without diving into the depths of our consciousness to do the real work of healing.

There is a correlation between spiritual bypassing and White privilege. It might be easier to focus on the positive aspects of spirituality when you haven't experienced institutional oppression, and sometimes encouraging others to "just be positive" is dismissive of the ways our systems keep certain others down. Toxic positivity is not always conscious. As White people, we sometimes have a difficult time facing the shadow because it means coming to terms with hard truths about how we've been to blame. Facing the shadow, then, is a radical act toward dismantling oppressive systems, and it begins with ourselves.

Facing the shadow is not a destructive but a creative act. Carl Jung writes, "In spite of its function as a reservoir for human darkness—or perhaps because of this—the shadow is the seat of creativity."

To illustrate, Jung noted that the snake was a common shadow vision cited by his patients. In 1932 he gave a seminar in Zurich, Switzerland, called "The Psychology of Kundalini Yoga," during which he recalled his conversation with one patient in particular, a twenty-eight-year-old woman who told him that she had a black serpent in her belly that was causing her illness.

"One day she came and said that the serpent in her belly had moved; it had turned around," Jung says. "Then the serpent moved slowly upward, coming finally out of her mouth, and she saw that the head was golden."

The snake is a collective symbol, particularly significant in Tantric Hinduism and Kundalini yoga, as it represents the primal energy that moves up the body as the practitioner makes progress toward enlightenment. The serpent is a feminine energy named Shakti that lies coiled at the base of the root chakra. She lies in darkness until she is activated. Ritual practices such as yoga enable the serpent's ascent to the crown chakra, at which point, the primal instincts in the individual meet with the divine.

In his private journal, Jung writes: "The serpent is not only a separating, but a unifying principle." Jung interprets his patient's experience as a confrontation with the shadow and the subsequent transformation of the shadow from a personal problem into a collective power. Transpersonal psychology has ascribed these theories to Western men, but the shadow is an ancient concept. It is the embodiment of the unknown, the forms we reach for when we haven't yet wrangled phenomena into equations. Shadows and demons have a rich history in not just individual enlightenment but also scientific advancement. We would have no science without the imagination that is spurred by the dark side of our humanity. The shadow is boundless potential. It's the dark energy of the universe—not empty, we know now, but *full* of mystery—that captivates and confounds quantum physicists.

So what does shadow work look like in practice? You might have heard the saying "You have to feel it to heal it." There are many ways to engage in shadow work, but at the root is a radical sensitivity to and honesty about how we are feeling and what we are experiencing. It's important to have safe containers to do this work in whatever form it takes, especially when facing old traumas. At first it's helpful to have a guide of some sort, whether a traditional therapist or a spiritual practitioner.

Shadow work is an individual and a collective pursuit. Healing ourselves is the first step toward healing the collective. We associate well-being with light, but the darkness is where we heal. We began in the dark of our mothers' wombs, and to the dark of the universe we will return.

To guys, I've invariably been the woman on the light side of things, the manic pixie dream girl, that character trope of the eccentric woman who shows the complicated or sad man how to enjoy life and live adventurously.

It was a role I chose unconsciously. In Miami culture, the woman was as valuable as her ability to make men's heads turn. As much as my parents centered my education and independence, I felt a thrill when men hollered at my body as I walked next to a busy street. To my inexperienced mind, it felt wonderful to be wanted. I learned how to be an object of desire, how to accentuate my curves and downplay my intelligence when flirting. Things that I would regard as assault now, like getting groped at a club, were badges of honor.

He wants me. I'm wanted.

I thought it was a power, a sixth sense of sorts, to reflect others' desires. It wasn't disingenuous per se to project a certain aspect of myself—we all do this to a certain extent at the beginning of relationships—but now I see I hid many parts of myself to fit the role of others' dreams. In relationships, things heated up quickly. I was attentive, downright doting. Partners would tell me they never thought they'd meet someone who *just got them* so well. That was the gold, to be told I was the ideal partner. I mistook my sensitivity for love. I could read people, feel what others were feeling. I convinced myself they were my own feelings.

It was always difficult to sustain, and inevitably, the dark, secret sides of me would rear their heads, and my partners would be taken aback. They were suddenly dealing with something they hadn't bargained for. Who was this person with such incongruent needs? They called me crazy for my strong emotions. I became resentful that they didn't want the full me.

The pattern went: strong attraction, rushed commitment, disillusionment, occasional violence, heartbreak, rebound. Over and over it repeated. I never stopped to think if I wanted any of it. All that mattered was being chosen by the man to whom I hitched my value.

When I met my last partner, we were both married to other people. The relationship started as platonic. I was in the middle of a crisis with my husband at the time, who was drinking himself to near death and becoming violent. I didn't think too much of the increasing attention I was receiving from this other man or the flirtatious way we talked, until his wife accused him of having an affair with me. She knew him well enough to know he had developed real feelings. It was overwhelming. I was suddenly "the other woman." I should have run from the situation then, but I was in a kind of lovestruck paralysis. It was a survival response almost, to become so still, to let things happen. It was saving me from complete breakdown.

One very windy day, he left me a cryptic clue that led me to find a note on my back fence, on a page torn from a very old book. When I opened it, it crumbled into dozens of tiny pieces before I could read it, and the wind sent them into a paper tornado above my head. I was completely charmed by it. Empty promises like that worked on me back then. It didn't occur to me that the magic I felt mostly had to do with me, assisted by some lucky weather. I was awakening to a pattern of abuse and the glimmers of the better life I deserved, but it was all mixed up in another man. Again.

My husband went into rehab, and we filed for divorce. I fell in love with the married man. We felt like soul mates sent to help each other out of relationships that had gone wrong. But I was perpetually anxious about the precarious feeling of it all. I hadn't sought therapy for my feelings about my short marriage and the abuse I'd sustained. I felt the suffering and vitriol of my new love's ex reaching me through the dark matter between us. For a time I tried to pretend I really was the lighthearted, adventurous woman, and I reserved my dark moods for my times at home alone. With him, I was happy. At home, I was sad. Never my full self, I thought I preferred this split state to another failed relationship.

Amid the chaos I fell in love with his children. There were three of them, and they reminded me of me and my siblings. I had decided I wouldn't have children from my own body, and I imagined that I might one day be a maternal character in their lives, maybe even a grandmother to their future children. They filled the world with creativity and possibility. I was especially close to his youngest, the boy, who held my hand and occasionally called me mom by accident. Every time he did, I felt bad for feeling good about it. He was the way I had been as a child. He saw the little lines on bugs and hid away treasures from his walks. His moods would take hold of him. He so strongly felt his emotion, whether it was joy or excitement or rage.

When the boy died, I let all the oranges on my tree fall to the ground and rot, releasing a stringent alcohol into the air.

In the earth a few yards from the tree, I'd buried a dog, who died the month before the boy. I'd been inside my house and heard a squealing of tires and the thump of a big body being hit and the raw screams of all the members of a family. My spine tingled like cold water being poured down my back, and I was already calling 911 as I ran out my door toward the sounds. A group of kids had been playing outside, and I was sure that one of them had been hit. But then I saw the yellow fur. It was a Labrador, a hit and run. I canceled the call and stopped running. As I walked up to the family, the dog was taking her last few breaths. They were renters, so I helped them carry the dog to my yard. I dug her grave and covered her with the petals of my camellias, which had newly bloomed.

"Thank you," her owners said. And I thanked them, because the dog would feed my orange tree. "The earth needs our bodies," I told them. I could tell by the way they looked at me that they were trying to figure me out. I had a moment of looking at myself from the outside, and I realized how strange it is in our culture to see any beauty in death.

When they were gone, I performed a smoke ritual for the dog's soul and drew a card from the Medicine Woman deck by Carol Bridges. It was the seven of pipes, which Bridges calls "spirit freed." The card depicts a person dancing while wearing an animal mask. Behind them, another form is dancing. Above, the spirit of an animal is flying off. I read the prayer in the accompanying book. It spoke of finding truth behind the masks of creatures, and of facing loss and letting go.

"I am able now to confront my fear of loss. In every creature, I find a friend hiding behind a mask of a beast, a mask I have created by my fear."

I didn't know then how much I would return to this card, again and again, over the course of the following year. The next month the boy died, and a couple weeks later, the world shut down because of a virus. One night my boyfriend and his older daughter and I huddled on his bed and cried. She said that maybe her brother's death caused a rip in the universe that everything was gradually being sucked into.

Nearly a year later, the oranges have come in brighter and sweeter, and this time I catch them before they drop to the ground. I eat them right here, spitting the seeds out and pushing them into the dirt with my bare toes. This is how we birth things, from the things that used to be.

Poeta Goddess is making something right now, I'm sure of it. Right now she is finishing a drawing that she saw in a vision, in a dream. She will print many copies of it. She will put each copy in a brown envelope and fill the envelope with a sprinkling of gifts, a sticker, a tiny note, fairy dust. She will address the envelopes, making little hearts above the *i*'s, one to each subscriber of her Patreon monthly mail. She will stack them until they are ready to send. They will travel across the country like brown doves, into the mailboxes of souls who want to learn to love themselves better. Some of them will really need these missives, will see theirs in their box a little late, perhaps on a Sunday because they spent the whole week crying and let the mail pile up. They will spot the brown paper under a bill and feel a little spark because they forget about it every time, until it turns up. They will hold it up from the rest, to the light. They will carry it inside, maybe place it on their altar to open later. When they do they will look at the image a long time and they will know that they are not alone, that something as small as this piece of paper connects them to something bigger, to other seekers like themselves.

Creative force is healing. Poeta Goddess calls her process "art as alchemy." She channels her images and words from Spirit with the intention to heal ancestral trauma. She started drawing and writing in order to reframe her experiences as power rather than victimhood. On a personal level, she transmutes her pain. On the collective, she hopes her art will help change the American myth of the undocumented woman of color as other.

Poeta Goddess believes that as a feminist artist, it's her responsibility to present the shadow side of the world. To her, activism and spirituality go hand in hand. "If you're not fighting for what's best for all people, what is the point of your spirituality?" she says.

Kimberly's great-grandmother on her dad's side, Socorro, was a community healer and tarot reader. She died two years before Kimberly was born. Her daughter Antonia, Kimberly's grandmother, was also a healer and reader. Kimberly grew up thinking this was common and that art and healing were one and the same process. Then she started to hear the term bruja used to describe the process of reclaiming ancestral power.

Kimberly has grown a large following on social media with Poeta Goddess. Since launching it a couple of years ago, hundreds of people have told her how much her artwork has helped them. She was floored. She thought she was only drawing for herself, but now she sees that her art is a form of curanderismo, a vehicle for healing.

To Kimberly, this is what being a brujx feminist means. It means being fiercely honest about your shadow side and the ancestral trauma of your line. It means unapologetically awakening to and reclaiming your power from patriarchal systems. It means transforming abuse through creativity, finding lessons in difficult relationships. It means not taking shit from anyone because you're here to carve a radically creative existence for yourself. Above all, it means not giving up on yourself, no matter what's happened or how broken you feel. You're here to forge a healing path that others might follow, however messy your process seems. Your brokenness will help someone else, someday.

Know that even in your darkest moments, you are guided, and because of what you've gone through, you will eventually guide others.

Kimberly hopes Poeta Goddess will help people find their own special powers, their own alchemical process. She wants you to feel something when you look upon her work. It's up to you what you feel. We've been told our feelings are second to our thoughts. But feeling our feelings without judgment is the only way we can become whole.

"Art has the power of invoking emotion and creating a portal of meditation and healing," she says. "I want my art to be a portal where you can get lost, navigate, heal, daydream, call upon your spiritual team and talk to your ancestors."

Kimberly's figures are mostly naked. Looking on them, I remember I grew up being very comfortable with nudity. They remind me of sharing a kind of sacred space with my mother and aunts while they showered and dressed. I learned shame later, when nudity became tied to sex. Sex changed everything. I know that this is part of my ancestral trauma. So many of the women of my family have suffered loss within their sexual relationships, and I repeated this pattern. Sex and violence have been intertwined in our stories. I didn't have a model for healthy sex growing up. I am learning to forgive myself for this, and to take responsibility for breaking the pattern.

This is the power of our art. Writing is my medium, and through it I've been able to bring a lot of unspoken things to the surface, as unrefined as they may be at first. By integrating them into this larger story, I feel the bad emotions clearing. In this process, I feel my grief, and I hold myself like I would a child. I tell her that she is loved, and that everything will be OK.

I am still paralyzed in fear sometimes. Sometimes panic seizes my heart, and the room turns dark. The shadow woman returns. But she doesn't terrify me as she did when I was a child. She has come to represent for me the opportunity for reinvention. She is made of the parts of myself I have forgotten and repressed, and the parts of myself that are yet to emerge. She is the divine feminine. Not the one that is reduced to a gender essentialism that contrasts a necessary male. Not the "receptive" or "passive" divine feminine. I mean the one that is so full that she is scary to look upon—because she is everything I have the freedom to become. She isn't an object of desire. She is full of her own desires.

Almost every bruja I've talked to has a story like this, about going through darkness to arrive at an understanding of themselves and their calling. They might have a practical business within the larger spiritual products and services industry, but beneath it all is a personal revolution, a movement from split selves to wholeness. This feminism is the foundation of every authentic bruja business.

The brujx feminist is the other woman. She does not fit in. She doesn't stay on the track laid before her. Brave and naked, warrior and lover, dark and light, she honors her voyage and trusts that she is always guided.

THE MOON JOURNAL

Keeping a journal has been crucial for me in processing the events of the last few years, especially in 2020 when time seemed to blur together. It's always been hard for me to keep a daily journal, so I write on the new and full moons, about every two weeks. This is supplemental to the rituals I carry out on those days, and it makes the rituals more meaningful. I treat journaling as a ritual in itself. After a while you'll be surprised by how many dots you can connect from past moon entries. Stories start to form; lessons start to arise. And best of all, you'll see the progress you've made. We have a tendency to forget the things we used to worry about or want, and it's humbling to go back and realize that your present state is a manifestation of things you put on the page long ago. Keeping a journal is a deeply feminist practice, as it allows room for reflection, exploration, and growth. When you dedicate yourself to journaling, you allow room for your own truth. Without it I may not have become conscious to see the patterns that bound me or given myself space to break those patterns.

Find a journal that feels sacred to you in some way. Dedicate it solely to the purpose of ritual moon writing or drawing. You might want to anoint it with oil during one of your altar rituals. Devise a process that works for you. Maybe you open it before your closing meditations at your altar, or maybe you'd rather write or draw in bed before you sleep or first thing when you wake up. Follow your intuition. Don't force anything or get down on yourself if you miss a writing session. It's better to create something, however small, however long it's been since your last entry, than not do anything at all because you are fixated on consistency or perfection. Sometimes it's helpful to start with a simple prompt, maybe something tied to the moon: What makes me feel full? I use tarot cards as visual prompts that help me step out of my linear mind.

Think of using your moon journal as a meditative act. Treat your words and images the way you treat your thoughts. Simply observe them as you put them down. Do not try to grasp onto them or fix them or wrangle them into meaning. Be the witness. Let the words or images come as they are, even if they don't seem to make sense to you. As you get better at allowing things to flow, you might be surprised at how they feel like they're coming from somewhere other than your own thinking mind. When you get to this level, it's sometimes called automatic writing or automatic drawing, a kind of mediumship.

SAGITTARIUS: THE VISIONARY

Sagittarius is represented by the archer, the one with great sight who takes aim and fires off into the unknown. It is the visionary and philosopher of the zodiac. Sagittarians are optimistic and dream big, and since they tend to climb high, they can handle hard falls. They're more empathetic than they seem. Call on Sagittarius when you need to reconnect with the big picture and get fired up about a cause or about the good of humanity.

ELEMENT: Mutable fire

PLANETARY RULER: Jupiter

AFFIRMATION: "I see"

FOR YOUR ALTAR: Figs or olives, oak leaves, turquoise or sapphire, spiritual teachers, the archer, sacred texts or prayer cards, blue and purple stones, anything that helps visualization

JOURNAL: It's important to have a safe space when engaging in shadow work and traveling to old memories. It can feel like you're right there again. Before diving in, make sure you're ready and that you have mental health resources on call. Who can you ask to hold space for you? What tools can you use to avoid retraumatizing yourself? How will you care for your inner child after you've done this work?

EMPOWERMENT IDOLS

Emilia Ortiz, otherwise known as Ethereal (@ethereal.1) is unapologetically herself. I go to her page when I need a pep talk or a reminder that there is not just one way to be a feminist. Farah Siddiq (@farah msiddiq, farahsiddiq.com) posts wonderfully empowering affirmations, lines of poetry, and tips to help you visualize a more powerful you.

Being a bruja is about taking responsibility for yourself as much as it is about giving yourself permission to let go and trust the universe. If you want a dose of reality about how to balance these seemingly opposing energies, follow The Trap Witch (@thetrapwitch, thetrap witch.com). She is a spiritual coach that helps you claim your power while remaining honest about where you are on your path. And she will unapologetically tell you when you're working from an ego motivation rather than from love. Trust her when she calls you out—it's for your own good.

10

DRAMA AT THE BOTANICA

Valeria Ruelas describes her homeland around Chihuahua, Mexico, as cold and rugged and in the middle of nowhere. There her great-grandmother, Maria Luisa, was a curandera. She worked with herbs and performed limpias, energetic cleansings. When Valeria was a baby, Maria Luisa took her to the local botanica for supplies. She didn't call herself a bruja. In those days, *bruja* wasn't a word you'd use. When Valeria was two years old, Maria Luisa died, and the family moved to New Mexico. She remembers something of her great-grandmother, some shared bond that is felt deep inside like an early instinct.

Botanicas are spiritual supply stores commonly found in Latin American neighborhoods. The word *botanica* is related to botany, referring to traditional plant medicine. At botanicas, you'll find altar products like candles, herbs, incense, oils, and books. To many, botanicas are a staple of life, like a pharmacy. Going to the botanica is part of a regular week of errands. It fills the gaps for those who don't have access to medical care, or for whom seeing a therapist carries a cultural stigma. The botanica provides a safe space that extends homeland traditions, especially for immigrants or those living in exile. Usually, there is a spiritual practitioner available to dress candles and provide consultations for a wide range of physical, emotional, and spiritual problems.

As more people struggle to afford health care, the self-care industry grows to meet demand for holistic healing alternatives and preventive medicines. There is a greater need for places like botanicas that serve a wider, more secular audience. During COVID-19, self-care spending has skyrocketed, and influencers make self-care look trendy. "Self-care is not selfish" is a common meme. Except it sometimes is. To many Indigenous communities, the same products and practices that are now being consumed en masse were never a trend—they were necessary for survival.

The idea of self-care has roots in politics and activism. To philosopher Michel Foucault, self-critique and radical awareness are inextricable from the practices of self-care. To achieve true freedom and ethically participate in politics, we must reflect on our relationship to power. Foucault's self-care is a radical act that centers otherness, what is usually repressed in us by governments or social norms.

Audre Lorde's treatment of self-care spread the idea widely to feminists and activists. To Lorde, self-care is preservation in the face of systems that will never care enough for those on the margins of society. The commoditization of the concept by influencers and retail businesses has whitewashed it and diluted its power. There's opportunity for bruja-owned botanicas to challenge the mainstream notion of self-care as just another commercial self-help concept and return it to its activist roots. After all, botanicas have always existed on the margins.

Valeria's mom grew up in the Catholic Church, but Valeria carried her great-grandmother's gifts. She was attracted to the bruja, especially her association with the outcasts of society. In 2013 a friend who identified as a bruja and had natural gifts woke Valeria up to her own. This is how it usually works, she says. Someone will see something in you, and they'll say something or offer some resource that will open up the world of magic.

Valeria developed her intuition through tarot cards. She started by reading for herself, then for friends, and over time, people approached her more and more for readings. As her friend had done for her, Valeria mostly helps people come to their spiritual purpose, whether it's by connecting them with their spiritual guides or ancestry, or simply by providing a space for them to vent. She started calling herself The Mexican Witch, and she gradually grew a sizable following.

I was attracted to The Mexican Witch's exuberant and colorful Aquarian energy and her body positivity. She's inspirational without being saccharine, and she is not scared to say what she means and to stand up against injustices. But she has this wonderful way of doing so without being harsh. In personal readings, she helps people have "slow, beautiful check-ins with spirit," centered on self-care.

Protection rituals are one of her specialties, and this she inherits from her patron saint, Santa Muerte. Santa Muerte is the Mexican saint of death and the champion of the outcasts of Mexico, of drug dealers and sex workers and people living in poverty. Recently, she's gained worldwide popularity, and people from all religions visit her altar in Tepito.

That's where the public worship of Santa Muerte started, in Tepito, Mexico, on Halloween in 2001. A woman called "Doña Queta," born Enriqueta Romero, set out a life-size statue of Santa Muerte, the skeleton saint. This was highly taboo at the time as her image had always been occulted behind the Virgin of Guadalupe and Catholics still associate her true form with evil.

This is what we do with death, because we fear it so. We associate it with evil, and we push it to the margins. It is a sign of our privilege to do this. For those who live closer to death, she cannot be ignored, and rather than being a fearful image, Santa Muerte is a comforting constant.

The worship of Santa Muerte has become the fastest growing new religious movement in the Americas, though it's condemned by the Vatican. This has not stopped many people from converting from Catholicism or carrying on a hybrid sort of worship of both the Virgin Mary and Santa Muerte. In contrast to the leadership of both the government and the clergy in Mexico, the movement's leadership has female devotees at its highest levels. In a country where the disappearance of people at the hands of the cartels and trafficking of women is commonplace, these women leaders risk their own safety to relay Santa Muerte's message of protection and hope. It's spread beyond Mexico. Arely Vazquez pioneered Santa Muerte worship in Queens, and another Enriqueta, Enriqueta Vargas, was a famous traveling evangelist for Santa Muerte.

The worship of the saint of death is deeply personal, and many people have stories of Santa Muerte calling them to her. Santa Muerte called Valeria out of the blue. It happened when she was in the midst of a deep depression. She was starting to think she had no reason to live. She hated her job. There was a lot of drama in her life. She was driving home from work one day, and suddenly she understood that she had to go to the botanica. She hadn't planned on going for any materials that day, and she didn't know what she was going to get, just that she really needed to go.

When she got to the botanica, she walked straight to a red-and-black candle for Santa Muerte. She bought it and took it home and created an altar to Santa Muerte and lit the candle. She didn't yet know how to dress a candle, but she used her intuition and made offerings. She instantly felt the negative energy clearing from her life.

"She might as well have gotten behind the wheel of my car and driven me there," Valeria says. "The way Spirit sometimes does things, you don't have a choice, you're dragged into it. I was pleasantly dragged into her practice."

From then on, magic became a healthy distraction, a daily medicine. Through magic, Valeria began to embrace her own power, to take care of herself, to disengage from others' dramas, and to love her journey, no matter how hard.

It's not an easy path, Valeria says. "We are here as the blood and sweat and tears of our ancestors. We're going to live through what they died for." Sometimes this is joyous, and sometimes this involves suffering. Either way, it's important to be fully present with yourself and your feelings, so you can clear traumas from your life and from your ancestral line in order to make room for blessings.

The boy died in early March 2020, on the very spot where he was born. I've seen in movies how people fall to their knees. They say I did that. That I howled and tore at my clothes, offered myself to the sky as sacrifice. I don't remember what my body did, just something inside snapping, then the feeling of falling and the deafening roar of an impartial universe.

Two of my friends, Annalise and Erin, were with me at my home when I found out. We had been eating dinner on my back deck. I remember their arms around me, a cradle of arms. They got me to bed, somehow. Erin stayed with me that night.

In my shock, I had fallen into an in-between space, a kind of trance. I tried searching for him in the dark. I put on my little light inside, as I had done when I was a kid. I automatically chanted a mantra I was familiar with, meant to help souls transition.

Erin chanted with me. We chanted until the room fell away. My voice was gone, and my body was gone, and I was just light for a moment. Erin says that a few minutes in, my voice became incredibly strong, unrecognizable, startlingly unlike my small and breathy voice. She became a little scared but kept chanting with me. She says it felt like we broke through some kind of sound barrier and she heard hundreds of voices mixing with ours. In her perception, a portal had opened, electric currents filling the room, and everything became light.

I remember light, too, nothing but light and no sense of the boundaries of my body, like I had expanded. Soon the light was interrupted by shadows. They came as they had come in childhood, and this time I let them, because I didn't want to end the chant prematurely. They multiplied, coming from every corner, covering the room, bleeding together. They became an encroaching wave of darkness. None of them were him. I pushed them away as I had always done when they tried to get in, until I couldn't hold them. I turned off my light and fell exhausted on the bed, where I would remain until late morning.

✦ ✯ ✦

In my moment of terrible grief, an old instinct kicked in. Maybe it's something that my great-grandmother passed to me, though she refused to teach me how to be a medium. Maybe it's a survival response to trauma, this instinct to lean toward the dead. Over the weeks and months that followed the boy's death, I read passages from the Tibetan Book of the Dead, searching for something that might make sense of this tragedy. Eastern traditions were my reference because they were well documented. But without a teacher, so much of the text remained obscured.

For many of us who grew up removed from our ancestral spiritualities in the United States, we have lost the wisdom of death rituals. I still find it difficult sometimes to reach out to the practitioners who work in the botanicas. I was conditioned to believe that botanicas were run by evil santeros, and just stepping inside would cause me to be cursed. I only realized recently how racist this stigma is, as botanicas are prevalent in Afro-Latinx communities and almost nonexistent in Whiter middle-class neighborhoods like my childhood one. So many of us were conditioned to think that Black spirituality is evil.

With the revival of ancestral spiritualities, there has been a wave of botanicas that reflect the aesthetic of the new generation of brujas. With this growth comes a wave of opportunities—and problems.

Valeria is brutally honest about the problems. "The spirits of these traditions are revolutionary Black and Brown people," she says. "People need to stay in their lane."

Especially when it comes to African religions, Valeria says. "The *lwa* are said to have caused the Haitian Revolution. These spirits literally hate colonizers, and you don't want to mess with them in the name of an image or a trend."

In New Orleans, where Valeria lives, the streets are full of spirits. The more that befalls the city—hurricanes, colonizers, epidemics—the stronger the spirits get. You can feel it in the air when you walk there, like maybe you could just reach out and centuries of concentrated magic will fall on your palm. That expectation has created an industry exploiting the culture of Voodoo.

Voodoo shops litter the French Quarter, dressed up souvenir stores for tourists interested in novelty, the commodities of spirituality. They're looking for zombies and witch doctors and dolls to stick pins in. They're not the biggest problem. Every place has its kitsch, and the inauthentic botanicas are fairly contained within the tourist trap areas.

The bigger problem is the increasing number of White shop owners, who would rarely, by the ancestral nature of these things, have a real stake in the traditions they're trying to peddle. They are White, and Voodoo is Black: a Black religion handed down by Black people for Black people. The White shop owners are mostly opportunists and gentrifiers, modern-day colonizers. They are bleeding to the edges of town, and they're everywhere on Instagram with their beautiful photos of bottles and herbs. They capitalize on the very traditions that their ancestors persecuted.

The White spiritual consumer has been trained that everything is for the taking, that everything has a price. Most are predictable. They'll go into a souvenir shop, grab a doll, and carry on to the next frozen-hurricane bar. But then there are those who are seeking something more "authentic," who have read all the books written by all the White researchers, who know that the dolls aren't actually the thing to look for, who have traveled—or even moved—to New Orleans for something real. Surely, they believe, they deserve to be let in on the secrets. They put in the time. They respect the real shit.

I know them, because I have been them. In Cuba I was a voyeur with good intentions and real problems looking for a little ancestral magic. It's not just White people who do this. It's all of us who go around saying we are reclaiming our ancestry, because our families are from here or there, because we know the spirits. And in the process, we try on histories and traditions that aren't ours.

The concept of reclamation is big in bruja communities. But how can we take back something that we never had? The occult is *occult* because certain religions had to be protected during periods of colonization and oppression. A lot of rituals stemming from these religions are now coming to the surface, because many people are seeking, and many people want to share. But some religions, especially Voodoo, in all its different origins and spellings, will always be secret to anyone who is not ancestrally connected to them. You can visit all the shops and buy all the products, and you'll even meet practitioners who will seem very inviting, but the lwa, the spirits of ancestors of Voodoo, will remain silent.

Of all the Afro-diasporic traditions, Voodoo is the most occult, and therefore the most misunderstood. To complicate things, there are many threads of Voodoo, and you'll see it spelled differently, because it's traditionally spoken rather than written: Vudú, Vodun, Vodon, Vodoun, Vodou, Voudou, and other variations.

Haitian Vodou, as it's most commonly spelled, is a Creole, or mixed, religion rooted in the Yoruba religion and African Vodun practices, which became syncretized with Catholicism to preserve the traditions that were threatened by European colonists and the turbulent Haitian government. Because of this, Haitian Vodou can never be separated from politics and the history of the slave trade.

Haiti was colonized by France in the 1600s, and the French Catholics' treatment of Africans was the most brutal in the Caribbean. The government violently kept enslaved people from practicing Vodou, banning meetings and enforcing severe punishments for "witchcraft" or "pagan" practices. The government was threatened by the power that

Vodou conferred to the people, as they resisted forced labor in favor of their own rituals, and the rituals' connection to the land encouraged family compounds to emerge as centers of power. Even after the revolution that freed Haitians from colonial rule, the religion was forced underground, and an anti-Vodou culture permeated Haitian government. Haiti's presidents worked with the Catholic Church to fight what they regarded as the "black magic" of Vodou, either through violence and imprisonment or by trivializing it as folklore.

In reality, Vodou's ceremonies and rituals have been lifelines for people who have had nowhere else to turn for help. Ceremonies are open to everyone, and all problems are taken on as the work of the community. Rituals are designed to align participants with the lwa, or spirits, who act as intermediaries between Bondyé, the supreme creator, and humanity. The body ritual is central to healing. Long histories of trauma are expressed through the body through dance and possession. In fact, the word Vodou refers to a mode of dance.

People initiated into the religion of Vodou call it "the way of the lwa." The lwa are ancestor spirits, sometimes likened to orishas. One of the most well-known lwas is Papa Legba who, like Santeria's orisha Elegua, is the first and last lwa to be called on during ceremonies, as he serves as the interlocutor between humanity and other lwa. He is associated with roads and rules communication and speech. Like so many other African deities, he has been syncretized with the beloved Saint Lazarus to keep him safe.

Although the saints serve similar purposes to orishas and lwas, persuasive campaigns by colonial powers have somehow protected the pagan-like rituals of Catholicism while demonizing the healing systems of Vodou as witchcraft.

Most people in the United States are more familiar with images of black magic as it relates to Louisiana Voodoo, which is distinct from Haitian Vodou or Dominican Vudú or other religions throughout the Caribbean. Louisiana Voodoo emerged as a hyperlocal response to slavery and colonialism in the Mississippi Valley, concentrated in New Orleans. While it's influenced by Haitian Vodou, it is a system of its own, with its own history, and it pulls more from African folk practices of rootwork and divination than it does from the Afro-Caribbean diaspora via the transatlantic slave trade. For instance, there is a greater emphasis on amulets and charms, like the gris-gris, in Louisiana Voodoo.

The fetishization of Voodoo images has created stereotypes and misinformation that persist today. Voodoo is erroneously associated with evil dolls and zombies. Priests and priestesses have become "witch doctor" caricatures associated with the devil. But in traditional African religions, folk magic was distinct from witchcraft. It referred to any means of influencing fate through natural orders and was considered a part of traditional healing.

Certain practitioners of this magic *were* considered destructive. "Sorcerers" and "witches" were historically people who used magic to harm others or to bend nature exclusively to their own will. When death resulted from this kind of magic, the sorcerer or witch was usually punished by the community through exile or death. This distinction between "good" and "bad" magic varied depending on context. But in Europe, what would have been considered traditional healing across African religions was often labeled with the blanket term of witchcraft.

At the heart of Voodoo is connection to your own history as a form of surviving and even thriving within oppressive systems. You don't need in on the secrets of any other besides your own. You have the power to channel your own past and connect to your own nature.

In New Orleans, Hoodoo is just as big as Louisiana Voodoo, and it's more open to outsiders. It's not a religion but a spirituality specific to the region, developed by enslaved people in the southern US. It's sometimes called Conjure, and it mixes traditional African folk magic, or rootwork, with Indigenous American and European influences. It can be practiced in tandem with Voodoo or Christianity, but it stands on its own, and it does not call on the lwa or on saints. It is still a primarily practiced by people of color and should not be greedily or thoughtlessly appropriated, but White people are invited on occasion to learn and use the folk magic of Hoodoo with respect.

As Valeria lives and practices in New Orleans, she observes a lot of disrespect, and she is an ally to Black spiritual practitioners. When she calls people out, she gets her fair share of "hater-ade," as she says. It's part of the deal when you have a large platform on which you are courageously honest and naked (sometimes literally!). Once, she called out somebody publicly about cultural appropriation, and the person reported her for discriminating against her for being White, and Valeria's account was temporarily banned.

To Valeria, a bruja is many things, but at the core, she is one who performs the justice work that other spiritualists fail to address. "We're brujas, because we are done with people taking our stuff away, our wealth away. It's our time to be the most present and powerful in this world."

To many of us whose ancestors grew up with little or were disenfranchised in some way, our relationship with money can be really complicated. There might be shame around making money because of what we know about markets and how they have excluded people of color in the past. To Valeria, being a bruja in business, a "brujapreneur," is about stepping into financial and career success, moving from a place of lack to a place of abundance.

It's not an easy balance to strike, remaining true to your spirituality while forming a business around it, but Valeria is an example of how to be ruthlessly honest in the process of coming out of the broom closet and how to perform as an ally. Being in business as a bruja is a kind of perpetual coming out, as you strike a balance between your spiritual practice and your livelihood within a gig economy that by its nature is inconsistent and unstable.

A harrowing 2020 has made most people reevaluate their relationship to work. Maybe you lost your job, or you started to work from home, or you had to keep going to work, somehow, amid so much grief and stress. Many of us have had to adjust in some way. Some of us never had sure footing.

During lockdown, brujas sent messages of hope and hosted workshops and created altar products to help us get through. Without the pressure to be out in physical spaces, the online community has grown and strengthened. In IGTV and Zoom meetings, there's been more talk about mutual aid networks, how we might support each other in the gig economy and create our own safety nets. I see in these conversations the beginnings of a new kind of economy, one underwritten by feminist and environmental principles, that shifts power and money into the hands of Indigenous peoples and women of color.

There's a lot of rhetoric out there about "getting back to normal," but for many people, things haven't been normal for a while. If this virus has taught us anything, it should be that the way we were living is unsustainable, and we have to change the way we think about business. For all the progress we think we've made as a society, for all the ways we think we've protected ourselves from the harsh reality of the world out there by accumulating material wealth, we are still a part of nature, and Mother Nature is showing us just how hard the stuff of evolution can be.

We are in a collective period of shadow work. Having delayed reckoning with the ills of our society, we in the global north have had to face them all at once as things fall apart closer to home. Environmental degradation, economic disparity, systemic racism: these are old problems that we've been pushing aside, that can no longer be ignored. When we put off doing the shadow work for years and years like we've done, something will happen to force us to face the shadows; 2020 will happen, again and again, if we don't make changes.

As brujas increasingly monetize their skills, they will need to adapt to this changing world. There are a lot of pitfalls to owning a spiritual business, not least of which is cultural appropriation, especially by White people. Certain Indigenous magical products, like sage and palo santo, have been near fetishized, and they are becoming overharvested. Big businesses like Sephora, Anthropologie, Free People, and Urban Outfitters have been called out for selling "starter kits" for witches including bundles of white sage. They have defended themselves by promoting "wellness" and suggesting that there is no reference to ceremonial smudging belonging to Indigenous communities, as though the product itself could be separated from ceremonial history. To Indigenous communities, it's not just that retail chains are profiting from this but also that they're perpetuating the notion that Indigenous cultural practices are trendy, when in the past they were banned by government measures, like Canada's Indian Act, which gave the Canadian government authority to dictate the practices of Native peoples and is still in effect today. These trends can also be detrimental to the environment. The mass mining of crystals and gemstones, which often leads to water contamination, soil erosion, and land degradation, is an example of the hypocrisy of a consumer-driven spirituality.

There is a fine line between cultural appropriation and devotion. Christy Lendechy of Bruja's Botanica offers products to support the worship of Santa Muerte. She recently posted a shirt with the words PROTECTED BY SANTA MUERTE on her Instagram. Her intention was devotional and inspirational. Shortly after, she was contacted by a business that has merchandise with the same "slogan." In good faith, she took down the shirt, but the other business never provided proof of the trademark.

Christy believes "Protected by Santa Muerte" should be considered a prayer. She thinks it's going against what Santa Muerte stands for to try to own it exclusively. The online community rose up in defense. Devotees everywhere were offended, and they bought up Christy's shirt in protest.

"It was a beautiful thing to have that support that I wasn't expecting," Christy said. "Even though it is primarily an online community, it's not to be underestimated. The presence is very strong."

These boundaries are important. When you come up to them and define them and decide what side you're going to be on, you find out what you're about. Being a bruja in business is more than making money. It's standing for your beliefs and defending the spiritual integrity of the work. Bruja's Botanica products are consciously made with a larger story in mind, and Christy reposts images of her clients wearing or using them, creating one of the most recognizable bruja brands in the community at the moment.

Spiritual communities are not immune to infighting, and since Santa Muerte in particular attracts so many different people, there is often a lot of conflict revolving around her worship.

Valeria posted a warning on her Instagram about Santa Muerte devotees who use the saint of death's image in service of violent aims. While Santa Muerte is for everyone, that also means that anyone can use her for nefarious purposes. Her worship is not for the weak of heart, and Valeria urges caution for those eager to connect with other devotees.

For as fierce as the conflict between individual practitioners can become, the larger sentiment in the bruja world is collaborative rather than competitive. Christy is currently working with photographer Monica Serrano on a visual project about Santa Muerte devotees in the United States, featuring brujxs such as Olde Ways, the Death Witch, Winkx Tess, and Tender Bruja. Christy hopes the project will show the in-betweeness of the Mexican American experience and foster a sense of belonging among Santa Muerte devotees in the States. She plans on opening a brick-and-mortar in Compton, her hometown.

As people continue to search for help facing death and trauma, Santa Muerte is an increasingly popular symbol of protection and comfort. Death is the great equalizer, connecting us all to each other and to the spirit world.

When we get caught up in trends and competition, we can forget that we're in this bruja life for healing above all else. Let's not sweat the small stuff. Instead of beating each other up, let's help each other and remember that we are here for love. We are all learning as we go along. You might someday buy into a superficial trend that's bad for the environment or support a White appropriator, but as long as you are committed to learning with love in your heart, you won't hurt the ancestors. They know their own.

And yours will always be waiting for you to come on home.

After the boy's wake, I helped his father clear out their family home. I spent a long time sitting on the spot where he died in the master bedroom. His sisters found him first. Then his parents rushed in. They couldn't resuscitate him. I'd learn of the terrible sounds of the ambulance sirens and the girls' screaming. I've somehow created a memory of it, though I wasn't there. We still don't know what happened. I told myself that it's always an accident when they're that young. The spot in the room was full of energy. Eleven years earlier, his mother had given birth to him right there, and I'm told it had been a difficult delivery.

I sat on the spot and chanted for him.

The boy had an amazing memory. He told me once that the first dream he could remember was about being in a dark ocean. He was with his mother and they were struggling to swim. Then a dolphin came by, and he grabbed hold of its fin with one hand and his mother with the other, and the dolphin pulled them toward light.

More than a year after his death, I can still sometimes hear his voice in the early morning when the room is blue gray, as clear as if it were in the room with me, that undeniable little ring.

I had hoped that in our grief, my relationship with his father would strengthen. But I was Lilith; I was Kali; I was the witch. The one who didn't belong in the story of creation.

In December 2020, as the boy's twelfth birthday approached, I had a breakdown. I couldn't sustain being split as I'd been. I was exhausted after years of being a supporting character in someone else's story: I had nothing left to give.

The birthday was significant, because the boy had left behind a shoebox that said something like "Don't open until your twelfth birthday," and I had been waiting to see what was inside. I needed a ritual of closure. My boyfriend and the boy's mother had already looked inside, together. They planned a remembrance ceremony to which I was not invited. The date got closer, triggering me. I felt acute panic and grief. It felt just like the night I found out he died, as if no time had passed. I was terrified. I called my boyfriend for support, but he wouldn't come.

It is a law of relationship physics that love ends the way it started. This one had its genesis and death in emotional breakdown. As horrible as the breakup felt, I was finally reeling back a thread of myself that I had lent out for too long.

I had the presence of mind to buy a little potted Christmas tree for my house before I ended the relationship. It's a Norfolk pine and can live in the Florida climate year-round. It was the first time I'd gotten my own tree in the three years I'd lived in my house. It took me a long time to thread the jingle bells and tie them on the fluffy fronds of my warm-weather pine. It didn't smell piney, but I had a Christmas-tree candle lit nearby, and when I was done, looking at it with its multicolored lights and shiny baubles, I felt almost happy.

When I first met the boy, it was like remembering. He was so much like I was as a child, always dirty with little rocks in his pockets, telling story after story, and putting his treasures in shoebox capsules. When we went on hikes, he kept me company, because I was much slower than his father and sisters. We stopped often to pick berries and look at bugs making their way slowly across our path.

I never saw what was in his birthday box. When I feel loss about that, I remember my own secret treasures and how they're probably still under my childhood tree, carefully hidden at the foot of the weeping willow.

An altar is really a reminder for care of the self. I leaned on that in my grief, went online and found things to perform the rituals I needed just for me. That's what bruja businesses are doing—sharing the ways they got through the worst things. That's what you're buying when you order an altar item or a service: experience. The power of objects or spells cast intentionally, magical relics of a passing moment.

Through the holidays, I sat by my altar and my grief, and I told myself my life had prepared me for this. I talked to my bees. The constant hum of them grounded my anxiousness and lifted me from hopelessness. Bees are at peace with death. There are tens of thousands in one colony, and they each live just a few weeks. About one thousand die every day. They drop out of the sky and land where they are. Or they are unceremoniously carried off by other bees when they get too weak.

Their bodies return to the earth. That's the law of conservation. When an organism dies, the atoms that made up its biomolecules break down to simpler molecules and return to the air, the water, the earth. The energy that moved within each being is recycled into the environment. Nothing is lost. Do you remember learning this in science class, long ago? You know you're a witch when suddenly this knowledge turns everything to magic. The little dead bird on the sidewalk, the grandmother who passed this past fall. Now they're in the leaves and in the thread of your sleeve.

FIND YOUR BOTANICA

We *all* have ancestors, so we can all access ancestral magic. But not all ancestors are for everyone. I think it's beautiful that we are changing the view of magic, redefining ancestral wisdom as resistance and power. *How* we do this is what matters. We have to acknowledge our privilege every step of the way. What a great privilege it is to openly identify with ways of knowing that used to be persecuted.

First, we educate ourselves. We learn the difference between ancestral religions and the traditions of folk magic. We learn as much as we can about our own ancestors and what they believed and practiced. If we can't or don't feel connected to our ancestors, we respectfully approach teachers of traditions to which we feel called. We ask for permission and wait for invitation into their ancestral knowledge. We put in the time and the work before expecting that we'll automatically become initiated into their traditions, whether we share ancestry or not. And we accept when we are not invited. Really. We don't get angry or make excuses. We say thank you and walk away.

Second, we consume wisely. We do not take thoughtlessly. We do not appropriate from cultures that are not ours. We show appreciation for businesses run by people who have ancestral connections to their work, who are trying to help people instead of just profiting off a fad.

As a regular spiritual practitioner, it's important to cultivate relationships with providers of sustainable resources for your magic. You might try visiting a spiritual supply store in your neighborhood if it's available to you, but now there are so many online botanicas that didn't exist when I was a kid. This will allow you to do your research and find a place that aligns with your practice. Here are some things to keep in mind or ask when looking for your place:

* Where do they source their materials? Are they nonappropriative, sustainable, cruelty free, and nontoxic?

* Do they offer spiritual consultations?

* Are they connected to a particular tradition?

* Which parts of their business are open to me, and which practices do I have to be initiated into before seeking?

* Do I feel safe here? Is there a good presence when I walk in or enter their website?

* Do they offer accessible and affordable classes or workshops?

* Do they make promises about outcomes? If so, are they realistic and attainable?

CAPRICORN: THE AUTHORITY

Capricorn rules the tenth house of career and authority. Capricorns are the most ambitious in the zodiac. They set goals that would scare off most others and work consistently toward them. Sometimes this takes decades. Though they might seem set in their ways, they are often pioneers. They measure success not by money nor status, though neither is ever in short supply, but by the groundbreaking quality of their work. Call on Capricorn when you need to build big structures or when you need to stay the course.

ELEMENT: Cardinal earth

PLANETARY RULER: Saturn

AFFIRMATION: "I succeed"

FOR YOUR ALTAR: Hemlock, iron or other dark metals, ascended masters, the goat, anything dark or in raw form or unfinished, guide-books or encyclopedias

JOURNAL: What do you want to build in this life?

BRUJX BOSSES

The best brujx bosses are those who push boundaries while carving out a place for themselves in the spiritual market. Firme Arte (@firmearte, firmearteonline.com) was one of the first brujx businesses on the scene. They are a queer Indigenous sibling duo. I followed them when they were just starting their monthly brujx boxes, a take on the sub-scription makeup and clothes boxes you get by mail. I remember being so excited about this. Each month, you get an assortment of altar items based on the astrology of the moment. There are now many magical subscription boxes out there, but Firme Arte manages to keep their lines of products authentic, because their motivation is more than making money. Besides their products, they focus on queer health and social justice, including the rights of incarcerated people. They make a Santa Muerte candle that the Mexican Witch swears by.

These brujxs will help you embrace the magical boss within you through sacred ritual: Behati Life (@behatilife, behatilife.com), J. Allen Cross (@oregon_wood_witch), Brujeria 'n' Chill (@brujeria_n_chill), Keiko (@theafrowitch), Brujas Morenas (@brujasmorenas), Brujitxs del Barrio (@brujitxsdelbarrio), Christina Arenas (@christinathelightworker), and Nicole Bloodmoon (@blood.moon.bruja).

11

THE MOON COVEN

Cindy Rodriguez remembers fields of *hierba luisa*, the lemongrass that grew wild on her grandparents' property in the Quechua-Kichwa territories, also known as Lima, Peru. She ran barefoot with cousins. One cousin picked the hierba for tea. The bright smell of the grass takes her back there, to the mountains and the stars and the folk music of her family.

Living in New Jersey, Cindy felt disconnected from the land. She describes her life there as "corre corre," always on the go. She got caught up, and she didn't visit Peru for many years. Then in 2014 everything fell apart at once. She lost her job. She broke up with her boyfriend of ten years. She suffered a constellation of physical symptoms. She was thirty-one, and she felt that she'd hit bottom as she moved in with her mother.

She had only talked about her ancestral spirituality with her mother in colonized terms. She had rejected the family practices that seemed like nonsense to her. She was a journalist trained to accept only what she read in books. She was always looking for facts, and the things her family believed in weren't based in facts, to her.

But back at her mother's house, her misery was so acute that her mother couldn't just stand by and watch. She told Cindy about a spiritual bath she could take to cleanse herself of everything that had died in her life.

At that point, Cindy was willing to try anything. She suddenly found herself in her mother's bathtub, holding two gallons of green water. Her mother had instructed her to take a shower and pour the liquid over her head. At the same time, she was to pray to San Miguel, saying her deepest wishes out loud. As she followed the instructions, she was surprised at all the things she wanted. She wanted to heal. She wanted to find her purpose. She wanted to see the world. She had never said any of it aloud, maybe because she was scared that she would never have these things.

When she was finished, she had to air dry. She couldn't use a towel, her mother said. So she just stood there, naked and cold, feeling mostly absurd, but also something else she hadn't felt in a long while: faith.

She woke up renewed and interested in what it was about the *baño* that actually worked. She started to talk to other friends who had bruja bloodlines, and she realized that there was much under the surface of their lives in the United States. She had been feeling empty, but in speaking with her friends, she realized their past was so full of rituals they could reach to for help with feeling connected. One of the friends is Nathalie Farfan, and together they started the podcast *Morado Lens,* in which they explored their bruja identities. It felt like coming out, both scary and exhilarating.

In the midst of her transition, Cindy found herself in nature more and more. Hiking provided a way to reconnect to the land. She would take her journal out and sit and write. "The more I did it, the more I reclaimed parts of myself I was sure were long gone. I fell in love with the process," she writes.

Cindy is a high achiever. She has big goals and a tendency to be impatient with herself. Hiking and journaling became her ways of slowing down, of enjoying her life instead of worrying about her progress, especially in relation to others. She realized that in her hectic life, she had been comparing herself to others' achievements, especially other women. She knew that she was not alone in this. The expectation to succeed kept everyone separate and in competition, but she saw that so many women, especially women of color, were struggling with feeling disconnected from their roots. Like her, many had run into problems.

Cindy thought that other women would benefit from being outdoors as she had. In Latinx communities, hiking is not a popular pastime, especially not for women. We are conditioned to always look clean and put together. My own mother reprimanded me when I returned home from long stretches outside. My clothes were always dirty, and I often had a scraped chin or knee. She tried to teach it out of me, pouring hydrogen peroxide on my wounds as a compassionate punishment.

"See? It hurts, right?" she would say. The pain was worth it.

Cindy knew that the discomfort the outdoors provided was somehow connected to her ancestral roots. There was wisdom in it, in her body so close to nature. She wanted to share this with others, so she started Reclama and began to lead spiritual hikes and retreats.

"I've learned that when we allow ourselves to unapologetically take up space in the outdoors, we affirm how we take up space in other parts of our lives," she writes. "Creating this space for WOC [women of color] out in nature has given me life in ways I didn't think were possible."

Hiking has been my most enduring hobby. When I was a kid, I would sneak out of my bedroom window at dawn, before my parents woke up to stop me. I would walk all day long, sometimes for twelve hours at a time. I was like a cat prowling my territory. Every day, I pushed it, daring a few steps outside the boundaries my parents set. I often got lost. I found treasures and buried them in secret places. I barely ate. Sometimes, I went up to friends' windows and begged a grilled cheese sandwich. But I was mostly sustained by the air and the trees and my imaginary friends.

As an adult, walking long distances has kept me open despite heartbreak. When I go too long without a long hike, I feel all my heart energies are blocked, and the first few hours or days into a hike are incredibly painful. It breaks me open. I feel it in my chest, and I often cry.

I think it is a mistake to think the wilderness is out there. What is wild to us will always be home to someone—to plants, to vast networks of fungi, to animals, to the first peoples whose energies remain even after they've been killed and relocated. The real wilderness is in our bodies. There's a whole universe inside, waiting to open.

I imagine what it would be like if I made a pilgrimage with other women the way Cindy has done. If we seasonally met in secret sisterhood, gathering within circles of stone, around open fires, by the hidden banks of rivers, on the bald patches of mountaintops. Cindy says that women walk away from the Reclama retreats empowered, more reassured about creating camping experiences with their own families as well. She shows them how to make a fire, cook for a group, and power off their phones so they can ground their bare feet into the earth. "We let go and we forgive," Cindy says. "And most importantly, we reclaim what's ours."

★　✹　★

In 2016 my friend Kelly opened a yoga studio, and we started a free monthly full-moon circle for women. I noticed immediately that the attendants were younger, browner, and queerer than the average yoga studio member. There wasn't anything quite like it in Tampa, at least not as consistent, and women came from all over to meet. The circle grew and grew over the following four years. Sometimes there were more than fifty women packed in the tiny space, and we'd have to make concentric circles.

At first, I had a hard time speaking in public. I would feel panic and get red and barely get a few sentences out before I had to stop. Over time I felt my voice strengthening, and now I can speak to any group without much trouble. These are the unexpected ways we heal in circle. We wrote in our moon journals. The entries helped us process difficult moments and emotions. Looking back on my entries, I see that they were the seeds for the topics that I would write about for years thereafter.

Moon circles had been gaining popularity in larger cities, and other yoga studios in the area took cues from us and started their own. In our circle, women confessed to each other about relationship or career troubles. They came out about their sexualities and gender identities. They processed grief. They made the intentions to start businesses or circles of their own, which would thrive over the following years. They returned month after month to recharge and share their progress.

The feeling in our moon circle was collaborative instead of competitive. Just by being together in this safe container, we were breaking the binds that a patriarchal capitalistic system had created. We didn't talk about politics, but what we were doing felt radical—just being, a secret society without the audience of men.

The moon provides a natural and consistent way to connect to magic. The full moon is when we share what's been welling up inside as we prepare to release our emotion over the waning period. The new moon is a time to clear out what we don't need so we can set intentions for the month ahead. Sometimes called the void moon, it is the darkest point of the month, allowing us to tap into a generative space without distraction.

Astrology is our love language. We point to our birth charts and say, "Here, this is who I am and what I want." It's a form of therapy to trace our stars. The houses of astrology are the big areas of our lives, twelve of them, and maybe someday they'll all be in balance. In our journals we log the movements of the planets through the houses. We take turns reading the words aloud to the circle, and our words together form poems.

It's the first time I felt like I belonged to a bigger network. The group was always changing, flowing. They were my soul family, these women who shared a love of the moon. In circle, I repaired the relationships that had gone wrong in the past, when I was competing or trying to own something.

Kelly and I set the tone for our rituals and discussions. We had forged our friendship by choosing each other over men. I met her when I was in a relationship with a guy who told me he had fallen in love with her. People were always falling in love with her, regardless of their gender or sexuality, because she helped them connect to something bigger than themselves, and they mistook this for interpersonal chemistry. When he told me how he felt, I knew that his feelings were misplaced, and despite my heartbreak, I was actually grateful that something came along to test my relationship and show me its weakness. I broke it off with him and chose her, instead. I knew from the moment I met her we had things to create together.

Soul mates don't have to be sexual, but I think they are all romantic.

What we call love is something that we have inside and that we choose to share. We have it the whole time, if we stop competing and sit and feel it. It's right there. Love flows through us when we sit in circles. We don't try to hold onto it or make it into something more.

This love is a river, and grabbing onto it is like trying to stand in a heavy current. In circle we learn to just let go.

In circle, I learned that anxiety is what you feel when something is wrong. Anxiety is the mark of an unsustainable relationship. It's a little warning bell if we choose to hear it. I learned that true love is the comfort you feel when you sit with yourself, when you connect without thinking and let yourself be weird, when you don't have to explain yourself too hard. The ones who are open to your love will always understand and accept you. You might still feel the anxiety, but suddenly it doesn't feel like you have to fix anything.

If love is always there, always flowing, then relationships are simply the containers we choose to hold love. Each container has different boundaries that we agree upon. The moon circle is a container. Work is a container. Home is a container. Bed is a container. Art is a container.

What are your containers? Are they helpful? Are they beautiful?

Sometimes the container is weak. It breaks, and our love flows out. Sometimes it takes a while to call the love back to our heart center, but it is always there. If you return to yourself, moon after moon, you will remember this steady love that is yours. If you return to your intentions, moon after moon, you'll see your progress. The things that are worthwhile emerge slowly. The slow things are usually the ones that last. In circle, we remind ourselves that we have time to create everything we want for our lives. Creativity requires time and rest and love.

Don't let fear of loss take hold of you. Many ancestral traditions subscribe to the concept of the evil eye. It's the idea that someone could hex you out of envy. The evil eye can disrupt your plans, it is said, so it's best not to say aloud what you are creating.

I reject this notion. It is meant to keep us separate and in competition. If I hadn't told circles and circles of women what I wanted over the years, I wouldn't have the best things in my life. My home. My writing. My friends. It is because I told others my deepest wishes that they came true. Radical authenticity and radical honesty are what we need of each other now.

I admit, committing to openness within your chosen containers is not without risk. There have been people who were envious, and there were hexes thrown my way. They might cause temporary setbacks, but when you set an intention with an open heart for a reason not driven by ego, the intention takes root no matter who doesn't support you. When you proceed with your intention with discipline and sustained effort, it grows. When you nurture it with love, it blooms.

Hexes are actually blessings, because if they work and your intention falls apart, it was probably not the right one for you. Maybe you were rushing or unfocused, or you weren't operating from a place of love. Take responsibility when things go wrong, and return to your intention. Revise and reframe it and try again.

To let the evil eye stop you is to believe in our separateness, to fall victim to the toxic masculinity that can pervade even the most feminist of spiritual circles. The bigger the intention, the more pitfalls there will be. But the bigger the intention, the more worth the wait and the work. Keep going and believe and reach for support when you need.

To risk. To show up. To allow ourselves to emerge slowly,

imperfectly. To cry and rest and laugh and scream. To learn all the ways we can make magic together, organically. This is why we hold circle. We are each so different, trying to figure out our unique gifts and how we might sustain ourselves, how to be whole on our own. We hold each other and teach each other that it's important to have love for ourselves before we can join in partnership. But by virtue of being in circle, we also reject the notion that we must be fiercely independent to be successful.

We need each other.

In the winter of 2021, Cindy started the *Reclama Journal*, a digital quarterly magazine about working with the seasons and filled with how-tos, moon rituals, interviews, spiritual baño & tea recipes, quotes, personal essays, and a digital moon cycle calendar. During the pandemic, our circles have moved online, and Cindy saw an opportunity to build a new container for connection even when we can't get together.

In the first edition, Cindy features articles about self-care as a BIPOC practice that resists spiritual bypassing, the bruja's role in protests like the ones at Standing Rock, and the cultural appropriation of Indigenous resources. Years ago it might have been taboo to invite political discussions into spiritual spaces, but now any talk of spirituality that isn't grounded in activism feels more like escapism. The convergence of COVID-19 and new waves of protests have brought into relief the intersecting problems in our country around racism, income inequality, and environmental emergencies. The protests have created conditions for collective grieving and inspired new therapeutic avenues.

Cindy makes note in the first edition that some of the proceeds from subscriptions will go to the Black Lives Matter (BLM) Global Network Foundation. More than any other recent movement, BLM invites religious pluralism, including African spiritualities and pagan religions.

Bruja feminists have increasingly appeared at protests, showing that their spirituality and social justice are intertwined. On June 5, 2020, witches on social media came together under the banner "Witches to Action," which included this message by Maria Brink:

> Global action will be taken on the supermoon of June 5 by witches, shamans, brujas, rootworkers, spiritualists and every other practitioner and/or occultist. On the supermoon of June 5, we call everybody to focus your intent, do spellwork, light a candle, do what you find necessary to send protection, do healing and bring justice to injustice everywhere. Let's help end this sh*t. From the inexperienced to the experienced, let's all join together.

BLM has done a lot to diversify witchcraft on social media. A meme with a Black Panther image and the text "Black witches to the front" circulated around the same time as the protests. Accounts and stores and publications that had predominantly featured White witches made more concerted efforts to diversify and invited Black witches and brujas into the fold. And BLM even posted toolkits on their website to center spiritual self-care.

In spiritual communities, Black witches and brujas are not minorities. They constitute the majority practicing ancestral traditions, just as Black and Brown people are the leaders of intersectional feminism. They are the helm of spiritual activism that employs daily ritual toward activist aims. When you get up in the morning to meditate, when you chant mantras during a protest, when you pray for those who are being oppressed, you are participating in activism.

It's a kind of shadow work in itself for institutions, even relatively radical ones like organized witchcraft, to admit that they have been excluding people of color and to make moves to change. As witchcraft continues to mirror feminist movements, it will have to adapt to remain relevant during revolutionary times. Bruja feminists can rise as examples of how to practice magic in a more socially conscious way. As more and more entrepreneurs flock to the spiritual market, we need leaders to show us how to engage in business responsibly and how to continue to center social justice even when we want to make a living off our products and services. We should not forget that people often seek these magical practices out when they are most vulnerable and in need of healing. Through magic, we can build an organic network of practitioners who care about changing the world. Connecting with groups toward mutual aims bigger than our individual selves helps us transcend our troubles and help others.

This is the kind of network Cindy is building with Reclama. When I met her, she felt like a cousin to me. Our stories are similar in many

ways. We are both writers. We see the big picture of this bruja movement. We have great ambition, and we are enthusiastic and maybe
move a little too fast sometimes, so we need to consciously slow ourselves down. We've both found ourselves suddenly alone, and we have
turned to walking in nature to soothe our grief.

When my ex's son died, I walked. For weeks it was all I could do.
I walked ten miles a day around Tampa. We were in lockdown for the
virus, and there was nothing to do and nowhere to be. So I walked
alone. I let myself cry for hours.

I associated walking with the boy and his family. The previous summer, we had walked 161 miles on the Appalachian Trail from Rockfish
Gap to Harpers Ferry. During the trip, I had the first indication that my
relationship might not last. On the second day of the hike, I had fallen
on a rock, and as I would later learn, I'd torn my patellar tendon. I was
in massive pain, but I limped on anyway. I decided to tough it out and
walk with them.

I used a walking stick I named "Wandering Wanda," a thick one
with a notch at the top I could put a lot of weight on. I had expected the
trip to be physically hard, and though I hadn't expected to be injured,
once I got going, the pain wasn't unbearable. It was the psychological
challenge I hadn't bargained for. I was raw. I fell behind the group, and
the symbolism of that tore me open. Childhood feelings of loneliness
rushed through me. Since I was alone on the trail so often, I took the
opportunity to cry openly, sometimes loudly. If my ex or the kids heard
me, they'd think I was crying because of my knee pain.

Alone on the trail, I came to understand that I longed for a home

I had yet to make. I'd spent so much time in my younger years constantly running from a home I'd deemed unstable. I was the first in my family to apply to college, and getting the acceptance letter from the University of Florida had been the happiest moment of my life. Since then, I had never settled down; I never stayed for longer than a couple of years in one place.

I wonder if it's in my blood, to keep moving, to never settle. We are a family of exiles and immigrants, after all, of people always on the edge of some frontier. Maybe it's why the wilderness renders me so vulnerable. To my grandparents, the woods had human eyes and human dramas. The woods are where the Revolutionary Armed Forces of Colombia lived, armed insurgents ready to kidnap their children. The woods are where Fidel Castro strengthened his army before striking their town and starting a revolution that pushed them from their homes forever. The woods aren't a safe place. The woods aren't for recreation. The woods are the difficult past.

Sometimes the boy would fall behind too, because he was tired, and we walked together. Sometimes we walked silently, both crying, and sometimes we stopped to look at a bug or to pick berries, and my heart would swell looking at him. I realized I loved him more than I loved anyone, even his father, and I felt lucky to know him. It was the closest I might ever get to feeling maternal toward someone, and I thought that if the relationship ended, at least I would have that.

I lost them all.

At the end of 2020, I was so alone and depressed I thought my heart would stop beating. But my friends wouldn't let it. They came, one by one, to help. They left food and talked with me for hours and told me I would be okay even though I didn't feel like I would ever be okay. Some of them were friends from childhood. Some were my first friends in Tampa, like family. Some were acquaintances from circle who became friends in my time of grieving. They were lifelines, and somehow amid my despair, there was a tiny, warm light that I knew would grow with time. I knew I was lucky to have these friends.

More than friends. My heart's coven.

JOIN A COVEN

Some of us are solitary witches, and some of us like sharing our magic. One is not better than another. If you crave a steady circle of magical friends, it might be time to join a coven, start your own circle, or strengthen bonds within an existing community. Take a look at events in your area. Is there a spiritual group you're interested in joining? Are there moon or tarot circles at your local yoga studio? Maybe there are magic-adjacent places, like art studios or workshop spaces you might start visiting to make new friendships. If you don't live in a place where this is possible, or if you'd rather start a little more anonymously, there are many online groups and gatherings that will welcome you, especially since COVID-19. Be creative and put yourself out there. You might be surprised at where you end up. A note of caution: be wary of transexclusionary radical feminists (TERFs), conspiracy theorists, cults, or anyone selling teacher trainings at exorbitant rates.

If you're more of a hedge witch (solitary practitioner) but want to take your practice to the next level, maybe you can carve out your niche and share your gifts with the world, through in-person or online workshops. Whatever you choose, it's helpful to narrow down your strengths, so you can more easily connect with others in your spiritual community through your offerings. It might take a while to open to what those are, but over time, you might find that you gravitate toward a particular set of gifts.

What kind of witch are you? Here's a nonexhaustive list of the kinds of magical practices you can explore. Keep in mind that they may overlap.

* Divination Magic: Tarot, dreams, palms, pendulums, tea leaves, and other kinds of readings

* Cosmic Magic: Astrology and the stars, moon rituals

* Green Magic: Nature, plants, rootwork, earth rituals

* Energy Magic: Crystals, sound healing, Reiki (lightwork)

* Folk Magic: Curanderismo/shamanism, mediumship, herbal remedies (often overlaps with green magic and energy magic)

✳ Sex and Relationship Magic: Glamour, tantric energy, love and boundaries

✳ Chaos Magic: Sigils, intention rituals, alchemy, ancient texts, spellwork

✳ Technopagan Magic: Technology and cyberspace as the primary vehicles of ritual

✳ Hereditary Magic: Santero, mambo, houngan, etc. (requires initiation)

AQUARIUS: THE SEER

Aquarius is the ruler of the eleventh house of friendships and humanitarian networks. Many astrologers believe that we are entering the age of Aquarius. In contrast to the age of Pisces, which was marked by the story of Christ and religions revolving around charismatic leaders, the age of Aquarius is about decentralized power and organic networks of humanitarianism that address the shifting problems of our age. Aquarians are perhaps the strangest characters of the zodiac. They are future oriented and boundary busting, and they care deeply about humanity. Reach to Aquarius when you need a revolution in the way you operate or view your life.

ELEMENT: Fixed air
PLANETARY RULER: Uranus
AFFIRMATION: "I know"

FOR YOUR ALTAR: Hemp, adaptogens, cannabis and psychedelics, aquamarine, lapis lazuli, containers for fluids such as chalices, pioneer spirits and alien beings

JOURNAL: Who are my people? What networks do I want to connect to?

MAGICKAL NETWORKS

The Modern Witches Confluence (@witchesconfluence, modernwitches .org) is an online network of modern witches from different traditions who are sharing their wisdom and craft. They offer online events, workshops, and courses for all levels. Every year, there is an annual gathering (virtual since the pandemic) with keynote speakers. Attendees learn divination practices, ancestral magick, and ways to hone psychic skills and have access to collective rituals and healing sessions.

Astrology and tarot have brought witches of color into the vast community of psychic readers. Check out these wonderful readers of color for new spins on ancient art forms: Astro Sagas (@astrosagas, astrosagas .com), Luz Astral (@luz_astral, luzastral.com), Esoteric Esa (@esoteric _esa), Kirah Tabourn (@thestrology, thestrology.com), Taylor Ursula (@thatssopisces, thatssopisces.com), Loli Moon (@mysticmoonmedicine, mysticmoonmedicine.com), Liliana (@hijaquecura), Daizy October (@thatafromystic, theafromystic.com), Diana Rose (@ddamascenaa, ddamascenaa.com), and Tatianna Tarot (@tatiannatarot).

12

SHADOW WORKERS

The room is that kind of blue right before the sun comes in. It's humid.
The air is static. My back is pulling down into the bed like I swallowed
a weight. Sinking. I can only shift my eyes. That's what I'll do, back and
forth, scanning the room. I know what's here. In the corner. A shadow
that will come if I don't get my eyes on her. There. A dark stain. The
color pulled off the wall. A pooling of some substance. A liquid and a
smoke at once, swirling into form. I'll keep the corner of my eye on her.
She doesn't take full shape when I look just off center. I can keep her
there. I can't look away, or she'll come onto my chest and try her way
in, and my body will float.

Don't think of that.

Hold the corner. Pretty soon she'll tire and return to her real place,
and I can wake from this in-between. And I'll still make the dawn. I'll
slip out of bed and straighten the covers and open the window and
crawl out into the park before my parents wake up.

I can hear the drizzle out there. I'll go to the willow tree. If nobody is looking, I'll walk right through the leaf curtain. It's dry by the trunk. Dig up the treasure box and add the new rock to it. Take off my shirt and shorts and fold them, so they don't get wet, so Mami won't get upset, and wrap myself around the trunk and smell the ground, the green smell that happens right at first, before it rains too hard.

Maybe he's here, the boy. He'll catch me some bugs, and when the rain stops, we'll climb the branches. I know he's not really there, the way the shadow isn't really there. Not all the way. They come from somewhere else. But I *feel* them almost all the way. The way the boy talks, a ringing sound. The shadow, the way it feels, sucking the energy out.

Wait.

Where is she? Not in her corner. Oh god. My heart. Hurts. Hurts. Deep breath. Not really real. Not really real. Try to move. OK. Move. Move a pinky. There she is. The foot of the bed. OK hold her now. Don't look away. Don't let your mind go away. Try to scream out for Mami. She is getting up. I hear her next door. Try to call her. She'll be in the hallway soon. At the end of the hallway is the door of the master room.

She's on me now. She's trying to get in. I must have left again. It's too hard to hold her. Get off now please. Get off. I always go somewhere else. I always do that. Why can't I stay and hold her? She's pulling at me, and I'm moving up to the top of my skin. Hold on. Hold. I'm not inside anymore. I am above her. She is below. Her arms are thrashing, a statue of smoke. She has the space to get in now. And I am at the ceiling. The popcorn feeling of it that I like to touch when we paint the walls and I'm all the way up on the ladder. It feels so nice up here. The ceiling is white, like clouds. I can see the clouds through it, they're starting to get pink. I think I'll float here.

I think I'll float.

I think.

I . . .

*　🌟　*

When I saw the shadow as a child, I thought I had been possessed by a demon that expelled me from my body. I thought I'd died. I floated to the ceiling, and when the fear dissipated, I felt the greatest peace. When I woke up, I was confused and a little sad that I was still there in my room. I didn't want to be dead, but I wanted to return to that peace.

Wherever the boy is, I know he is OK. I expected him to be my descendant, that I would one day live on the altar of his memories. Now, every memory of the short time we spent is a precious shard, so incomplete and fragile. My altar objects are placeholders for them, and I protect them with the maternal love I didn't get the chance to show him, a fierce potential energy that flickers between shadow and light. To love is to simultaneously feel the beautiful and terrible force of this grief. When I think I won't be able to open again after so much loss, when I find myself wishing for the peace of nonliving, I remember the boy's innocent bravado and how much more time I have to find my own courage in this life.

I reach to shadow workers for help when the grief comes. They know what sacrifice is. The ones who work with death and loss, they all lost something big. As Tampa grows, spiritual people are connecting here more and more. I recently met Lisa Rodriguez, an Afro-Caribbean psychic medium who told me that I could talk to the dead if I'd train my gifts. Lisa has one grey eye, like the blind seers in myths.

"Spirit removed my eye so that I could see better," Lisa says.

In 2012 Lisa landed a great job at a firm, and she was making more money than she ever had. She was hot. She was partying every week. She felt like she had finally made it and that nothing could get in her way—until the pain came. It struck behind her left eye and immediately debilitated her. It was a pain that she says she wouldn't wish on her worst enemy. Doctors ran tests, but they couldn't find the cause of her rare case of sudden onset blindness. Lisa was hospitalized for months as she underwent corneal surgeries. In that time, she lost her job and the future that she'd been banking on. Following the surgeries, she was confined to dark rooms. She thought she was being punished.

It was in that darkness that she found her real power. As she lost one sight, another emerged. She came from a lineage of spiritual practitioners, so she always had the gift, but after she lost her eyesight, messages from the spirit world started to come through more strongly. Lisa could no longer deny this gift, could no longer be distracted by the material world. She was a spirit medium.

Now Lisa is in her forties, and she owns Hip+Indie Botanica. She visited me one afternoon with a friend of hers, a young Black woman whom she was mentoring at the time. The young woman told me that she looks up to Lisa.

"She sees more in me than I see in myself," she said. She is many generations removed from her homeland, and she doesn't know her own ancestral spirituality, so Lisa is teaching her the Afro-Caribbean cultures and cosmologies.

Lisa and another local energy worker, Rev. Milagros Reynoso, led a circle for women of color on the winter solstice at the end of 2020. Together, they cleared the energy for a better year ahead. Black and Brown women are the spiritual teachers of the bruja future. They fill in the gaps for those separated from their homelands and ancestries. When I was growing up, there were no teachers to turn to. Now it's up to my generation to establish mentorship programs for spiritual seekers.

The world needs more Black and Brown female leaders as we continue to face catastrophic crises. Black women organizers turned Georgia blue in the 2020 election, then flipped the Senate. Black feminist ecological thought forms the most relevant ecocriticism of the moment, as African-descended women from across the diaspora are at the helm of environmental justice advocacy. But we can't expect them to take on the world for us. It's up to White allies to bear the weight of reeducating ourselves to support Black and Brown healers like Lisa, Milagros, and Sabel, who embody resilience, power, sex, joy, and radical magic. Their magic is not a commodity for us to use up.

There is a Scorpionic power about Sabel Santa that I noticed right away. She wears black, exclusively. She looks good in it, and she knows it. Black is the perfect color, because it contains all possibilities, as does Sabel. She is pansexual, because her love is boundless, but she is also unknowable. She is an open book, and she is the part of the ocean that eats all light. She will invite you in, but not before warning you. She has walked between worlds, and there are things she can't unsee, can't protect you from. She has integrated with her shadow self, and she wants you to face yours too.

Making friends wasn't always easy for Sabel. Her mother moved the family back to the mainland United States, and Sabel went to high school in Virginia, where she attended ESL classes to relearn English. Nobody spoke to her, and she felt like an outcast. A couple of years earlier, two White high schoolers had committed one of the deadliest school shooting in US history in Columbine, Colorado, and people were freaking out about goths. So Sabel couldn't dress in her trademark all black, because she was afraid to be associated with the trenchcoat mafia. Going to school felt like walking a tightrope. She longed to connect to the witches of her imagination. She didn't fit in with the White kids, and the Black kids didn't speak Spanish like her or have similar cultural backgrounds. She went looking for practitioners of the old ways like the ones she grew up with in Puerto Rico, but all she could find was White ladies to read her cards.

Her family eventually settled in Miami. There she met other Afro-Caribbean immigrants. With them, she felt the most belonging and understanding, these self-labeled brujas who contained so many traditions and nationalities. Over time, her magical practice became more and more social. She joined Eleventh House, a directory of mystical healers practicing around Miami. Through this network, she began offering astrological birth chart readings, using the symbolism of the stars to help people understand themselves and work through problems.

By 2017 she was part of an online community of spiritualists, and she was invited to hold an in-person workshop during a monthly market at Catland Books, a metaphysical shop in Brooklyn. She was excited to be included. It was energizing to notice increased interest in her practices among White people. Still, Sabel wondered where the magical resources were for people of color, something that spoke to their unique backgrounds and traditions. On the one hand, there were these trendy witch shops in gentrified neighborhoods, which, at least at the time, catered mostly to a young White market. On the other hand, there were the botanicas, the old-school spiritual stores of the Afro-Caribbean diaspora that didn't always reflect the feminism of the new generation of brujas.

Back in Miami, she visualized how she might link this trend to her ancestral spirituality. She started Brujx School, a series of workshops and community classes to educate budding practitioners of color and allies about "decolonized magic," rituals that evolved from African and Indigenous traditions rather than European ones. Through Brujx School, Sabel has hosted classes, including Brujería 101, Tarot as Resistance, Sex Magic, Moon Magic, and Rituals for Queer Health, that mix popular new age topics with these traditions. The classes form a curriculum for students that centers ritual as a kind of performance art and elevates QTBIPOC art as magical practice.

"Art and magic are the same," Sabel says. "Art is the manipulation of energy for expression. Magic is in anything. It can be found in a stick in the ground."

Sabel focuses on education, creativity, and empowerment. To her, magic is more than a trend. It doesn't come from a static object. It certainly doesn't come from a forty-nine-dollar bundle of sage from Mary Kate and Ashley Olsen's line of witchy products. She knows that when you use an object that's been appropriated from Indigenous peoples and overharvested for mass consumption, you're killing any chance of real magic, because magic is not a possession, but a movement—a movement between worlds, between identities, between languages. Magic is always of the moment and inextricably connected to what came before, whether we remember our past or not.

In February 2020, just before the coronavirus lockdown, Sabel's mother died of cancer. She was in her fifties. The previous November, Sabel had left her community of Miami mystics and moved to Jacksonville to help her mother in her final days. The grief has surprised her, the ways it keeps unexpectedly asserting itself as a force, "like the pull of gravity."

"Grief is a box of chaos," Sabel says. "Sometimes you crack the lid and peek in and say 'nope!' Not ready to deal with that. Sometimes the wind knocks the lid open when you're not expecting it, and your whole day is gone. And sometimes you put yourself in a room with the box and take a deep breath and open that lid."

She speaks of her old self, the self before her mother's death and the virus and the protests, as if she were a different person. She thought she could "manifest" anything she wanted as an individual, and for a short time, it seemed like she could, as she helped build a community of brujas in Miami and became recognized and sought out for her services.

Now she sees how grief turns you away from individual concerns, as you realize you are so small in such a large universe, connected in ways your mind could never fully grasp. Magic is not about controlling your life, she says, but is a means of letting go into uncertainty. When she accepts sickness and death, her pain isn't unbearable, but becomes a channel for transcendence.

You have to face your shadows, or they will grow and grow.

How you lean into that work looks different for everyone. For Sabel, it's been working through the grief of losing her mother while remaining connected to the things that carry her memory. Each object contains atoms that used to be part of something bigger, maybe even part of a human. It holds memory, and sometimes you can feel the hum of what it used to be. The bruja is the guardian of this memory, neither ignorant of nor above physics, but a conduit of natural laws, the ones we have formulas for and the ones that still resist formulation.

Sabel posted an IGTV video called "Las cosas de mi madre," a piece of performance art cataloging objects that her mother left behind. Sabel describes the objects in Spanish as they appear on the screen: a collection of mermaids, five plastic bags in which to vomit, a hair dryer, a bottle of Frangelico, a favorite book, a nearly dead orchid, twenty-six hospital bracelets, a seat for the shower, a paper face mask. It goes on like this for a couple of minutes, these heirlooms both sacred and mundane.

The objects paint a life, one of pain but also beauty, and you can't help but feel your heart swell with compassion while you imagine Sabel caring for her mother in her final days, gently, with a patience she didn't know she had. You can't help but turn to the few artifacts you have of your own family members, to try to squeeze some truth out of them. Maybe they are roots we can stick in the ground, and maybe something will grow from them. Maybe magic is an unbroken line of lives, suffering and joyous, who keep on surviving through the flesh of their children.

That's not the "love and light" spirituality that makes life seem like an Instagram feed. The real spiritual work is in the painful things that we suppress or try to conquer—an untimely death, a violent event. Every now and then, a bomb will go off or a storm will rip through, reminding us that there's no running away from the systems of oppression and inequality that pattern our lives. Maybe it's not an acute event that wakes us. Maybe it's a long-term haunting, a struggle with mental health, a mystery that reminds us there are secrets left to be uncovered. Maybe it's the shadow that keeps showing itself in our dreams, night after night. Whether or not we are aware of them, we tread over the traumas of our past as we walk through our lives. Some are generations old, still threatening us with mouths agape.

In one of her virtual rituals, Sabel stands in a white nightgown in a yard, just an ordinary fence behind her. She raises her arms above her head slowly, gracefully, then drops them, dead weight, her head falling, defeated. She repeats. She brings her hands to her heart and looks up and to the side. And then her arms in front of her, one by one, and back to her heart. Repeat, repeat, the tempo builds. Sharp exhales. Slapping chest. Pained face. Head swinging side to side. Grief expressing. Arms at her heart. Holding herself, heaving chest. Then slowly, one arm down to her side, across and back to her heart. The other arm follows. Both arms open like wings now, open heart. Wind is blowing and she with it. Arms to the sky, this time floating down slowly, head rising once more. Tender.

The caption of the video reads: "A closeup of fear. The attempt to open yourself up again after heartbreak is one of magnificent bravery. Be kind to your heart. It will take time to heal. The fear is there to protect you, but don't let it control you."

People are continuously seeing organizations they counted on failing to support them: their careers, their governments, their own families. They are looking for new leaders, for new ways of making meaning. In times of turmoil, what we have called the "dark ages," humanity has historically turned to magic, that space between the known and unknown where we allow imagination to reign. We have been taught, especially in Western culture, to see this in opposition to science, but it is part of the scientific process itself, to create connections (hypothesize, if you will) in the face of uncertainty. The darkness is not devoid of answers, but quite the opposite. It is pregnant with possibility.

It's surreal to Sabel, to have experienced such a hard loss as the community stalls in the midst of a pandemic and wakes up to the ways Black people have suffered in this country. She does what she can to share her perspective, what her energy allows. She summons the strength of her ancestors. She takes something she learned from her grandmother or her mother, something maybe she wasn't taught but has the power to channel from them now that they're gone, and she creates something new. She transmutes grief into a gift for those who are hurting and seeking.

I still don't know exactly where the dead go or how to speak with them at will, but I know a little more about grief now. How it doesn't follow any rules. How you can feel numb for a while, so you say you're fine, and then one day out of nowhere you're knocked into chaos, and your day is gone. Is this what my great-grandmother felt when she lost her daughter, what Sabel feels having lost her mother so young? Is this what so many people in the world are dealing with at this moment, as they lose loved ones too soon to a virus with no cure?

Sabel wants us to know that our traumas are also our strengths, and the path of survival and growth are the same. We must each walk our own path, meeting fear with courage, undoing the traps we've created, letting our shadows free. It's a lifelong process, because life has a way of keeping the challenges coming, especially when you're committed to the spiritual path.

In February 2021 Sabel was in Austin, Texas, when a snowstorm took down the power grid. She sat in her freezing apartment for days, alone, without her phone. I had booked an astrological love reading with her as a belated Valentine's Day gift to celebrate my status as a newly single lady, and as I tried to get in touch with her, I realized that she had been affected by the storm. Days later, when she could finally respond, I texted her, "You and storms!"

"Storms are such a big part of my life," she texted back.

Sabel will ride out the storms. She is a bruja. That's what she does.

Having been so recently separated from homelands and from native cultures, brujas preserve the wisdom of the ancestors who gradually fade with each death, as descendants assimilate to new worlds that don't make much room for magic. As the world shifts in response to so much loss, to pandemics and uprisings and mass migrations and catastrophic weather, the wisdom of the ancestors is emerging from hiding and offering itself up to the new generation of spiritual workers. They are guardians of ancient memory, each developing their own practices, whether on the land of their grandmothers or stranded on pavement where thousands of strawberries used to grow.

Outside of my house are three old oak trees that are dying, I've been told. They are water oaks, planted in the early 1900s all around Tampa, and they're coming to the end of their lifespans. Many people cut them down at this point, so their limbs don't fall on their houses. On the first night I slept in my house, my head was at the window facing the center tree. I had a dream that the trees' limbs became yellow ribbons, and the ribbons came through my window and wrapped me up.

Just after the lockdown, I had another dream, that men had cut the three oaks down with chainsaws as they prepared the property for "landscaping." I came home to find the men with the machinery in their hands. I cried and cried, and it was a deep cry like a howl, and my heart opened up with the grief I'd been holding in all year. When I woke up, I felt cleansed.

Trees communicate a lot at the end of their lives through a type of mutual aid network. Underground, intricate and vast fungal networks help them "talk" with each other. They tell of the hardships they went through and transfer their resources to their young. As they decompose, limbs dropping here and there, the fungus produces mushrooms that envelop the limbs and break them down, bringing them down into the soil. When you cut a tree down and cart it off to a dump, you block a natural cycle that benefits the tree, the earth, and the underground network that talks to other trees on other properties, and you block the benefits you might have received from that communication.

This is the gift of death: wisdom.

My house sits on the edge of the cycle of life and death. Little creatures crawl under my house to die, and mother cats seek refuge under it to birth their babies. If I don't clear the air every few days, a veil of nature falls over it quickly. A feral hum takes over, and everywhere there are flies. The spirits of animals patter through the house and jump onto my bed at night. I am inclined to let them, to learn to live among them. I've taken to asking the house and the little piece of land for permission for everything I do.

I'm recommitting to spirit and nature again. For years, I've focused on accomplishing big things: getting a PhD, buying a house, writing a book. It's easy to forget what motivated me in the first place—how to live a life full of love while keeping my eyes open.

In the new simplicity of my days, devoid of the rush of activities and meetings, I am starting to feel a call toward death work. I'm not sure what form it is going to take, whether it's the mediumship of my great-grandmother or helping people transition as a death doula. It's exciting not to know. I am listening to my intuition, letting it unfold before me. Who knows where I'll be when I'm an old lady?

When I returned home from Miami following my grandmother Ninoska's funeral, I lit my altar for all my grandmothers. It was Samhain and the Day of the Dead—neither of which they observed themselves—and as I placed objects on the altar, next to the Buddhist statue of Green Tara, I realized how cobbled together this spirituality of mine is. Nobody taught me how to do this, so I've borrowed from here and there as I've studied different traditions. At first I felt like I had no right to do this, but over time I learned there is no shame in referencing other spiritualities in the absence of your own, as long as it's coming from a place of respect and well-informed connection.

For a long time, I didn't practice any spirituality, because I didn't feel like I knew enough. I didn't write my grandmothers' stories, because I thought I would get the details wrong. Then, when I was struggling with mental health, I found yoga and learned about Hindu and Buddhist deities. I saw how versions of the same stories were just slightly different, as they were initially passed down orally. Imagine if they hadn't been passed down, simply because the details were unknown or inconsistent. When I realized the power of building on my spirituality over time, I came back around to the Virgin Mary of my childhood, who had always been on the altars in my families' homes and whom I associate with my grandmothers.

This cobbled altar is like my story and the story of my family, discovered piecemeal, filled in with what I have on hand. To finally have it all on the page after so many years of trying and trying to write it, there's healing in this.

It feels strange and nice to place things on the altar for grandmothers I haven't seen in so long. For Ninoska, I brought back white flowers from the funeral and placed them in water. I bought a lottery ticket and placed it under a candle. Like her grandmother Cancianila, she loved playing the lottery and would fantasize out loud about how she would spend the money if she won. I've caught myself doing this lately.

I dress the altar for my other grandmothers too. The little obsidian pin that my great-grandmother Elvira gave my parents at my birth is a protection against the evil eye. Most Cuban babies receive one when they're born, but this one means more to me than the average charm, because I remember the story of my father, how he couldn't open his eyes when he was a kid in Cuba (OK, so *sometimes* that shit is literal).

I've always thought faith a sappy word, and as a kid I rejected it as a challenge to Catholicism. "Have faith" sounded to me like "you have no control" or "give up." The call for faith clashed with the expectation that we can have anything and that our work will pay off. As I've grown and experienced failure and loss, I've realized that there is so much wisdom and power in letting go. Faith is not a cop out but an act of courage.

It's incredibly brave to let go and let your ancestors hold you. It is also an act of love to open yourself to them, to let them enter you, to let them fulfill that purpose. I started on my spiritual path because of my grandmother Elvira, who had a clear connection to the spirit world with her work, but in the process, I've arrived at the story of another grandmother, who recently left this world. When you let go in the process of spiritual exploration, surprising things like this happen. Stories mix together. Lessons appear.

In writing all these stories, I see now that so many of them are about the mother-child connection, cut too soon. Whatever my shadow is, it is this disconnect, these broken lines between mother and child that haven't been mended. It is the guilt about leaving home. It is the ghost of colonialism, as both the colonized and colonizer runs through my blood. It is a potential that I have yet to acknowledge, an initiation that has never taken place.

It is never too late to have faith.

I call on my guardian ancestors now.

I channel Elvira, who lost her daughter, who lived to see so many beloveds die, who lived to be old old old. I write you, Elvira. I continue your story. From you I call on my ability to see the world of the spirits.

I channel Elsie, whom I never met, whose womb became sick when she left her home, who died before she could see her grandchildren. I write you, Elsie. I continue your story. From you I call on my love of learning.

I channel Cancianila, whom I never met, who worked in a circus and lived without a man, who lost her daughter. I write you,

Cancianila. I continue your story. From you I call on my love of adventure and breaking boundaries.

I channel Ermelinda, whom I never met, who died giving birth. I channel you, Ermelinda. I continue your story. From you I call on my kindness and my mothering nature.

I channel Ninoska, who lost her mother, who is the wounded child that I feel inside myself. I write you, Ninoska. I continue your story. From you I call on my innocence and my vulnerability.

I channel my grandmothers who lived so I can exist. They all run through me now, imperfect like me, threads of unfinished stories. Protect me, all, and I will protect you. I might not know you, but I can feel you. I am you. I build what you started with these words. When I can't get the truth from the living, I can channel you, the dead, the knowing. We never lose each other. We become each other and keep going. We free each other through living our lives.

I hope that one day I'll be very, very old, as some of you never got to be, holding the hands of my descendants when they visit, answering their questions, guarding them.

I don't try to keep the shadow from advancing now. I walk right up and touch it, and it morphs into a primal form that shines brightly, some ancient part of me stirring. Maybe the shadow was never a thing to be feared. Maybe it was always an invitation, an initiation.

I feel a door opening where a shadow used to stand in the corner of my room, a straight line to another world, where the ancestors speak.

START A MENTORSHIP

I wish I'd had a guide when I was exploring my spirituality as a kid. This is an exciting time, because now we have so many ways to connect with one another. The best and most enduring way we can participate in a spiritual life is through a mentorship relationship. What do you want to learn? If you have a particular lineage or practice in mind, reach out to an established teacher, and ask them if they are taking on students. You might read up on them or their practice, including their books if they are published. Or you might take their workshops or group classes before requesting one-on-one time. Talk to other students, and learn about their experiences. Know what you are seeking. Is your exploration for your own personal path of practice, or do you want to train to be a teacher? Some programs of study offer certifications, such as yoga-teacher training programs, while others are more organic. Use your intuition about what is right. How does it feel to be around this teacher? Be wary of people who say they will heal you instead of teaching you ways to heal yourself. Beware of the cult of personality or people who seem too into their own aesthetic. There are a lot of charlatans out there. Real healers are regular people who are also healing themselves, and they will be transparent about their own struggles along their path.

If you are a teacher, you might think of ways to expand your offerings to others. Perhaps you can develop a series of workshops or develop a structure to take on one-on-one mentees. If you are thriving, clear a pathway for others to get to where you are. Stay humble and keep learning, even if you are very successful as a teacher. Teachers need teachers too. Always remember to honor your teachers, and give credit where credit is due.

PISCES: THE DREAMER

Pisces is the final sign of the zodiac, ruler of the twelfth house of spirituality and the unconscious. Pisceans are the most intuitive and ethereal of all the astrological archetypes. They are in tune with dreams and what lies beneath the surface. They can be surprisingly sensual. Connect with Pisces when you need a dose of psychic power, or when you need to be reminded of the spiritual power behind your worldly affairs.

ELEMENT: Mutable water

PLANETARY RULER: Neptune

AFFIRMATION: "I believe"

FOR YOUR ALTAR: Sacred smoke, seashells, ashes or fossils, sages or saviors or martyrs, the fish, anything that imparts ancient wisdom, pale blue and lavender stones

JOURNAL: What does your ideal world look like?

THE BRUJA FUTURE

There are practitioners out there inspiring witches of color to transcend the bruja collective from a passing trend to an enduring movement. Sacred Sisters (@sacredsisterscircle, sacredsisterscircle.co) is a space for ceremony and ritual, offering a circle and ceremony facilitation course with best practices for those who want to host their own spiritual circles. Spiritual Black Girls (@spiritualblackgirls) offers a joyful appreciation of African traditional religions and a free spiritual planner and prayer book for the year. The Ancestor Project (@theancestor project, theancestorproject.com) provides resources for responsibly conducting ceremonies with psychedelics. And Black Healers Connect (@blackhealersconnect) spotlights practitioners of color.

adrienne maree brown (@adriennemareebrown, adriennemaree brown.net) is a writer and organizer who inspires spiritual activists everywhere with her powerful words and vision for a magical liberated future.

The future is bruja.

INCANTATION

Emerge

my inner voice says,
I want you to go in the water,
not to kill yourself,
but just, imagine you're under

I look at the ripples
in the dark of night,
lights reflecting on the surface,
imagining myself
at the bottom of this river
and not able to breathe

I remember
the Dragon King's Daughter
who can breathe underwater

INCANTATION

according to the parable,

she was denied enlightenment

since she was only 8 years old,

female and half-beast

I remember my friends

who said talking to their childhood selves

helped them heal and move forward

I am the Dragon King's Daughter

sitting at the river bottom

looking up at me

standing on the sidewalk

my inner voice says,

what would you say to her?

I say,

you are equal

—Yuki Jackson, Mark of the Beast, pt. 8

ACKNOWLEDGMENTS

During this book project, I was grieving and the country was in lock-down for COVID-19. Some days, I could barely get a paragraph on the page. Other days, writing was the only thing that kept me going. I want to thank all who supported me and rooted for this book when it was hard for any of us to see the future. You've shown me how sharing our grief can open us to deeper love. Let's keep taking care of each other.

I feel deep gratitude for all the brujxs and spiritual practitioners who shared their stories, offered their services, and inspired me to write this. Special thanks to Kimberly Rodriguez, a.k.a. Poeta Goddess, for creating the beautiful cover image for the book.

Thank you to Jane Dystel for seeing the promise of this book when it was just a paragraph in an email. And to my editor, Kara Rota. I have little point of reference, but I do believe you're the best editor in the world. Also, thanks to Frances Giguette, Melanie Roth, Sadie Teper,

ACKNOWLEDGMENTS

Michelle Williams, Alayna Parsons-Valles, Stefani Szenda, Natalie Rodriguez, and all the folks at Chicago Review Press for bringing this book to life.

The seed of this project began in my PhD program and would not have been possible had my dissertation committee not let me explore things that academia largely considers unacademic. Thank you to Drs. Mariaelena Bartesaghi, Art Bochner, Carolyn Ellis, and Heather Sellers for teaching me how to navigate my different writing voices. And to Drs. Elizabeth Bird, Joey Burchfield, Sheila Gobes-Ryan, Lawrence Morehouse, and everyone at Florida Education Fund for keeping me steadily funded throughout the years.

As a first-generation American, my family lifted me up so I could live my life doing what I love. Thank you to my mom, Gloria Martinez, my dad, Rudy Monteagut, and my brothers, Rudy and Michael Monteagut, for supporting this little black sheep, even though it's really hard to explain what I do when people ask. Thank you to Ricky Martin, Andrea Auza, Alika Brackett, and especially my new sister, Ally Cardona, for loving my people so I don't have to worry about them so much. Thanks to Marcela Montoya, who will always be my stepmom. To all my cousins, aunts, and uncles for keeping the family traditions alive back home while I wander. And of course, to my ancestors and helping spirits.

To my chosen family, I hope I can repay the kindnesses you generously offered when I had little to give in return. Thank you to my OG Tampa family, Karoline Povil and Dennis Alvarado Lopez, Andrea and Brett Kuhlman, Rachel Wilson and Izzer Skizzers, and Krista Jacobson and sweet Ellie; my spiritual superhomies, Kelly Watson and Prem

ACKNOWLEDGMENTS

Thomas, Meghan Hornstrom and Cameron White, Melissa Carroll, Carey Lewis, Micaela Lydon, and Ali Norman; my séance sister, Annalise Mabe, and Ryan Cheng; my Cancerian babies, Emily Norton and Zac Bowe; my constant counselor, Anna Oliver; my friends who live elsewhere but are never far, Richard Boggs, Cara Brunvand, Daniel Buquet, Mallory Danley, Dr. Alyse Keller, Navied Mahdavian, Melanie Osborn, and Summer Wallace; my childhood friends who won't let go, especially Cristina Rivera; and my newest friend, Dan Xie, for keeping me organized.

Thanks to Ben Montgomery for showing me the path to writing for a living, and to his girls, Asher and Morissey, who continually inspire me to be better, and to Bey. In my heart, we are always walking on a trail together.

Above all, I thank Dr. Erin Scheffels, my soul sister, for reading every single word I have written over the last eight years, for going through the hardest shit by my side, and for being Nala's second mom. She saved the world a lot.

FURTHER STUDY

BOOKS

ANCESTRAL WISDOM AND INSPIRATION

Anzaldúa, Gloria, and Carmen Valle. *Borderlands/La Frontera: The New Mestiza*. San Francisco, CA: Aunt Lute Books, 1987.

Avila, Elena, and Joy Parker. *Woman Who Glows in the Dark: a Curandera Reveals Traditional Aztec Secrets of Physical and Spiritual Health*. London: Thorsons, 2000.

Bird, Stephanie Rose. *Healing Power of African-American Spirituality: A Celebration of Ancestor Worship, Herbs and Hoodoo, Ritual and Conjure*. Newburyport, MA: Hampton Roads, 2022.

Dorsey, Lilith. *Orishas, Goddesses, and Voodoo Queens: The Divine Feminine in the African Religious Traditions*. Newburyport, MA: Weiser Books, 2020.

Estés, Clarissa Pinkola. *Women Who Run with the Wolves: Myths and Stories of the Wild Woman Archetype*. New York: Ballantine Books, 2003.

Harjo, Joy. *An American Sunrise: Poems*. New York: W. W. Norton & Company, 2020.

Murrell, Nathaniel Samuel. *Afro-Caribbean Religions: An Introduction to Their Historical, Cultural and Sacred Traditions.* Philadelphia, PA: Temple University Press, 2010.

ACTIVISM, CULTURE, AND PHILOSOPHY

brown, adrienne maree and Malkia Devich-Cyril. *We Will Not Cancel Us: And Other Dreams of Transformative Justice.* Minneapolis, MN: AK Press, 2020.

Kaba, Mariame. *We Do This Til We Free Us: Abolitionist Organizing and Transforming Justice.* Chicago, IL: Haymarket Books, 2021.

Lorde, Audre. *A Burst of Light: And Other Essays.* Mineola, NY: Ixia Press, 2017.

Prescod-Weinstein, Chanda. *The Disordered Cosmos: A Journey into Dark Matter, Spacetime, and Dreams Deferred.* New York: Bold Type Books, 2021.

Ricketts, Rachel. *Do Better: Spiritual Activism for Fighting and Healing from White Supremacy.* New York: Atria Books, 2021.

Sparkly Kat, Alice. *Postcolonial Astrology: Reading the Planets through Capital, Power, and Labor.* Berkeley, CA: North Atlantic Books, 2021.

Taylor, Sonya Renee. *The Body Is Not an Apology: The Power of Radical Self-Love.* 2nd ed. Oakland, CA: Berrett-Koehler, 2021.

Womack, Ytasha. *Afrofuturism: The World of Black Sci-Fi and Fantasy Culture.* Chicago: Chicago Review Press, 2013.

FOR YOUR PRACTICE

Ajana, Paris. *Little Book of Rootwork: A Beginner's Guide to Hoodoo.* United States: Berkeley, CA: Ulysses Press, 2021.

Cross, J. Allen. *American Brujeria: Modern Mexican American Folk Magic*. Newburyport, MA: Weiser Books, 2021.

Diaz, Juliet. *Plant Witchery: Discover the Sacred Language, Wisdom, and Magic of 200 Plants*. Carlsbad, CA: Hay House, 2020.

Herstik, Gabriela. *Bewitching the Elements: A Guide to Empowering Yourself through Earth, Air, Fire, Water, and Spirit*. New York: TarcherPerigee, Penguin Random House, 2020.

McQuillar, Tayannah Lee. *Astrology for Mystics: Exploring the Occult Depths of the Water Houses in Your Natal Chart*. Rochester, VT: Inner Traditions International, Limited, 2021.

Ruelas, Valeria. *Cosmopolitan Love Potions: Magickal (and Easy) Recipes to Find Your Person, Ignite Passion, and Get over Your Ex*. New York: Hearst Books, 2019.

Spalter, Mya. *Enchantments: A Modern Witch's Guide to Self-Possession*. New York: Lenny, 2018.

PODCASTS

Bae, Juju. *A Little Juju Podcast*. https://itsjujubae.com/podcast.

Bonman, Joi, and Praxie A. Osong. *Lil' Black Witch*. https://thelil blackwitch.com/podcast.

Buchanan, Nikki. *How to be Magical*. Produced by Soul Things Botanica. https://anchor.fm/howtobemagical.

Burke, Tara Rin. *The Witches Muse*. https://thewitchesmuse.com.

Da'Tella, Kay, and Delayna. *Brujas after Dark*. https://anchor.fm /brujasaf.

Dickens, Risa, and Amy Torok. *Missing Witches*. https://missing witches.com/category/episodes.

Grossman, Pam. *The Witch Wave*. https://witchwavepodcast.com.

Kroll, Marcella. *Saved by the Spell.* https://savedbythespell.com.

Lanyadoo, Jessica. *Ghost of a Podcast.* https://lovelanyadoo.com /ghost-of-a-podcast.

Mama Rue. *Mama Rue's Ancestral Musings.* https://open.spotify.com /show/3I6EC1kK5GSOOa8geG8sdc.

Rosella, Corinna. *Rise Up! Good Witch Podcast.* https://www.riseup goodwitch.com/podcast.

Vanderbeck, Paige. *The Fat Feminist Witch.* https://thefatfeminist witch.com

OTHER RESOURCES

Allied Media Projects. https://alliedmedia.org.

Ancestral Voices. Ancestral Voices Home Study Course. https:// ancestralvoices.co.uk/courses.

Delgado, Sofia. This Witch Magazine. https://www.thiswitch magazine.com.

Hood Herbalism. Hood Herbalism Course. https://hoodherbalism. com/hood-herbalism.

Modern Witches Confluence. https://modernwitches.org/confluence.

Nicholas, Chani. Chani App. https://chaninicholas.com/chani-app.

Rodriguez, Cindy. Reclama Journal. https://recla.ma/journal.

UCLA. The Archive of Healing. https://archiveofhealing.com.

NOTES

1: The New Brujas

One of the bombs caused property damage: Manuel Suarez, "Puerto Rico is Hit by Five Explosions," *New York Times*, May 26, 1987.

During this time of great political: "Why Witchcraft Still Enchants Us," October 26, 2020, in *The Takeaway*, produced by NPR, podcast.

Pam Grossman, author of Waking the Witch: Pam Grossman, "Yes, Witches Are Real. I Know Because I Am One," *Time*, May 30, 2019.

A March 2020 Atlantic *article:* Bianca Bosker, "Why Witchcraft Is on the Rise," *Atlantic*, March 2020.

Witches took to IGTV and TikTok: Morgan Sung, "In TikTok Protest, Witches Cast Spells to Hex Cops," Mashable, June 5, 2020.

There was even suggestion that one of Kamala: Jessica Bennett, "Kamala Harris Will Make History. So Will Her 'Big, Blended' Family," *New York Times*, January 17, 2021.

2: Occult Powers

The Taíno were the largest group: Edmund S. Morgan, "Columbus' Confusion About the New World," *Smithsonian Magazine*, October 2009.

Millions of Africans were enslaved: Nathaniel Samuel Murrell, *Afro-Caribbean Religions: An Introduction to Their Historical, Cultural, and Sacred Traditions* (Philadelphia: Temple University Press, 2010).

But when Castro solidified power: Carlos Moore, *Pichon: Race and Revolution in Castro's Cuba* (Chicago: Chicago Review Press, 2008).

The misa espiritual *(spiritual mass):* Diana Espírito Santo, *Developing the Dead: Mediumship and Selfhood in Cuban Espiritismo* (Gainesville, FL: University Press of Florida, 2015).

However now scholars believe that the Taíno: Haruka Sakaguchi, "Meet the Survivors of a 'Paper Genocide,'" *National Geographic*, October 14, 2019.

3: The Ancestral Curse

This conocimiento, *or "way of knowing":* Gloria Anzaldúa, *Borderlands/La Frontera: The New Mestiza* (San Francisco: Aunt Lute Books, 1987).

NOTES

"You might be processing": Trauma Aware Care (@traumaawarecare), "You might be processing what your parent(s) didn't," Instagram, December 17, 2019, https://www.instagram.com/p /B6MPH1vgVq_.

"If trauma can be passed": Xóchicoatl (@lamalayerbalove), "If trauma can be passed down generations so can healing," Instagram, December 12, 2019, https://www.instagram.com/p /B5-dTkDAFWg.

"Your feeling deeply": Dr. Rosales Meza (@dr.rosalesmeza), "Beloved, the emotions you are feeling are an invitation," Instagram, December 25, 2020, https://www.instagram.com/p /CJPWeOQAKZO.

Ancestral trauma can be transmitted through: Olga Kazhan, "Inherited Trauma Shapes Your Health," *Atlantic*, October 16, 2018.

This has been documented in refugees: Cindy C. Sangalang and Cindy Vang, "Intergenerational Trauma in Refugee Families: A Systematic Review," *Journal of Immigrant and Minority Health* 19 (September 22, 2016): 745–754; Anne Ancelin Schutzenberger, *The Ancestor Syndrome: Transgenerational Psychotherapy and the Hidden Links in the Family Tree* (New York: Routledge, 1998).

4: Guardian Spirits

Though she was never canonized: Antoinette Gimaret, "La réception ambiguë d'une figure mystique au xviie siècle," *Revue de L'Histoire des Religions* (September 2012).

In 1890 a chapter was established in Bogotá: July Andrea Garcia Amézquita, "Pagando Penas y Ganando el Cielo: Vida Cotidiana de las Reclusas de la Cárcel El Buen Pastor 1890-1929," *Historia y Memoria* 10, (Universidad Pedagógica y Tecnológica de Colombia, February 10, 2014): 19–42.

In 1862 the Morrill Act: Bennett Leckrome, "Why New Research Calls Some Flagships 'Land-Grab Universities,'" *The Chronicle of Higher Education*, April 8, 2020.

Over the last few years, they've been attracting: Janel Martinez, "Why More Afro-Latinas Are Embracing African Spiritual and Wellness Practices," Oprah Daily, September 25, 2020.

There's a woman called "La Cachetona": Libardo José Ariza Higuera, "En El Corazón Del Buen Pastor," *Antípoda, Revista de Antropología y Arqueología* 23, (Universidad de Los Andes, August 10, 2015): 45–54.

5: Joy as Resistance

In 2017 a pilot program in El Paso: "Family Separation Under the Trump Administration—A Timeline," Southern Poverty Law Center, June 17, 2020, https://www.splcenter.org /news/2020/06/17/family-separation-under-trump-administration-timeline.

The New York Times *reported:* Matthew Haag, "Thousands of Immigrant Children Said They Were Sexually Abused in U.S. Detention Centers, Report Says," *New York Times*, February 27, 2019.

The Human Rights Watch: Kids in Cages: Inhumane Treatment at the Border Hearing Before the Subcommittee on Civil Rights and Civil Liberties of the Committee on Oversight and Reform, 117th Cong., House of Representatives, July 10, 2019 (statement of the Human Rights Watch).

NOTES

Besides the fact that these child immigrants: Yuki Noguchi, "Unequal Outcomes: Most ICE Detainees Held in Rural Areas Where Deportation Risks Soar," NPR, August 15, 2019.

As Gloria Anzaldúa writes: Gloria Anzaldúa, "El Mundo Zurdo: The Vision," in *This Bridge Called My Back: Writings by Radical Women of Color,* ed. Cherríe Moraga and Gloria Anzaldúa (New York: Kitchen Table: Women of Color Press, 1985).

Chiquita creates a space: Audre Lorde, "The Uses of the Erotic: The Erotic as Power," Fourth Berkshire Conference on the History of Women, Mount Holyoke College, August 25, 1978.

"Recognize that pleasure is a measure": adrienne maree brown, *Pleasure Activism: The Politics of Feeling Good* (Stirling, UK: AK Press, 2019).

She said, "Sometimes we are held down": Evan Rachel Wood, "Evan Rachel Wood Reveals her Experience with Domestic Violence," *Nylon,* February 2021.

6: Abuelita Medicine

In the mid twentieth century, White people: Richard Rothstein, *The Color of Law: A Forgotten History of How Our Government Segregated America* (New York Liveright Books, 2017).

By the time the market stabilized: Emily Badger, Quoctrung Bui, and Robert Gebeloff, "The Neighborhood is Mostly Black. The Home Buyers are Mostly White," *New York Times,* April 27, 2019.

"Some of us have survived many apocalypses": La Loba Loca, "Sprouting Gardeners: DIY Plant and Garden Tending for the Apocalypse," (recorded e-class, April 2020), https:// lalobaloca.bigcartel.com/product/sprouting-gardeners-diy-plant-garden-tending-for-the -apocalypse-e-class.

The COVID-19 pandemic has triggered: Kimiko de Freytas-Tamura, "How Neighborhood Groups Are Stepping in Where the Government Didn't," *New York Times,* March 3, 2021.

I stand on land stolen from the Tocobaga: "Hillsborough River Watershed Excursion," Southwest Florida Water Management District, https://www4.swfwmd.state.fl.us/hill.

One poster responded, "Orishas are demons": Angela Caruso Soiferman in Seminole Heights Community, "We've lived in our house on the river," Facebook, December 14, 2020, https://m.facebook.com/groups/552339598261548/.

In July 2020 Trump gave a speech: Stephen Groves and Darlene Superville, "Trump Scores Protesters 'Merciless Campaign to Wipe Out Our History' in July 4 Mount Rushmore Speech," *Associated Press,* July 3, 2020.

7: Queer Magick

"I AM / VAST I / AM LIGHT": Edgar Fabián Frías (@edgarfabianfrias), 2020, "I AM EVERYTHING I AM NOTHING," Instagram, December 1, 2020, https://www.instagram .com/p/CIR4H9eAhSL.

"I AM ALLOWED / TO MUTATE": Edgar Fabián Frías (@edgarfabianfrias), "Full Moon in Gemini," Instagram, November 30, 2020, https://www.instagram.com/p/CIPYEpNATsk.

"THERE IS LOVE / WAITING FOR US": Edgar Fabián Frías (@edgarfabianfrias), "CN: This Post is A Spell," Instagram, July 16, 2020, https://www.instagram.com/p/CCtyQctFNbN.

NOTES

A recent Pew Research Center survey: Caryle Murphy, "Lesbian, Gay and Bisexual Americans Differ from General Public in Their Religious Affiliations," Pew Research Center, May 26, 2015, https://www.pewresearch.org/fact-tank/2015/05/26/lesbian-gay-and-bisexual -americans-differ-from-general-public-in-their-religious-affiliations.

Scientists have begun to study: James Doubek, "Scientists Talked to People in Their Dreams. They Answered," NPR, February 27, 2021.

Gloria Anzaldúa writes about this: Gloria Anzaldúa and Carmen Valle, *Borderlands/La Frontera: The New Mestiza* (San Francisco: Aunt Lute Books, 1987).

8: White Witches

"Me llamo Ismael": Lorraine Monteagut, "Second-Generation *Bruja*: Transforming Ancestral Shadows into Spiritual Activism," (PhD diss., University of South Florida, 2017).

Cubans love to play with words: Yoani Sánchez, "Leaving Home Coming Home," *New York Times*, November 27, 2013.

According to demographers: Kim Parker, Rich Morin, and Juliana Menasce Horowitz, *Looking to the Future, Public Sees an America in Decline on Many Fronts*, Pew Research Center, March 21, 2019, https://www.pewresearch.org/social-trends/2019/03/21/views-of -demographic-changes-in-america.

"what if radical movements erred": adrienne maree brown (@adriennemareebrown), reposted from Margaret Killjoy (@margaretkilljoy), "what if radical movements erred," Instagram, May 19, 2021, https://www.instagram.com/p/CPEy29Kg4HB.

9: Brujx Feminisim

A plaque discovered in Syria: Janet Howe Gaines, "Lilith: Seductress, Heroine or Murderer?" Bible History Daily, Biblical Archaeology Society, April 14, 2021, https://www .biblicalarchaeology.org/daily/people-cultures-in-the-bible/people-in-the-bible/lilith.

Facing the shadow is not a destructive: Carl Jung, *Memories, Dreams, Reflections* (London: Fontana, 1983).

"One day she came and said that the serpent": Carl Jung, *The Psychology of Kundalini Yoga: Notes of the Seminar Given in 1932 by C.G. Jung* (Princeton, NJ: Princeton University Press, 1996).

In his private journal, Jung writes: Carl Jung, *The Red Book (Liber Novus)* (New York: Philemon, 2009).

Shadows and demons have a rich history: Casey Cep, "Science's Demons, from Descartes to Darwin and Beyond," *New Yorker*, January 8, 2021.

"I am able now to confront": Carol Bridges, "Spirit Freed," *Medicine Woman Tarot Deck* (US Games Systems Inc., May 10, 2011).

10: Drama at the Botanica

The idea of self-care has roots: André Spicer, "'Self-care': How a Radical Feminist Idea was Stripped of Politics for the Mass Market," *Guardian*, August 21, 2019.

287

NOTES

Haiti was colonized by France: Nathaniel Samuel Murrell, *Afro-Caribbean Religions: An Introduction to Their Historical, Cultural, and Sacred Traditions* (Philadelphia: Temple University Press, 2010).

Certain Indigenous magical products: Haley Lewis, "Indigenous People Want Brands to Stop Selling Sage and Smudge Kits," *Huffington Post*, November 30, 2018, https://www .huffingtonpost.ca/2018/11/29/indigenous-people-sage-and-smudge-kits_a_23602571.

11: The Moon Coven

Cindy Rodriguez remembers fields: Cindy Rodriguez, *Reclama Journal*, January 2021.

On June 5, 2020, witches on social media: Josh Johnson, ABC News Radio, June 5, 2020, http:// abcnewsradioonline.com/music-news/2020/6/5/in-this-moments-maria-brink-calls -witches-to-action-to-bring.html.

12: Shadow Workers

Sabel posted an IGTV video: Sabel Santa (@santasabel), "La Cosas de Mi Madre," IGTV, April 23, 2020, https://www.instagram.com/tv/B_Vf4dsgc1j.

In one of her virtual rituals: Sabel Santa (@santasabel), "Love: A Physical Exploration of the Heart," IGTV, May 15, 2020, https://www.instagram.com/tv/CANuRiKAWff.